The RISE and FALL of BRITISH INDIA

imperialism as inequality

Karl de Schweinitz Jr.

Routledge
LONDON and NEW YORK

First published in 1983 by
Methuen & Co. Ltd
Reprinted 1985

Reprinted 1989 by
Routledge
11 New Fetter Lane, London EC4P 4EE
29 West 35th Street, New York, NY 10001

Printed in Great Britain by
J. W. Arrowsmith Ltd, Bristol

British Library Cataloguing in Publication Data
De Schweinitz, Karl
The rise and fall of British India
1. India–History–British occupation
I. Title
954.03 DS463
ISBN 0–416–33530–6
0–415–04505–3 (University paperback 804)

Library of Congress Cataloging in Publication Data
De Schweinitz, Karl, 1920–
The rise and fall of British India
Bibliography: p.
Includes index.
1. Imperialism–Case studies 2. India–History–British occupation, 1765–1947. I. Title.
JC359.D36 1983 325'.341'0954 82–20868
ISBN 0–416–33530–6
0–415–04505–3 (University paperback 804)

The RISE and FALL of BRITISH INDIA

Imperialism as inequality

Contents

Preface

In writing this book I am doubly presumptuous, first for addressing the matter of imperialism about which in the last century there has been a crescendo of commentary and learned exegeses and, second, for looking to India's history for the institutional substance of my argument when I have neither the formal credentials of an Indian scholar nor the insouciant assurance of James Mill that that is all to the good. My argument, however, addresses an aspect of imperialism that has been neglected, namely its coercive impact on the imperialized. This neglect, oddly enough, reflects the tendency of the theorists and historians of imperialism to assume that its grim underside is self-evident and what needs explanation is its causes.

I come to this matter from a long-standing interest in political economy. I believe Carlyle's characterization of it was well-founded in that resources are made scarce by the demands imposed upon them and that however societies resolve the consequent choice dilemmas they must in some degree constrain individuals. Outside the Garden of Eden coercion is at a discount. My assessment of it in imperialism therefore starts from the premise that we are concerned with a special manifestation of a general problem.

My choice of the British in India for the historical basis of my argument needs no defense. It is a long and varied history of the encounter of quite different peoples in vast and changing settings which has generated an inexhaustible literature the reading in which is its own reward. My obligation to the legion of Indian,

African, and Asian scholars, both in the East and West, who have made that history so vivid is profound. Without them it would have been impossible to season the insights of economics with non-western experience. Of that splendid host I am especially indebted to three persons who read previous drafts of the entire manuscript. A. G. Hopkins of the University of Birmingham rendered me invaluable service by calling attention to problems I had overlooked and the references which helped me cope with them in revision. John R. McLane of Northwestern University gave me the careful reading of an Indian scholar of Bengal. He also was extremely generous in sharing with me the extensive resources of his personal library. Rhoads Murphey of the University of Michigan, whose knowledge of Asian, especially Chinese and Indian, institutions has been enriched by intermittent residence in various parts of Asia going back to the middle years of World War II, was at once supportive and insistent that the development of my thesis needed greater focus and coherence. Needless to say, none of these scholars is responsible for the way in which I have responded to their criticisms.

It would have been very much more difficult for me to do the reading and write the initial draft of the manuscript had I not had a leave of absence from Northwestern University during the academic year 1978–9. I am grateful to Dean Rudolph H. Weingartner of the College of Arts and Sciences and Dean David S. Ruder of the Law School for releasing me from my normal academic obligations and financing the 'leisure' for the enterprise. My thanks also to Ved Mehta for permission to quote an extensive passage from 'City of the Dreadful Night'; to the *New Yorker Magazine* where it first appeared; and to Farrar, Straus & Giroux who reprinted it in his *Portrait of India* in 1970. Finally, I thank V. S. Naipaul for permission to use a similarly long passage from 'India, New Claim in the Land' and the *New York Review* which published it in June 1976.

KARL DE SCHWEINITZ JR.
Evanston, Illinois
1982

I

Imperialism

On 13 April 1919 General Reginald Dyer ordered British troops in his command to fire upon a crowd of some 5000 Indians who had gathered peaceably in an open area in Amritsar called the Jallianwala Bagh to listen to nationalists speak about independence, a goal whose time appeared to have come. The command was not preceded by a warning or an order to disperse. Nor did General Dyer call a cease-fire, when men, women, and children in their frenzy to escape the fusillade piled up at the bottlenecks of the narrow alleys which were the only means of getting into and out of the Jallianwala Bagh. The firing started at 5.00 p.m. and stopped at 5.15 p.m., by which time the Indian sepoys had exhausted their ammunition. The troops then withdrew, leaving behind, according to the official report, 379 dead and at least 1200 wounded, none of whom was given medical assistance. In testimony before the Hunter Committee that was subsequently appointed to investigate the matter, General Dyer acknowledged that had he been able to maneuver the machine guns of his detachment through the narrow alley leading to the Jallianwala Bagh he would have deployed them too for maximum effect.

In the days following the massacre at Amritsar martial law was imposed there and throughout the Punjab until 6 June. As the top military leader in the district General Dyer was thus not restrained by the rule of law. His hostility to the local population had been exacerbated by the disorders that preceded his ill-fated command, especially an attack on a European woman – a Miss Sherwood – apparently for no other reason than that she was European. He ordered any Indians that entered the street where the attack occurred to crawl on their hands and knees.[1]

The occasion for these actions by a member of the British Imperial Command in India was real enough, at least as seen through the eyes of imperial proconsuls who had been governing India for the British Crown for more than sixty years and were the successors to the servants of the British East India Company which had played the critical role in the establishment of Great Britain's imperial presence in India. World War I and the rhetoric of self-determination propagated by Woodrow Wilson stimulated the expectations of Indian nationalist leaders for independence that had been nurtured in the development of the Indian National Congress. The exigencies of waging the war, however, had led the British government to enact in 1915 the Defence of India Act, which among other things restricted civil liberties and increased the authority of the Indian government to deal with subversion. Upon the expiration of the Act at the end of the war, the British government recommended that these restrictions be continued and in March 1919 they were duly embodied in the Rowlatt Acts. The response of the Indian nationalists was immediate. Gandhi, whose satyagraha movement later became such a powerful force in the mobilization of nationalist India, called for a *hartal*, a day of non-work in mournful commemoration of the British frustration of nationalist hopes.[2] In some parts of India, including the Punjab, there were disorders and clashes between Indians and civil authorities, leading to bloodshed and a number of deaths. For some of the English, these events raised the specter of the Sepoy Mutiny of 1857 and the fear that these disorders were not merely spontaneous riots, but the early warnings of rebellion. Apparently one of this persuasion, General Dyer seemed to believe that forceful action at Amritsar would cool the ardor of Indian nationalists for disobedience to the British Raj.

One century earlier on 16 August 1819, yeomanry charged a large crowd of men, women, and children that had assembled peaceably at St Peter's Fields outside Manchester, England to listen to Henry Hunt, a radical orator of the day, speak on political issues that were aggravating the unenfranchised classes. Although those responsible for organizing the meeting had received no word from the local authorities that it was an illegal gathering and indeed had gone to great lengths to ensure that the crowd was orderly and well-behaved, the authorities, fearing that Hunt was a threat to the peace of the community, ordered the yeomen to arrest him. While making their way through the crowd to the platform, they apparently lost their nerve and rode into it swinging their sabers with abandon. Eleven people were killed and more than 400 injured, the massacre at Peterloo, as it came to be called, no doubt doing more in the long run for the democratic cause than anything Hunt might have said in his oration.[3]

Amritsar is a page from the history of imperialism, Peterloo from the history of the British democratic movement. There are many other obvious differences. The assembly in the Jallianwala Bagh was very much smaller and the casualties there very much higher than the assembly in St Peter's Fields. General Dyer consciously used his overwhelming fire-power to teach the Indians a lesson; the yeomanry may really have been panicked by the tremendous multitude.[4] The English were not much concerned about the massacre at Amritsar since many of them thought General Dyer was protecting the legitimate imperial interests of Great Britain in India; they were outraged by the massacre at Peterloo. Both, however, were incidents in the effort everywhere in all societies for governors to use force in the control of people they believe or fear are dangerously hostile to the values they serve, an infinitesimal sample of an infinity of such historical events, many of which may never be known, but all of which survive in the memories of their victims and those who identify with them.

These brief accounts of Amritsar and Peterloo underscore my concern for imperialism as an aspect of a general problem, namely the use of force or coercion in social organization. Traditional analyses of imperialism stress causal factors in the explanation of why, for example, the British governed India in the nineteenth century or the European powers competed so vigorously for the territories in sub-Saharan Africa during the last quarter of the nineteenth century. Some of them find the explanation in economic factors and others in non-economic factors. Whatever caused imperialism, its agents coerced subject peoples in varying degrees and thus depressed the latter's sense of well-being and/or freedom. Coercion, however, is a ubiquitous phenomenon, as we have every reason to know in the twentieth century. It may be gratuitously random or originate in the intimacy of personal relationships. It may be directed against traditional or established institutions by those who themselves feel unconscionably constrained by their norms. And, as our opening vignettes of law and order show, the officers of the status quo may demonstrate their forcefulness to those they suspect of wishing to break down those norms. Moreover, if there are many occasions for the use of coercion, it may manifest itself in many ways, from the physical threat to life and limb to the withdrawal of love or other highly regarded values. Imperialists hardly coerce societies that otherwise would be free of it. Among its many roots, none can be deeper than the scarcity of resources which afflicts all societies. We therefore start our analysis of imperialism by assessing the role of coercion in economic organization.

Scarcity, force, and freedom

The wants of society are greater than the capacity of resources to satisfy them. This primary assumption of economic analysis is not a figment of the economist's imagination. For most of history and in most parts of the world, poverty and subsistence have been unpleasant facts of life which few people expected to transcend. In the western world these limited expectations were given powerful doctrinal justification in the stern Old Testament injunction to Adam, 'In the sweat of thy face thou shalt eat bread, till thou return unto the ground; for out of it wast thou taken: for dust thou art, and unto dust shalt thou return.'[5] Whether or not this grim wisdom eased one's passage through a subsistence world, it was not more ineluctable than eastern wisdom in these matters which enjoined Hindus, for example, to abide by the rules of caste, however frugal or limiting they might be, if they wished a better incarnation in the next transmigration of souls.

Poverty is not synonymous with scarcity. When in the late

eighteenth century and with increasing vigor in the nineteenth century economies in northern Europe and North America began to industrialize, there was a promise of an end to the former but little reason to believe that the latter would be relegated to the dustbin of history. As per-capita output increased, the wants of society increased in at least equal measure. Many of these new wants may have been less urgent than subsistence needs and some no doubt were frivolous. None the less, their satisfaction required the utilization of scarce resources and thus confronted society with the continuing need to organize itself for making difficult economic choices.

The necessity for deciding what to produce, how to produce, and for whom raises difficult ethical and political problems. If there is not enough to go around, on what grounds does one decide who shall receive what? And having decided that question, how does society ensure that its decisions are accepted by those who have received less than they want?[6] Economics projects a picture of active, Promethean, calculating decision-makers who endlessly scan relative prices as they search for better means of maximizing utility and profits. Why should such people live comfortably with the constraints of scarcity? What makes them observe the rules that must be laid down to abort the chaos of a Hobbesian war of each against all?

In a preindustrial world where the rate of economic changes is slight, the economy overwhelmingly agrarian, and subsistence the norm, expectations may be very limited. A hierarchical social order may forestall those Promethean drives that we associate with economic growth, as the great majority of people defer to the few in authority who monopolize its economic and non-economic perquisites. Economic decisions are made implicitly in the traditions and rituals of social organization, whether class, caste, or guild. The economic order is difficult to distinguish because there is little differentiation of function. Work and leisure do not have the same meaning as they have in industrial society since they are intertwined in the geographical propinquity of home and workplace, into both of which religious observances and social obligations readily enter. Here the coercive impact of scarcity is in part sublimated in traditional relationships, which have as their rationale the repetition of historically sanctioned behavior including collective welfare through kin groups. It also may be manifest in the demands for service and tribute from headmen, princes, and kings. And in its grimmest, most fateful materialization, it takes the form of famines and plagues which periodically vent their Malthusian spleen.

In a world of economic change that has overcome subsistence and in which there is great differentiation of activities both among and within the subsystems of society, economic decisions no longer are made implicitly. Nor can they all be made in a small setting of face-to-face relationships. Rather an economic system must be organized which allows society explicitly to address the choices that scarcity entails and makes possible accommodation of production and consumption. When these do not occur at the same time or place, it requires an extraordinary flow of information and an extraordinary adjustment of individual behavior to match them. The price or market mechanism is, of course, one such system.

In contrast to a command economy in which a central planning authority articulates a public interest in complex planning documents and then contrives administrative means for accommodating individual behavior to those purposes, the price system depends upon exchanges of goods and services among individuals whose preferences for work, leisure, and commodities are the primary guides to resource allocation. The gross national product (GNP), which embodies the public economic interest, is, then, the summation of the many decisions made by individuals in firms and households and can be viewed as an additive function of their utilities.

In a perfectly competitive world in which individuals are highly mobile and informed and make decisions without regard to their impact on market prices, the GNP from an allocative standpoint is optimal. Households and firms maximize utility and profits in exchange, thereby indirectly maximizing society's benefit. Consumers achieve peak satisfaction from their limited money income by buying that combination of present and future goods and services which make their marginal utilities proportional to their prices. As owners of resources, they sell their services for the highest money income consistent with their preferences and capabilities.

The firms purchase that combination of inputs – the services of land, labor, and capital – that makes their marginal physical products proportional to their prices – rents, wages, and interest. They then produce a level of output that equates marginal revenue to the price of the product. Since they do not believe that their decisions affect the market price, price and marginal revenue turn out to be equal. Thus the perfectly competitive firm produces an output that makes marginal cost equal to price.

Finally, all markets, for both outputs and inputs, clear as prices change to make supply equal demand. In the process some industries will expand as firms are attracted to them by profit rates that are above normal and others will contract as firms are driven out by losses. In the equilibrium of the economic system, firms will operate at minimum cost and industries will earn the minimum rate of return necessary to maintain their various capacities. Because all firms have fulfilled the marginal conditions, it is not possible to shift resources from one use to another and raise the satisfaction society obtains from its scarce resources, *given* technology, tastes, the distribution of income, and the level of income.

While perfect competition may be imagined to operate autonomously and independently of the state, in fact it cannot do without it. Exchange cannot take place outside of an institutional framework which establishes ground rules for the transactors. We have already suggested that there is a tension between the condition of scarcity and calculating market behavior. One way that this tension may be managed is through the law of property which establishes entitlements in its use and the remedies for owners against those who violate them. The efficacy of law, however, depends on the ability of the judiciary to adjudicate the issues brought before it by the bar and to have its resolution of them accepted in society, all of which depends ultimately on the legitimacy accorded to the coercive powers of the state.

Moreover, exchange in highly differentiated economies and

societies is extraordinarily complex and typically cannot be consummated without there being a contract drawn up which specifies the conditions to which the contracting parties may be held and the penalties which may be exacted for non-performance. There is a tendency in neoclassical economics to view the modal exchange as an instantaneous transaction which requires little or no forethought or planning. One gets the impression that the economy consists of people who are buying and selling bread, aspirin, and similarly uncomplicated commodities. In any event contracts are unimportant in that world or are assumed to be drawn up and performed as quickly as a person can swallow a couple of aspirin.

In so far as economic decisions are not consummated instantaneously, there are more opportunities for unanticipated happenings which impose costs on individuals who may or may not have been part of the original transaction. As an increasing proportion of the GNP is allocated to the production of durable goods, consumption becomes more of a longitudinal phenomenon with a concrete history and an uncertain future. If defective parts of houses, cars, boats, or lawn mowers cause accidents, who is liable for the damages they entail? So torts and the law of liability grow along with the market.

Property, contracts, and torts are not the only armor in the legal panoply encasing exchange systems. Jean Valjean knew nothing of these, but for stealing a loaf of bread suffered the inexorable penalty of the criminal law. While property law may address easement problems and whether owner A may construct a fence so high that it deprives adjacent owner B of a view of a common resource such as a lake, it does not deter burglars who care very little how these matters are dealt with in civil law. In addition to sanctions against theft, the criminal law plays a part in the maintenance of general order in society, the breakdown of which disrupts the environment conducive to exchange. Riots, disorderly conduct, mayhem, and other actions which threaten the person reduce the scope of markets. In the extreme, rebellion and revolution destroy the legal foundations on which economic activity depends.

Moreover, as competitive conditions break down and the micro- and macroeconomic performance of markets becomes less satisfactory, government may be required to do more than maintain the efficacy of the systems of civil and criminal law. If the externalities of market conduct strain the capacity of the law of torts to modify them, administrative means may be used to influence the behavior of firms and households. Or, what historically has been a more important occasion for government intervention, aggregative instability – too much unemployment, too much inflation, or, as we know to our despair today, too much of both – may cause government to extend the uses of fiscal and monetary policies, incomes policy, or even wage and price controls.

The neoclassical view of freedom and coercion is part of the vision of exchange as a private activity relatively unencumbered by governmental authority. As Milton Friedman has put it so succinctly: 'The possibility of co-ordination through voluntary co-operation rests on the elementary – yet frequently denied – proposition that both parties to an economic transaction benefit from it, provided the transaction is *bi-laterally voluntary and informed*. Exchange can therefore bring about co-ordination without coercion.'[7] To put the proposition in the framework of freedom, individuals may or may not enter into an exchange. If they do, presumably they think they will benefit from it. It is the choice that they exercise to buy or not to buy, to sell or not to sell, that constitutes economic freedom. And it may be inferred that the quality of freedom is higher the better the alternatives that confront choosers in markets.

Freedom as choice has a distinguished paternity in John Stuart Mill's classic interpretation of it: 'The only freedom which deserves the name, is that of pursuing our own good in our own way, so long as we do not attempt to deprive others of theirs, or impede their efforts to obtain it.'[8] Pursuing our own good in our own way, of course, involves making choices among alternatives. In the classical view, and also in Milton Friedman's, the most serious threat to individuals' capacity for choice is the control that may be exerted over them by a paternalistic or authoritarian government, even if it is intent on improving the welfare performance of the economic system. Freedom, then, in this tradition, is the absence of external restraints in the realization of one's desires. For this reason Isaiah Berlin has called it negative freedom, or liberty *from* and observed that:

> Everything is what it is: liberty is liberty, not equality or fairness or justice or human happiness or a quiet conscience. If the liberty of myself or my class or nation depends on the misery of a vast number of other human beings, the system which provides this is unjust and immoral. But if I curtail or lose my freedom, in order to lessen the shame of such inequality, and do not thereby materially increase the individual liberty of others, an absolute loss of liberty occurs.[9]

This view of freedom, it is important to note, gained strength in the nineteenth century when the growth of the private sector in the British economy was indeed stimulated by governmental retrenchment as mercantilist prescriptive policies and subsidies to aristocrats and their retainers were cleared away. While the economy was being transformed, so too was the government, as it became less an institution of privilege and played more even-handedly the role of the night-watchman. The classical assumption, therefore, that private behavior was capable of realizing worthwhile social goals was grounded in the visible, material performance of the market economy.

The neoclassical rendering of economic freedom, however, tends to be more libertarian than the classical view because unlike John Stuart Mill it backs off from making qualitative judgments about individual choice. It does this by impounding tastes and behavioral propensities in that most convenient of Pandora's boxes, *ceteris paribus*. To take tastes as given is to say, in effect, that economics has no special insight into how they are formed. But this methodological convenience has a strong libertarian rationale in the query that it evokes – who is a better judge of tastes than the individual whose behavior responds to them? Certainly no external authority, least of all the state, knows better than the individual what is in his interests. The third martini at lunch and the second glass of milk are equally meritorious. The burden of proof for recommending changes in the performance of the private sector of the economy, therefore, falls heavily on those who presume to quarrel with the outcome of autonomous choice in households and firms.[10]

The liberation outlook of neoclassical economics is further reinforced by the simple commodity bias we have already commented on. The student being introduced to the subject is likely to be challenged by the problem of deciding in what proportions the rational consumer should buy apples and oranges or some such set of commodities which technically are not complicated and whose properties can be understood and appreciated through repeated and rapid use. The transactions in which they are bought and sold, therefore, may be bilaterally voluntary and informed. Somewhat less attention is paid to commodities and services whose exchange is complicated by the restriction in the flow of information about them. It is not customary for professors of economics to start the section on consumer choice in the beginning course in economics by discussing the rental market in the inner city.

Moreover, the market for labor, where choices are made infrequently and the worker is selling his willingness to abide by the orders of his employer, is treated as an analogue of the market for apples and oranges. There is the same emphasis on the mobility of knowledge and persons and there is thus posited an active chooser who reveals his preferences in market choice and so gets what he deserves. If he worked in a coal mine and died young from a respiratory disease or a cave-in, fire, or explosion, he assumed those risks in the light of his knowledge of alternative employment. Going into the mines was an affirmative, calculated free choice in no way different from the sale or purchase of apples or oranges.

Further, choices are made in peculiarly static circumstances. It is as if each person were born anew with every choice. Memories are of short duration and are acquired principally in learning through market transactions. There is little thought given to the influence of the experience people have with exchange on their normative perception of the performance of markets. Where transactions are not bilaterally voluntary and informed and some individuals and groups in society systematically bear the costs of such inequalities, economic choice may be felt less as freedom and experienced more as coercion.

Unlike neoclassical economics, Marxian economics treats coercion very explicitly. The capitalist epoch, it is argued, was preceded by a long series of historical events – enclosures, inflation, the depredations of privateers, the seizing of monasteries – which concentrated the ownership of capital and separated workers from the means of production. This Marx referred to as primitive capitalist accumulation, the explicitly coercive characteristics of which were to be contrasted to the less naked coercive relationships in mature capitalism where workers, no longer in possession of the means of production, had to sell their labor power to the owners of capital.[11]

Marxian analysis thus focuses on work and the organization of labor as the critical place for observing the restrictive consequences of economic systems. Choice, the substitution of commodity A for commodity B as the price of one changes relative to the price of the other in the never ending search for the peak of consumer satisfaction, is for the great part ignored. Marx did not believe there was much to explain about consumption. In his view, whether 'an egg cost(s) more than a cup of tea', to use Joan Robinson's derisive phrase, was not likely to concern a society which could afford very little of either.[12]

In paying scant heed to microeconomic transactions, however, Marx and his followers overwhelmed the individual in vast aggregates. Exploitation and coercion were expressed through the medium of classes. Capitalists coerced the proletariat, the homogeneity of both being presupposed by their relationship to the means of production. The market domination of the proletariat by the capitalists was reinforced by the latter's control of the state which used its military and police powers and its command of legislatures or law-making bodies to guard their interests. But the detailed workings of the system with its effect on the individual incidence of coercion were far from clear.

As for freedom in Marxian economics, it is the culmination of the historical transformation process. Society becomes free when it has surmounted scarcity and overcome class conflict, when, in short, it has reached communism. It is a utopian rather than a current condition, the achievement of which is the promise of the future and indeed a rationalization of the coercive burden of the present. It therefore is an absolute, indivisible value which appears to be coterminous with the whole institutional structure of society. Where neoclassical economics envisages freedom as the continuing opportunity to seek individual goals through market choice, Marxian economics conceives of it as a union, or reuniting, of the individual and society, a social condition in which individuals have spontaneously subordinated their self-seeking drives to the community interest.[13]

If neoclassical economics distorts our understanding of freedom and coercion by withdrawing the market from its institutional integument and analyzing it statically and ahistorically, Marxian economics inhibits analysis of them because it argues that coercion is so omnipresent a phenomenon in class societies that there is not much point in discussing the nature of freedom until the historical process has brought on the classless society. Yet both analyses are inside the puzzle of freedom and coercion because they influence people's views about what they are and how they can be maximized or minimized. By stressing scarcity, choice, and allocative efficiency and deemphasizing the parameters crowded into *ceteris paribus*, neoclassical economics tends to underscore the limits of human potential. It is choice at the margin that counts. The state should not make sudden or non-marginal adjustments in tax and expenditure rates; nor should it alter the ground rules of economic conduct except so far as such changes enhance opportunities for individual profit or utility maximization. It is in the private sector that freedom is realized and it is the coercive powers of the state that threaten it. In contrast, by stressing the growth and transformation of social institutions, Marxian economics urges upon its adherents the actions that will bring about the historical process it has adumbrated. While the state is an instrument of coercion, if it can be controlled in the interests of the proletariat rather than capitalists, its power can be used to realize the future order where individuals freely identify with society and so make the oppressive state redundant.[14]

Empire and imperialism

Neoclassical economics and Marxian economics both project a weak territorial or spatial sense, the one perceiving more critical relationships in individual-maximizing behavior, the other in the conflicts of social classes. In contrast, territorial aggrandizement has been central to imperialism as embodied in the empires formed in the history of the world. A reference to the British empire evokes an image of a world map with countries in Asia, Africa, and the Americas colored with the red that geographers once favored for distinguishing England's overseas territories. The governance of empire meant that the people indigenous to those far-flung territories were ruled by foreigners. So much is clear, and there can be no doubt that imperialism as a complex of forces that brought empires into being has something to do with the rule or control of one state or nation over another.[15]

If, however, we are interested in the impact of imperialism on the people so ruled, it is not so simple a matter. Suppose General Dyer had used the troops under his command at Amritsar as a police force to ensure an orderly entrance and exit for the crowd assembling in the Jallianwala Bagh, would that have been less imperialistic than the punitive action he ordered? Would it make any difference if a prudent use of the police power of the imperial state prolonged its rule for fifty years? For one hundred years? Or is imperialism indivisible and everywhere equally heinous? Suppose the imperial state tried to create an institutional environment favorable to economic growth that had been inhibited by the feudal policies of a predecessor indigenous ruler, how does one assess the coercive burden of imperialism? We argued above that the scarcity of resources has coercive consequences, notwithstanding the implication of the neoclassical competitive model that exchange is a voluntary method of economic organization. If that means that, no matter how the state affects the allocation of resources, some people will bear a greater burden of scarcity than others, is the imperialist-growth-oriented state merely gorging a different ox from the indigenous feudal state?

These questions are easier to pose than to answer and for the time being they must remain somewhat rhetorical. They have been asked, however, in the knowledge that imperialism now has pejorative meaning. Whether or not people are familiar with histories of imperialism, they think of it, if they think of it at all, as a process in which the strong oppress the weak. No one today takes pride in the imperialist label. No state accepts with equanimity the charge that it is behaving imperialistically toward another state, people, or nation. This has not always been so. Indeed the word itself is only of recent vintage. Even as far into the Victorian age as 1878 Lord Carnarvon was complaining that 'we have of late been perplexed by a new word "Imperialism" which has crept in amongst us. . . . I have heard of Imperial policy, and Imperial interest, but Imperialism, as such, is a newly coined word to me.'[16]

When the word imperialism first gained currency, its pejorative meaning was muted. It was derived from imperial which brought to mind empire and emperor. These words had an ancient lineage and were not common coin to be used casually by any regime. Rather they were reserved for particularly awesome, majestic, or tyrannical systems – Imperial Rome, the Mughal emperors, the Chinese dynastic emperors – whose special status was acknowledged throughout the world. In the nineteenth century, while England was acquiring the greatest of all modern empires, many Englishmen believed that its special quality, distinguishing it from lesser political orders, laid on British leadership a responsibility of trusteeship for the welfare of mankind. In the North American colonies before the demise of the first British empire, there was strong support for it as an institution through which the colonists could achieve their rights as Englishmen, Crown and Parliament willing.[17] And Edmund Burke during the trial of Warren Hastings, the first governor-general of India, following his impeachment in 1787 for misconduct while holding that office, articulated a theory of colonial trusteeship which no doubt was the more forcefully argued because of the recent failure of British governance in North America. Subsequently in 1835 the House of Commons through the Report of the Aborigines Committee reiterated the view of Burke that the British government was responsible for the welfare of its subject races even as it was responsible for the welfare of Englishmen. Thus as the word imperialism initially saw the light of day in the nineteenth century, it was associated in some people's minds with trusteeship and the governing of colonies for humane purposes, values that were given visibility in England by an extensive imperial literature, especially by Charles W. Dilke, *Greater Britain*, John R. Seeley, *The Expansion of England*, and J. A. Froude, *Oceana*.[18]

Moreover, in the far reaches of the British empire many of the Victorian proconsuls stunningly embodied these values. Lord Curzon, a viceroy of India, was not dissembling when he wrote, 'In Empire we have found not merely the key to glory and wealth, but the call to duty, and the means of service to mankind.'[19] So too Lord Cromer, the indirect ruler of Egypt from 1883 to 1906, in his view that:

> The British generally . . . possess in a very high degree the power of acquiring the sympathy and confidence of any primitive races with which they are brought into contact. Nothing struck me more than the manner in which young men, fresh from some British military college or university, were able to identify themselves with the interests of the wild tribes of the Soudan, and thus to govern them by sheer weight of character and without use of force.[20]

However sincere the protestations of those who carried the banner for imperialism, strong forces were molding a hostile point of view. The democratic tradition of the western world, so dramatically symbolized by the American and French Revolutions, was taking hold with increasing tenacity in Europe and North America in the latter part of the nineteenth century even as European imperialist expansion was at flood tide in Asia and Africa. If no society had yet achieved universal suffrage, many had extended the vote to middle-class men. In England the great age of political reform started with the First Reform Bill of 1832 and thereafter inexorably expanded the pale of the constitution so that the majority of adults had been enfranchised by the passage of the Fourth Reform Bill in 1918.[21] And what could have been more incongruous than the democratization of political processes at home while abroad viceroys and district commissioners governed foreign populations who had little or no say in the matter?

The incongruity of democracy at home and authoritarian rule abroad permeated the public mind slowly. The Boer War, the many disasters of which included the first concentration camps of the twentieth century, shook British complacency about the empire and impugned those imperial motives that Lord Curzon and Lord Cromer found so ennobling. Most people in Great Britain, however, like people everywhere, were more concerned with their immediate, familial, insular problems than the affairs of people many thousands of miles removed from them. These had been given increased urgency in the continuing industrialization of the British economy. The development of new techniques and new commodities destroyed old markets and old labor skills, disrupted stabilizing social relationships, and exacerbated economic inequalities. At the same time economic growth visibly increased the wealth of society and affected expectations. Some people, not excepting the poor, came to believe that poverty was not inevitable. Yet the promise and reward of economic growth could be at odds for a lifetime, leaving many with neither the assured status of an unchanging subsistence economy nor the material sufficiency of a changing industrial economy.

The nineteenth century saw the vigorous development in Great Britain of many organizations – trade unions, cooperatives, mechanics' institutes, self-help societies, and political action groups – which from different perspectives sought solutions to the social–economic problems that were sublimated in less dynamic economies. If it was a turbulent century, it was partly because of the self-consciousness with which so many different groups addressed these problems. The conflicts of society no longer turned primarily on the differences of élites struggling for control of an oligarchic political system; these conflicts now had a wide social base in the middle and working classes. The task of articulating interests, then, became more complex and gave scope to the myriad means by which individual beliefs and attitudes could be influenced and made to serve the purposes of organization.

Among these means, economic and political literature was important as it came to express ideas systematically that otherwise remained stillborn in people's minds as vague notions, feelings, or unarticulated intuitions. It provided the basis, as Schumpeter argued in *Capitalism, Socialism, and Democracy*, for the slogans and catchwords with which leaders of interest groups mobilized their constituents.[22] It also educated, informed, and shaped the preferences of leaders and constituents alike, all the more so when the issues at stake were not readily encompassed in personal experience. A worker may have been an expert on the impact of managerial employment policy on morale in the plant, but know little about the consequences of imperial governance on the peasant in Bengal or the fellahin in Egypt.

The literature of imperialism

The pejorative view of imperialism was forcefully expressed in a literature that originated in analyses of the economic crises of capitalism. Its great period of growth was in the early years of the twentieth century when Marxist writers especially were filling in the sketchy treatment of imperialism in Marx's own work. So familiar is this body of literature that we only need review the highlights that bear on the major concern of this book – coercion in economic relationships.

Marx's stress on coercive growth in capitalism picked up a strain of thought in classical economics that was becoming attenuated and, as we have seen, all but disappeared in neoclassical economics. The classical economists, notably Adam Smith, reacted against mercantilist thought, which was nothing if not an explicit rationalization of colonies, wages and price controls, production and sumptuary restrictions, and discriminatory tariffs. Designed to rig the terms of trade and maximize the accumulation of precious metals, mercantilist prescriptions were a crude economics of imperialism. Adam Smith placed the market and its extension at the center of his explanation of the wealth of nations and thus made way for an analysis of exchange that stressed the benefits it conferred on all transacting parties.

David Ricardo made these implications explicit in the theory of comparative advantage. Yet there lurked in Ricardian economics the specter of the stationary state. Focusing its analytical insight on the distribution of income among landowners, capitalists, and the working classes, it predicted a long-run decline in profits. Growing population increased the demand for subsistence, leading to an expansion of the intensive and extensive margins of cultivation, which in their turn caused an increase in the cost of production of grain, a rise in money wages and in rents, and therefore a decline in the share of net product for capitalists and in their incentive for accumulation. The scarcity of 'the original and indestructible powers of the soil' bound workers to subsistence and made capitalists hostage to the rising rents of landowners.[23]

It is this pessimistic prediction, so oddly out of sorts with the young, ebullient, industrial environment from which it emerged, that gave rise to a classical view of imperialism. It also appealed to Marx's transitory sense of capitalist institutions and so may be thought of as a forebear of Marxist theories of imperialism. The former was a pragmatic response to the prediction of declining profits. If the villain of the piece was a Malthusian growth of population relative to natural resources, there were two means of postponing the evil day, importing subsistence from areas of the world where there still existed favorable land–population ratios or exporting population to those same territories. Edward Gibbon Wakefield was the most zealous advocate of the second option during the age of classical economics in England.[24] His proposals for colonization in Australia and New Zealand attracted wide attention and gained the support of so eminent an economist as John Stuart Mill. They were all the more pleasing because they stressed choice and voluntarism in migration at a time when in Australia convicts, transported there for offenses against English law, provided the primary source of labor. None the less, colonization was not free of coercion. Though the indigenous population in Australia was small and primitive, it always had had access to the land until repressed by people from a different society with different motivations and skills as well as different intentions with respect to how land should be owned, controlled, and used. Thus classical economics somewhat circuitously lent support to imperialist ventures which were inconsistent with its primary outlook and orientation.

As for Marx, his *Weltanschauung* placed capitalism in a sequential process, each stage of which was better than its predecessor, until society attained surcease from the class struggle and release from the burden of economic necessity in communism.[25] Only then could society enter the era of history proper when mankind consciously controlled its destiny. The Ricardian stationary state pointed to the demise of capitalism, however much Ricardians' realization of this was lost in the false consciousness of the bourgeoisie. Critical in Marx's anticipation of the capitalist transformation was a theory of declining profits which, unlike the classical economists, he related to the periodic crises of the business cycle. It is in this that one finds the origins of Marxian theories of imperialism.

In the manner of some people of capacious mind and extraordinary originality and insight, Marx wrote many things that were contradictory, to the great benefit both of his critics and of his quarrelsome followers. Marx's explanation of the course of profits and the crisis is a case in point. He himself preferred an explanation of declining profits based in long-run secular forces centered on capitalist accumulation and technological change, apparently not realizing that while the former might work in the right direction the latter most likely would not.[26] Committed to an internally inconsistent theory of declining profits, he none the less made a number of observations attributing the crisis of capitalism to an inability of the market to buy the output it was capable of producing. In short, there are in his writings the elements of a theory of underconsumption. Both of these explanations of the crisis foreshadowed the theories of imperialism of his followers.

Meanwhile in the neoclassical renovation of economics, which was well under way at the time of Marx's death in 1883, there was little interest in the cataclysmic, disequilibrating characteristics of capitalist growth that captured his fancy. Moreover, neoclassical economics had purged itself of those concerns that had kept imperialism faintly alive in classical economics. Its methodological inward turn made it increasingly positivistic and bound by standards of proof and validty that had not inhibited the classical economists. It became less concerned with the interaction of economic and non-economic forces and more with purely economic relationships. Marginal utility analysis elevated demand to a coequal status with supply and, as we have seen earlier in this chapter, brought choice, exchange, and resource allocation as they were mediated by relative prices to center stage. Imperialism was scarcely in the wings; by the turn of the twentieth century it was a subject fit only for those outside the bounds of orthodox economics. Neoclassical economists paid scant heed to that burst of European imperial energy, subsequently called the new imperialism, that led to the scramble for Africa and brought Lord Cromer to Egypt and Cecil Rhodes to the Cape Colony.

If neoclassical economics was otherwise occupied, there was no lack of unorthodox economists, not to mention historians and students of international relations, ready to explain the new imperialism. Pride of position in entering the lists belonged to J. A. Hobson whose *Imperialism* was published in 1902. An iconoclastic non-Marxian English economist never welcomed into the academy, he was persuaded that capitalism suffered from underconsumption.[27] The imperialist division of sub-Saharan Africa was a consequence of this internal economic ailment which compelled capitalists and allied interests aggressively to look for markets overseas. In the following year Rosa Luxemburg's *The Accumulation of Capital* appeared.[28] A Polish-born member of the German Social Democratic Party, she seized on the underconsumption option in Marx as the basis of her analysis of imperialist expansion. Unlike Hobson, who thought that external aggression could be muted in redistributive reforms that strengthened domestic consumption, Luxemburg did not believe that capitalism could survive without being aggressive to less economically advanced societies and that when these had all been incorporated inside capitalist empires, capitalism itself would fall.

Marxists, particularly those of revolutionary persuasion, tended to be uncomfortable with underconsumption theories because of their reformist implications and there soon developed hypotheses about imperialism stemming from Marx's theory of the declining tendency of the rate of profit. Lenin, of course, was the most forceful advocate of this explanation. *Imperialism, the Highest Stage of Capitalism* was published in 1916 and drew heavily on the empirical data contained in Hobson's book and on the argument of the Austrian Marxist Rudolph Hilferding in *Das Finanzkapital* (1910) that stressed the increasing importance of financial capital and investment banking in the monopolistic growth of capitalism.[29] According to Lenin, the export of capital became the typical feature of the relationship of finance capitalism to the world economy, as the export of goods was typical of the earlier stage of competitive capitalism, the occasion for the change being the declining profit rate in maturing capitalist markets. With the export of capital there followed the political controls of empire as each capitalist system attempted to secure for itself international markets that were protected from the competition of rival capitalist systems. As the world economy was divided into combines of capitalism, so too were the workers divided between the metropolitan proletariat and the colonial masses, the former being bought off with some small part of the monopoly profits accruing to capitalists. Inevitably the competition of capitalisms became more intense as each one, in proportion to its strength, occupied as much colonial territory as possible. In time, the rivals turned on one another and precipitated the outbreak of world war. This, then, was the highest stage of capitalist development, the harbinger of its downfall.

Lenin's *Imperialism* hardly stemmed the flow of Marxian writing on the subject. Some later writers have laid greater stress on underconsumption as the source of capitalism's aggressive imperial expansion.[30] Others have emphasized the structural characteristics of monopoly capitalism that intensified the struggle of oligopolists for control of foreign markets.[31] Still others have underscored the role of the multinational corporation in creating dependency relationships between capitalist and Third World countries.[32] But they all explain the phenomenon as a consequence of some need of maturing capitalist systems.

Modern economists writing in the Marxian tradition have had to explain the resilience of capitalist markets which have continued to be the primary institution for organizing international economic relationships. They also have seen the decline of the old imperial systems since World War II and in their place the emergence of the formerly colonial territories as independent states. Moreover, where Lenin perceived a dichotomous world in which he anticipated that socialism would rise in the same proportion that capitalism fell, these writers view a world of mixed economies which make use of markets and public administration in varying and complex combinations. Capitalists are still at the old stand, though surrounded by a ubiquitous host of public officials. In the Third World, the new states can look to these old models for guidance or to the models of central planning that were initially invented in Russia in the years following the revolution of 1917. All this does not look much like the world predicted by Lenin, and writers in the Marxian tradition have attempted to account for this in theories of neoimperialism or neocolonialism, the implications of which are that though the details of capitalist domination have changed capitalist dominance none the less persists.

In addressing this theme many of these economists differ from their Marxian forebears in one important respect – they have been trained in the methodology of neoclassical economics. They know the price system as an allocative institution from the inside. What distinguishes them from orthodox neoclassical economists is that they make the class struggle a central feature of their analysis and so comprehend the price system or the market as an instrument for distributing economic and political power in support of a ruling class. They therefore have not been constrained by those methodological influences mentioned earlier in this chapter that have made neoclassical economics a self-contained discipline whose licensees are little concerned with the political implications of their models. This may be readily seen in their treatment of international trade and investment as manifestations of the continuing dominance by capitalist states of formerly colonial countries.

Everyone concerned with these matters knows that in the years since the great decolonization movement set off by the independence of India and the establishment of Pakistan in 1947 there has not been an appreciable reduction of the inequality of wealth between the old established states and the newly independent states. Independence did not assure economic growth; it was a good deal easier to break the imperial chains than it was to assimilate those behavioral patterns that generated it. Moreover, the conditions which had transmitted the growth impulse so strongly among western states in the nineteenth century seem to be attenuated in the non-western world. In trade, for example, the new states are predominantly producers of primary output, the demand for which originates largely in the developed economies. In the late twentieth century advancing technology and rising income in the latter have reduced the growth rate of this demand. Synthetic fibers, for example, have displaced some of the market for natural fibers. Low-income elasticities of demand for food products in the advanced economies limit the growth of the market for agricultural commodities. The relative growth of the service sector in the United States and other wealthy capitalist economies inhibits the expansion of the market for raw materials consumed by firms. Unless an underdeveloped economy is endowed with petroleum deposits, iron ore, or some such resource which is central to industrial technology, it may find that its primary output does not earn in trade the foreign exchange essential for its import needs.

Not only has the vigor of trade in certain primary products lessened since the nineteenth century, but population movements with their equalizing shifts of human capital have diminished. Indeed, there may be a perverse movement of people away from the less developed economies. Technicians, engineers, economists, mechanics, or doctors are not leaving the western world to settle in the non-western world. Cultural barriers deter migration from one to the other. So do low material rewards relative to what can be earned in the capital-rich west. But, of course, these factors do not prevent the reverse flow of people – the 'brain drain'. The western nations are pleased to accept skilled immigrants from the non-western world, though they are careful to keep out the teeming millions who can offer little more than a willingness to work.

Finally, private capital is not being invested in the less developed economies as it was in the nineteenth century. The rise to independence of the new states frequently has brought in its wake political instability where formerly the imperial powers maintained law and order. More important, the rate of return on investment, discounted for relative risks in different areas of the world, is higher in the more rapidly growing economies of the capitalist countries than in the formerly colonial countries. The private capital that is invested there is sponsored by multinational corporations (MNC) whose world-wide interests transcend the national priorities of the new states. Headquartered in the advanced economies, they are likely to invest in the expansion of those mineral resources, preeminently petroleum, so critical for the continuing growth of the industrial economies with only a mild interest in the development of the complementary human capital so critical for the early growth of the new states. If it is cheaper to import highly trained personnel than to train the local population in the needed skills, this will be done, though the creation of a foreign, technically trained advanced enclave in the midst of a less developed economy inhibits the forging of the lateral and backward linkages that might stimulate the transmission of the growth impulse from one to the other.

While all economists may not accept this account of international economic inequalities in every particular, they will agree that trade, population movements, and private investment do not stimulate economic growth as they once did. Economists of Marxian persuasion in addition blame the situation and the poverty of the Third World on capitalism. If the commodity terms of trade are secularly adverse to primary-producing countries, this is not merely the consequence of the international specialization of function among agrarian and industrial societies. It is the consequence of a nineteenth-century imperialism which stunted industrial and manufacturing development in the former by forcing the growth of primary sectors and of twentieth-century trade barriers in the advanced economies which rig markets against Third World manufactured goods. Private capital movements through the MNCs accentuate the growth of the foreign enclaves in the development of primary output and also of an indigenous clientele subverted by the material perquisities of the MNCs into accepting their values at the expense of the well-being of the more numerous members of society. Moreover, bilateral public capital movements from one state to another are motivated less by the economic problems confronting Third World countries than by the security and strategic interests of the advanced countries. They too nurture a local clientele which in fact is likely to be the same élitist groups that are beholden to the MNCs. Many former colonial countries, then, in this view, are led by élites who benefit from the dependency relationships which originated in the world economy in the imperial age and are being perpetuated in the neoimperial age by the capitalist states' careful and self-serving use of market controls and foreign investment. The extreme proponents of this view assert that the economic plight of Third World countries is a necessary condition for the continuing growth of capitalist economies.[33]

Economic explanations have not monopolized the controversy about the causes of imperialism. Schumpeter defined imperialism as 'the objectless disposition on the part of a state to unlimited forcible expansion', and accounted for it by the proclivity of a warrior class to wage war, not for economic, political, or religious reasons, but for the reason that this is what it did. It was an atavistic class whose grasp on society diminished with the rationality fostered by the spread of capitalist market behavior. This idiosyncratic view never gained the currency of political theories which stress the interest of the state in its security, that is, in the perpetuation of its governing capacity over present and future generations. Putting aside the familiar, but difficult, problem of how the interest of the state relates to the interests of the individuals comprising it, security not unreasonably can be seen as a source of aggression. Statesmen perceive a threat to it in the behavior of foreign governors who are similarly concerned for the security of their own state. As Benjamin J. Cohen has succinctly put it in what he calls a general theory of imperialism:

> Here is the real taproot of imperialism – *the anarchic organization of the international system of states.* Nations yield to the temptations to domination because they are driven to maximize their individual power position. They are driven to maximize their individual power position because they are overwhelmingly preoccupied with the problem of national security. *The logic of domination derives directly from the existence of competing sovereignties.* Imperialism derives directly from this crucial defect in the external organization of states.[34]

According to this theory, the scramble for Africa, for example, is to be explained by the decisions of European statesmen as they assessed their security interests in the light of the anticipated reaction of their rivals to alternative policies they might pursue. Great Britain occupied Egypt in 1882 because of its security interests in maintaining the lifeline through the Suez canal to India which was all the more important because of its concern over Russia's expansion toward the northwest frontier of India and its fear that the weakening Ottoman empire no longer could be relied upon to keep Russia out of the Mediterranean. Subsequently it gained control of Uganda and the headwaters of the Nile to forestall its occupation by France which had designs on it from its beachhead in West Africa. Moreover, it seized Kenya to protect the eastern flank of Uganda from the encroachment of newly formed Germany which had only recently entered the imperial sweepstakes. These actions, Professor Cohen is asserting, can be explained more persuasively by a theory of political oligopoly than by a theory which asserts, as in the case of Marxian theories, that what counts are the decisions made in the boardrooms of giant financial and/or industrial corporations, the security interests of the state merely being a screen for these more deeply rooted interests of private property and profits.

One may note that this theory without too much strain may accommodate what D. K. Fieldhouse has called the imperialism of the masses.[35] This refers to the jingoism and nationalist fervor of citizens for imperialist ventures and the glory that presumably strengthens their identification with the state. The concern of statesmen for security does not restrict their field of vision to the behavior of rival states; they may also detect internal threats to security from dissidents, radicals, or malcontents. Imperialism, especially if it is enveloped in a shroud of moral purpose or mission that stresses the benefits the more 'civilized' may bestow on less 'civilized' societies, may indeed infuse a citizenry with a subjective sense of their own uniqueness and perhaps make them more amenable to the demands that states impose upon them.[36] Or, in a somewhat cruder way, imperialist adventures and the external crises they generate may provide statesmen with a rationale for curtailing the dissident behavior of domestic groups that, for whatever reason, they find threatening.

None of these theories of imperialism is wholly satisfactory for investigating the coercive, dominating, and controlling face of imperialism. Neoclassical economics, of course, has no such theory, since any trace of force in its models has been dispersed and fragmented in the voluntarism of exchange relationships. Schumpeter's theory of imperialism hardly neglects force, but makes it the business of the warrior class and thus minimizes or denies its role in the market place.

Marxian theories of imperialism are very explicitly about coercion but they associate it so closely with a specific form of economic organization that the predictions they spawn are extraordinarily parochial. Imperialism is a function of capitalism and its geriatric ailments. So long as it prevails over them, so long will imperialism survive. By the same token, when capitalism fails, the world will be released from the agonies of imperial dominance, if, that is, the new social–economic order is socialist and motivated by welfare rather than profit considerations.

Political theories of imperialism are not so institutionally specific as Marxian theories and so do not exclude socialist or communist societies from being imperialists. Yet in being more general, they become vague about the phenomenon to be explained. If 'the logic of domination derives directly from the existence of competing national sovereignties,'[37] does this mean that as the number of sovereign nations increases the burden of imperialism becomes heavier? Are we to infer that there will be no surcease until the world is ruled by one state? And if that is a valid inference, why should it be so that the domination and force which appear to be the essence of imperialism will fade away in one world? Clearly there are empty boxes in this theory that need to be filled, not the least important being the sensibilities and reactions of the people who willy-nilly have been caught up in the dynamic forces which have transformed the world's economies and polities.

In this last respect all these theories are inadequate, because they have a Eurocentric bias that locates the critical decisions in the countries that have been the historical aggressors. If one becomes so engrossed with European capitalists and statesmen as the imperializers, one casts in the shadow the imperialized, namely the people against whom European states' aggressiveness was aimed. It is as if a play were to be performed with most of the cast missing. This may not be surprising. Until recently, the theorists of imperialism have been almost without exception western and knew relatively little about the non-western societies which suffered from western imperialism. Again, not surprisingly, when the west began to penetrate areas of the world with which they had previously been little acquainted, they were inclined to interpret what they saw through the conceptual and moral categories of their own societies.

Another view of imperialism

The Eurocentric bias of imperialism may be diminished by viewing it as a relationship in which A dominates, controls, or coerces B, preventing B from acting in its own interests or compelling it to act in the interests of A. This definition, too, has its share of empty boxes. While it may not be difficult to identify the As and Bs, the matter of interests, both substantively and as they may or may not be expressed, is complex enough to have created enduring analytical problems for political economy, welfare economics, and other social sciences.[38]

If the As and Bs are individuals as in market exchanges, interests inhere in the utility and profit maximization of households and firms. The extent to which they experience freedom in exchange, that is do not feel coerced by it, depends upon the assets they possess that can be applied to their various purposes. If these assets wealth, knowledge, and skills – are distributed unequally, the individual with less of them is not likely to be as inspired by market freedom, especially when transactions are complex in the sense discussed earlier in this chapter, as the individual with more of them. In short, coercion in market transactions is a function of inequality.

If the As and Bs are countries, states, or regions, England and India, for example, differentiated from one another in language, religion, ethnicity, or political organization, one confronts a potentially imperialist relationship. What would it mean, however, to assert that the interests of England dominate or control the interests of India? England and India are abstractions of the political, cultural, and historical imaginations of the individuals who dwell there (or, to make the matter more complicated, do not dwell there). While one may comprehend the purposes and values of individuals, it is not easy where these differ to understand how it turns out that they come to stand for a public, state, or collective interest. Or, conversely, how individuals come to identify with a collective purpose that has somehow become part of the public domain.

In the imperialist relationship one collective entity has come to dominate another. The consequent inequalities are more complex than in individual market relationships because of their public or quasi-public character and the necessity for organizing individuals in the pursuit of a collective purpose. One may account for this greater complexity conceptually by modifying and extending the assets that affect the purposes of individuals in exchange. For wealth, knowledge, and skills, substitute wealth, military power, knowledge (which includes technology), organizational capacity, and ideology. If country A has accumulated greater wealth than country B, maintains a stronger military establishment, is more knowledgeable about the natural and social worlds, has acquired greater ability in organizing reluctant subjects in private and public activities, and is animated by an outlook or ideology that more effectively rationalizes the control of foreign peoples, it may embark on imperialist ventures in B with verve and a clear conscience.[39]

How the inhabitants of B experience the coercive impact of the imperialist conduct of A can only be appreciated by viewing the inequalities of the relationship in concrete historical settings. I shall therefore explore imperialism as a paired relationship of countries – England and India – with quite different characteristics in widely disparate periods of history, the early seventeenth century, the second half of the eighteenth century, the nineteenth century, and the second half of the twentieth century. In examining the rise and fall of British imperialism in India, we wish to understand in what way the imperial proconsuls made the Indian environment in which the ordinary affairs of life were carried on different from what it otherwise would have been. If the testimony of those who bore the incidence of these changes was weak, we can none the less sense their impact by looking at the underside of the political and economic forces the theories of imperialism variously have held to explain the aggressive expansion of the west in the non-western world.

Moreover, since imperialism is so complex a phenomenon the coercive impact of which is embedded in specific histories, it is appropriate to recognize that there are imperialisms rather than a monolithic imperialism. By the same token, the imperial relationship may fade away in the social controls that characterize any society. While the analysis focuses on England and India, it will be relevant for assessing other imperialist relationships. I shall therefore conclude this historical essay with a chapter on the implications for other imperialisms of British imperialism in India.

Notes

1 Rupert Furneaux, *Massacre at Amritsar*, London, George Allen & Unwin, 1963, 13–32, 88–98.

2 Satyagraha literally means 'insistence on truth' and is generally rendered as 'soul force'. Vincent A. Smith, *The Oxford History of India*,

Percival Spear (ed.), 3rd edn, Oxford, Clarendon Press, 1967, note 1, 784.

3 Cf. G. D. H. Cole, *A Short History of the British Working-Class Movement, 1789–1947*, 2nd edn, London, George Allen & Unwin, 1948, 49–50; E. P. Thompson, *The Making of the English Working Class*, London, Victor Gollancz, 1963, 669–700.

4 The estimates of the size of the crowd assembled in St Peter's Fields varied widely from Hunt's 180,000–200,000 people to one magistrate's 30,000. For reasons that are not clear the figure most often cited is 60,000. Joyce Marlow, *The Peterloo Massacre*, London, Rapp & Whiting, 1969, 125.

5 Genesis 3:19.

6 Not the least interesting aspect of John Rawls, *A Theory of Justice*, Cambridge, Mass., Belknap Press, 1971, is his attempt to accommodate the inequalities occasioned by the scarcity of resources in a system that ensures basic individual liberties.

7 Milton Friedman, *Capitalism and Freedom*, Chicago, University of Chicago Press, 1962, 13. Italics in text.

8 John S. Mill, *On Liberty*, New York, Appleton-Century-Crofts, 1947, 12.

9 Isaiah Berlin, *Two Concepts of Liberty*, Oxford, Clarendon Press, 1958, note 1 10.

10 There is considerable question-begging in this analysis because the household and firm are conceived as individual decision-making units when in fact they are institutions of collective choice. In a household, for example, consisting of members of different ages, there are frequent occasions and circumstances in which a decision is made by one member in the interests of junior or senior members, a state of affairs that is not congenial to the libertarian view.

11 Karl Marx, *Capital*, trans. S. Moore and E. Aveling, 3rd edn, Chicago, Charles H. Kerr, 1906, 1, 784–7.

12 Joan Robinson, *On Re-reading Marx*, Cambridge, Students' Bookshops, 1953, 22.

13 The use of society or social interests in Marxian economics appears to be rhetorical, perhaps because in Marx's time a social or public interest may have seemed to him to be self-evident or, at any rate, much less difficult to identify than in a democratic age where the assertion of so many diverse individual interests makes the determination of the public interest problematical.

14 The danger inherent in this utopian outlook is well known and in this

respect Marx was very much in the tradition of Rousseau. 'Whoever refuses to obey the general will shall be compelled to it by the whole body: this in fact only forces him to be free.' J. J. Rousseau, *The Social Contract*, trans. Charles Frankel, New York, Hafner, 1947, 18. Karl R. Popper, *The Open Society and Its Enemies*, 5th edn, Princeton, Princeton University Press, 1966, and J. L. Talmon, *The Rise of Totalitarian Democracy*, Boston, Beacon, 1952, along with Isaiah Berlin, have made us very much aware of how deeply rooted in the western tradition this outlook is. In this section I have drawn heavily on my paper 'The question of freedom in economics and economic organization', *Ethics*, 89 (4), 336–53.

15 Definitions of imperialism abound and vary according to the writer's theory of and interest in imperialism. Joseph Schumpeter defined it as 'the objectless disposition on the part of a state to unlimited forcible expansion' (*The Sociology of Imperialism*, trans. H. Norden with an introduction by B. Hoselitz, New York, New American Library, 1974, 6). In contrast to this sharp, pithy definition, William L. Langer defined imperialism so inclusively that few states could be excluded: 'the rule or control, political or economic, direct or indirect, of one state, nation, or people over similar groups, or . . . the disposition, urge or striving to establish such rule' (*The Diplomacy of Imperialism 1890–1902*, 2nd edn, New York, Knopf, 1968, 67). We shall have more to say about Schumpeter's imperialism later in this chapter.

16 Quoted by C. A. Bodelsen, *Studies in Mid-Victorian Imperialism*, Copenhagen, Gyldendap Forlagstrykkeri, 1924, 127. Lord Carnarvon may have been a bit disingenuous in this observation. He was Disraeli's colonial secretary and, as James Morris noted, though he seemed at first to have difficulty in understanding imperialism, later 'he sorted it out in his mind, and cogently explained it to others' (*Heaven's Command, an Imperial Progress*, New York, Harcourt Brace Jovanovich, 1973, 388).

17 Richard Koebner, *Empire*, New York, Grossett & Dunlop, 1965, 85–104.

18 It is difficult to know how this literature affected attitudes about imperialism. The reading public represented a small proportion of the British population, though it no doubt played a disproportionate part in the public dialogue on the great issues of the day. It is far from clear, however, that in Victorian England imperialism and colonialism were among these. Debates in the House of Commons on the colonies were likely to be conducted with most members absent.

Moreover, if one believes that the great Victorian novels reflected the critical problems of the society, one is forced to conclude that interest in imperialism was non-existent. At the most the colonies in that literature were far off-stage, a distant world to which the dramatis personae could be banished if it were convenient for the development of the novel. No one in Dickens, Thackeray, Eliot, or Trollope brooded about the imperial relationship.

19 Quoted by A. P. Thornton, *The Imperial Idea and Its Enemies, a Study in British Power*, London, Macmillan, 1959, 72.

20 Earl of Cromer, *Ancient and Modern Imperialism*, London, Longmans, Green, 1910, 75.

21 The fourth Reform Bill extended the franchise to women for the first time, but only to those aged thirty or over. It was not until 1928 that women were on the same footing as men and could vote at twenty-one.

22 Joseph Schumpeter, *Capitalism, Socialism, and Democracy*, 3rd edn, New York, Harpers, 1950, 145–55.

23 David Ricardo, *On the Principles of Political Economy and Taxation*, (ed.) P. Sraffa and M. Dobb (eds), Cambridge, Cambridge University Press, 1953, 67.

24 Edward Gibbon Wakefield, *A Letter from Sydney: The Principal Town of Australasia*, New York, Dutton, 1929.

25 The literature on Marx is so vast that no one work or writer dominates it. For the man and the philosophical foundations of his analysis one may recommend Isaiah Berlin, *Karl Marx – His Life and Environment*, New York, Oxford University Press, 1959, and David McLellan, *Marx before Marxism*, New York, Harper & Row, 1970; for his economics Joan Robinson, *An Essay on Marxian Economics*, New York, St Martin's Press, 1966, and Paul M. Sweezy, *The Theory of Capitalist Development*, London, Dennis Dobson, 1946. One can, of course, read the three volumes of *Capital*, but since the Charles H. Kerr edition runs to more than 2400 pages, it is a forbidding task and there is no assurance that the number of pages read will correlate positively with an understanding of Marx's analysis. The first volume, however, the only one Marx saw through the press, is a classic well worth reading, especially if one already has a feel for his economics.

26 Joan Robinson, op. cit., 35–42, and Paul Sweezy, op. cit., 100–5.

27 J. A. Hobson, *Imperialism: a Study*, 3rd edn, London, Allen & Unwin, 1948. In *The General Theory of Employment, Interest, and Money*, New

York, Harcourt Brace, 1936, John Maynard Keynes amended handsomely for the neglect of Hobson by the establishment as he included him in the 'brave army of heretics . . . who, following their intuition, have preferred to see the truth obscurely and imperfectly rather than to maintain error, reached indeed with clearness and consistency and by easy logic, but on hypotheses inappropriate to the facts' (371).

28 Rosa Luxemburg, *The Accumulation of Capital*, trans. A. Schwarzschild with an introduction by J. Robinson, London, Routledge & Kegan Paul, 1951.

29 V. I. Lenin, *Imperialism, the Highest Stage of Capitalism*, New York, International Publishers, 1939; Rudolph Hilferding, *Das Finanzkapital*, Wien, Verlag der Wiener Volksbuchhandlung, 1923.

30 Paul A. Baran and Paul M. Sweezy, *Monopoly Capital, an Essay on the American Economic and Social Order*, New York, Monthly Review, 1966.

31 Harry Magdoff, *The Age of Imperialism*, New York, Monthly Review, 1969.

32 Stephen H. Hymer, 'The efficiency (contradictions) of the multinational corporations', *American Economic Review*, 60 (2), 441–8; id., 'The multinational corporation and the law of uneven development', in J. Bhagwati (ed.) *Economics and World Order*, New York, Macmillan, 1972, 125–6.

33 Andre Gunder Frank, *Capitalism and Underdevelopment in Latin America*, New York, Monthly Review, 1969, 113–40.

34 Benjamin J. Cohen, *The Question of Imperialism, the Political Economy of Dominance and Dependence*, New York, Basic Books, 1973, 245. Italics in text.

35 D. K. Fieldhouse, *Economics and Empire, 1830–1914*, Ithaca, Cornell University Press, 1973, 69–76.

36 For an analysis of the possible conflict between optimal resource allocation in the conventional sense and the use of scarce resources for building support for the state see Karl de Schweinitz, Jr, 'Growth, development, and political monuments', Muzafer and Carolyn Sherif (eds) *Interdisciplinary Relationships in the Social Sciences*, Chicago, Aldine, 1969, 209–24.

37 Cohen, op. cit., 245

38 The literature on individual and social choices in economics is vast. For seminal contributions on the subject see Kenneth J. Arrow, *Social Choice and Individual Values*, New York, Wiley, 1951, and A. Bergson,

'A reformulation of certain aspects of welfare economics', *Quarterly Journal of Economics*, 52 (2), 310–34. See also Kenneth J. Arrow and T. Scitovsky (eds), *Readings in Welfare Economics*, Homewood, Irwin, 1969, and Dennis C. Mueller, 'Public choice: a survey', *Journal of Economic Literature*, 14 (2), 395–433.

39 See Karl de Schweinitz, Jr, 'What is economic imperialism?', *Journal of Economic Issues*, 15 (3), 675–701.

2

The connection established: England and India in the early seventeenth century

At the time Europeans opened the all-water passage to Asia in the late fifteenth century, Asian goods had been reaching Europe for centuries by various routes that converged on Mediterranean ports or ports near the Mediterranean where they could be transshipped in vessels plying the coastal waters of that great inland sea. The efficacy of these routes changed from time to time depending on the goods being carried, the hazards of robbery, and the tribute or taxation imposed by rulers in the regions through which merchants passed. The more than two hundred years of Mongol domination of the Eurasian steppes stimulated the use of overland routes by caravans using pack animals, the danger of bandits and other predators being reduced inside the Mongol empire. These, of course, were costly and suitable only for commodities whose value was high relative to their weight. Wherever possible rivers and inland or open seas were used. Sometime before the Christian era Arabs had learned to sail with the monsoons, moving southeast across the Arabian sea to India and Ceylon and even beyond to the East Indies in the summer and returning with the northwest monsoons in the winter. In the first century before Christ, a Greek named Hippalus learned the art from the Arabs and became the first-known European to make a landfall on the west coast of India.[1]

By the fifteenth century a highly developed and complex system of trade had developed in Asia connecting China, Japan, and the Malay–Indonesia archipelago with India, the Middle East, and the Mediterranean. In the western reaches of the system, small pedlars buying and selling in the markets of the Levant and Persia moved overland to India or Hormuz at the entrance to the Persian Gulf. There they met Muslim traders who had entered Asian water routes 'as merchants, not as conquerors' and 'accommodated themselves readily to the conditions of the localities where profitable trade was to be had'.[2] Some of them were Indians from Gujarat in the northwest corner of India where it abuts the Arabian Sea. Others were Arabian. The former dominated the long distance carrying trade from west India and the Malabar coast to Malacca on the north side of the straits between the Malay Peninsula and Sumatra. By the end of the fifteenth century Malacca had become the great entrepôt of the Far East. The silks and porcelains from China and the spices from the Celebes and the Moluccas and the other islands in the Indonesian archipelago were warehoused there pending the northwest monsoon that propelled the ships carrying them to west Asia. In the long transit from Malacca they traded at ports along the convoluted coastal routes that terminated in Calicut and Cochin on the Malabar coast where the Indian pepper markets were located and in Surat on the Gulf of Cambay, an important market for Gujarati cotton goods. These entrepôts were pivotal in the exchange of European and Asian goods.

While the west coast of India was the more important link in the trading system connecting Asia and Europe, there also were trading expeditions from Bengal and from the Coromandel coast to Malacca. These too were largely conducted by Muslims, though some Hindus participated in the trade, caste proscriptions against movement overseas apparently being weaker than in western India.

The pepper, spices, silks, and other Asian commodities destined for Europe that were received in Indian ports could be carried west by trading caravans through India and Persia. Or they could be transshipped to Hormuz, there to be moved to the Levant by the network of small pedlars. Still another route lay through the Gulf of Aden and the Red Sea to a point close enough to the Nile for a land crossing and a trip downstream to Cairo and Alexandria.

By whatever means Asian goods reached Europe the risks were

great. The theft of cargoes was a perpetual danger along the trade routes, whether overland or water, and at the frequent transshipment points. Floods, typhoons, or sandstorms could destroy or impair the value of commodities in transit. And the taxes or tribute imposed on merchants and pedlars by the political jurisdictions through which they passed, 'protection costs' as Niels Steensgaard calls them, tended to be higher than transportation costs.[3] Moreover, the extraordinary gap in time and space between production and consumption meant that the investment in tradable commodities that would embark on the odyssey across Asia was made in the face of great uncertainty. Tastes in a traditional subsistence world changed slowly, but none the less still had to be reckoned with. The market in Europe for silk, for example, became more discriminating as consumers came to learn about the fabric through use. Even at those exhausting distances market choice mattered. If, in consequence, the cost of Asian commodities was high in Europe and their markets limited, they still might deteriorate from shocks – famine, plague, and so on – that periodically devastated European economies.

Before the voyages of discovery and the opening of the oceans to trade, the Italian city–states, especially Genoa and Venice, grew wealthy in this market on the strength of their strategic position between Europe and western terminuses of the Asian trade routes. Vigorously commercial and active developers of maritime technology, they were frequently at war with one another in the competition for shares of the Eurasian trade. Initially Islam had been a boon to these merchants because it inhibited Muslim merchants in the Levant from venturing into Christian territories. But when the Turks captured Constantinople in 1453, thus making the Byzantine capital a Muslim city, Genoa and Venice lost an important outpost in what was becoming an increasingly hostile world. The city–states were soon to enter a long period of decline as the maritime strength of the west passed first to southwest and then to northwest Europe.[4]

With the historical trade routes connecting Europe and Asia clogged, if not blocked, in the Middle East, the interest of Europeans in the all-water route to the Indies became all the stronger. To outflank Islam served not only Christ but Mammon as well. If the markets of Asia could be reached without passing through Muslim lands, Christian merchants might reap what hitherto had been harvested by Muslim traders. It surely was not fortuitous that the fall of Constantinople was so closely followed by the first voyage to the New World of Christopher Columbus in 1492 and the first voyage to India of Vasco da Gama in 1497.

The East India Company and the English economy in the early seventeenth century

The East India Company, chartered by Queen Elizabeth in 1600 at the close of her long reign, was the commercial organization empowered to expand England's share of the fabled Asian trade. It was granted a monopoly in the Indies for an initial period of fifteen years, its shareholders, as in any capitalist enterprise, motivated by an interest in the profits that could be gained in the Asian trade. Most of them were London merchants fully alert to the risks they were incurring, which accounted for the manner in which profits were to be distributed from its first venture. With the capital contributed by the shareholders, the Company bought five ships, outfitted them, hired crews, and purchased an inventory of commodities for trade. The acquired cargo of pepper and spices from the Indies was to be sold in London after the return of the fleet and the original contribution of the shareholders paid off plus a profit, if any, in proportion to the value of their shares.

It would be abusing the hindsight of history to assert that the formation of the East India Company was a wily imperial move consummated two centuries later by British dominion in India. The shareholders would have been aghast at the thought of supporting an imperial venture, if by that was meant the occupation and the rule of foreign lands. This is not to say that they were any more sensitive to the rights of foreign peoples than any other Englishmen or, for that matter, Frenchmen, Spaniards, Portuguese, Indians, or Chinese. Rather in 1600 it would not have been apparent to them that ruling foreign countries helped much in turning a profit. Apparently, however, they had little objection to the use of force. The outbound cargo of the first voyage was not right for the East Indies, Sumatrans, for example, not being taken with 'skillfully wrought iron . . . East Anglian woolen vests', and 'hard-wearing Devon trousers'.[5] Lacking vendible commodities, the captain of the fleet did not hesitate to attack a Portuguese galleon whose rich prize included a more suitable stock of merchandise. It is not recorded that the gentlemen of the East India Company were so far shocked by this looting that they declined to accept their share of the profits when the first fleet returned to England two-and-a-half years after its departure.

If the Company was not established with imperial designs, it was none the less the first effective organization in using English resources for the development of trade with the Indies. While England was several years behind the Dutch in this regard and a century behind the Portuguese, in little more than one hundred and fifty years it had replaced them as the dominant European power in the east. England's venture to the Indies, then, was part of a European movement which had its origins deep in the historical struggles and economic drives of European peoples. It is a critical piece in the puzzle of imperialism that there were no similar commercial movements mobilizing the energies of Asian, sub-Saharan African, and American peoples. We do not know of merchants in India who were importuning the emperor Akbar, whose reign from 1556 to 1605 coincided with Queen Elizabeth's, to grant them the privileges of trade in European countries. Still less do we know of such an interest among the Chinese of the emperor Wan-li, their contemporary in the Ming dynasty. The west went east by sea, the east did not sail west of the Cape of Good Hope. In consequence the site of modern imperialism was in the non-western world.

The first expedition sent out by the English East India Company in the opening years of the seventeenth century could not have made a great impression on the English public. As an Atlantic state, England, like Spain its arch rival and frequent enemy, looked to the west to realize its mercantile ambitions. The interposition of the New World between Europe and Asia may have delayed the opening of a viable western route to the latter, but it played upon the imagination and offered opportunities to talents and energies that were unappreciated or overly constrained in post-Tudor English society. The Spanish had a century's head start on the English who did not establish their first colony in North America until the tenuous founding of Jamestown in 1607. Thereafter the tide of colonial expansion ran strong as the Stuarts granted various charters to English colonists who settled the eastern seaboard north and south of Jamestown. By the standard of eastern voyages, the trip to the New World was short. In 1492 Christopher Columbus had taken only two and a half months to reach the Bahamas from Spain; by the seventeenth century the voyage from England to North America took about two months.[6] The colonies in Virginia or Massachusetts were extensions of England whose less venturesome inhabitants could without unseemly difficulty remain in touch with their pioneering relatives. The inaugural expedition of the East India Company endured so long that, however much its return rewarded the London merchants who held shares in the Company, it could not serve as a focus for a continuing and abiding public interest in India. The Company had entered upon a lonely venture.

Moreover, in the sixteenth century before England embarked on colonization in the west and trade in the east, the drama of its survival in the struggle with Spain was played out in the Atlantic and surely did implant in the English mind a consciousness of that ocean as both a threat to and protection of its security. When Shakespeare in *Richard II* had John of Gaunt utter his impassioned love of England,

> This happy breed of men, this little world,
> This precious stone set in the silver sea,
> Which serves it in the office of a wall,
> Or as a moat defensive to a house,
> Against the envy of less happier lands;
> This blessed plot, this earth, this realm, this England,[7]

he hardly had in mind the Indian ocean. And his readers or audience would have had in vivid memory the recently defeated Spanish Armada (1588) that had brought naval warfare so close to the shores of England. So too would they know of those dauntless men – Francis Drake, Martin Frobisher, Richard Grenville, and John Hawkins, among others – who sailed the Spanish Main seeking the treasure that an indigenous slave population mined for their Spanish overlords.

Drake especially excited the English imagination. Whether he was viewed as hero or buccaneer, he symbolized the aggressive, expansionist, maritime drive of the English nation. In a voyage lasting three years from December 1577 until September 1580, he circumnavigated the globe in the *Golden Hind*, thus becoming the first sea captain to accomplish this feat in his own ship.[8] He also accumulated rich prizes along the way, as he preyed on Spanish galleons whenever the opportunity presented itself, so that when he returned to Plymouth his backers, not least of all Queen Elizabeth, were amply rewarded for their patience – for their abstinence, as Nassau W. Senior would have put it. It has been estimated that the value of the prizes was £600,000, of which the queen might have received as much as one half, 'more than the total of Exchequer receipts for a year'.[9] The venture has lost none of its luster or tarnish through the years and John Maynard Keynes conjectured that

> the booty brought back by Drake in the *Golden Hind* may fairly be considered the fountain and origin of British Foreign Investment. Elizabeth paid off out of the proceeds the whole of her foreign debt and invested a part of the balance (about £42,000) in the Levant Company; largely out of the profits of the Levant Company there was formed the East India Company, the profits of which during the seventeenth and eighteenth centuries were the main foundation of England's foreign connections.[10]

Marx might have agreed with Keynes, since Drake's exploits were a prime example of primitive capitalist accumulation, the coercive process he believed so essential for the formation of the capitalist class.

Whether or not Keynes and Marx were correct in this, there is no denying that Drake used military force to fill his hold with treasure during his great feat of circumnavigation and in subsequent forays against the Spanish. We do not think of Drake's conduct in these matters as imperialistic. Depending on our individual standards, we may view it as theft – hijacking in contemporary practice – an act of war, or privateering. In contrast, we are inclined to view the role of the Spanish in acquiring gold and silver in the mines of South America as imperialistic. The reason for these different outlooks is important to bear in mind. In the one case, Drake was assaulting the ships and towns of what then was the most powerful state in Europe, often taking advantage of the main chance rather than acting systematically pursuant to instructions from a state or monarch of which he was the agent. Indeed Drake was an annoyance to some of Elizabeth's advisers who were more fearful of the Spanish threat than he was, and he himself was far from sure how the queen would receive him upon his return to England. In the other case, the Spanish systematically organized slaves to mine gold and silver in territories claimed by conquest and legitimized by papal bull, and then arranged for transporting the precious metal to Cadiz and Seville in convoys of galleons.[11] The critical difference between the two cases turns on the inequality mentioned at the conclusion of the previous chapter, the degree to which the interacting parties were differentially endowed with assets that could be used to achieve their several purposes. We shall not develop this point here. It will suffice to suggest that in the relationship between the Spaniards and the Peruvian Indians there was a marked asset imbalance in favor of the former that did not characterize the relationship between the Spaniards and the English. As we examine the historical encounter between England and India, however, we shall give institutional substance to the asset inequalities that define the imperialist condition.

We have noted that in the seventeenth century the ventures of the East India Company were secondary to the colonization of North America and the West Indies which formed the heart of the first British empire. But this is a relative matter and it is certainly true that the fortuitous intrusion of the American continents in the English understanding of the geographical nature of the globe did not diminish their interest in the Indies and Asia. In this respect England was no different from other European states which had a stake in the development of the Asian trade, and the East India Company was not the first systematic attempt to gain part of it. Keynes, in the quotation above, referred to the Levant Company, which was a joint-stock company founded in 1581 to trade with the eastern Mediterranean countries at the western terminuses of the Asian trade routes. Prior to the Levant Company, the Muscovy Company was formed in 1553 as a joint-stock venture of merchants to ply a route from Asia to England that went from the Caspian Sea through northern Russia to the White Sea and then around Scandinavia.[12] Popularly and appropriately known as the Muscovy Adventurers, their imagination ran ahead of their technical capability to master that formidable northern route, their place in economic history being preserved more by the innovation of the joint-stock venture than by the robustness of the rate of return.

The East India Company and its predecessors were a manifestation of the organizational ingenuity of English commerce in establishing a continuing exchange relationship with the Indies and wherever in Asia pepper and spices could be secured. Moreover, though far from being an industrial economy of the sort that took shape in the latter part of the eighteenth century, late Tudor England was already affected by those propensities so important in industrialization, the willingness to save and accumulate, the belief in empiricism, the interest in technological change, and the capacity to reorganize economic and social institutions. Where the Portuguese had concentrated their innovative capability in those activities which related to the discovery of the all-water route to the Indies,[13] the English capacity for innovation was more diffuse, affecting a wider range of occupations and engaging more varied economic interests.

The population of England in 1600 cannot be determined with great accuracy, the first census not being taken until 1801 and there being at that time no counterpart to the Domesday Book, that remarkable cadastral survey conducted by William the Conqueror which provided some clues to the size of the population at the end of the eleventh century. Then it may have been 1,500,000. By 1500 the population of England and Wales may have been as high as 3,000,000, by 1700 perhaps between 5,000,000 and 5,500,000.[14] At the end of Queen Elizabeth's reign, when the English were preparing to compete for trade in Asian waters, their population may have been three to three and a half times larger than the Portuguese.

The population was, of course, predominantly rural, with London as a commercial, administrative, and metropolitan center with as yet no competition from those great industrial cities that proliferated in the midlands and the north of England during the industrial revolution. In 1600, London may have had as many as 150,000 residents.[15] In the countryside, more heavily wooded then than it is now after centuries of enclosures, the feudal land tenures in the manorial system as interpreted by the common law were changing, with freeholds and copyhold tenures steadily replacing villeinage tenures which had imposed on tenants obligations for services and duties to landlords that increasingly seemed inconsistent with the Tudor understanding of English freedom. By the time of Charles I there were no bondmen in England and possessors of land under a copyhold had protection in law against lords who violated the holders' rights, or so thought Sir Edward Coke.[16] In any event, the idea of private property as a complex of rights which the barons of England had secured against the arbitrary demands of the monarch in Magna Carta in 1215 was being realized far beyond the holder of the privileges of the manor. The English yeoman was coming of age and was still another portent of the peculiarly strong sense in England of the private realm with its concomitant limitations on the power of the state. I have made these observations about private property because they stand in sharp contrast to the way in which land tenures were organized in India and will therefore become relevant when we come to examine the interaction of England and India.

Just as the population was rural, so was the economy. The most important industry was the manufacturing of cloth, especially woolen and worsteds, which was carried on throughout England in household industry, sometimes as a primary occupation and other times as by-employment when primary agricultural work permitted. In pre-Tudor days the output of wool above household-consumption requirements was exported to the Low Countries and Italy where the cloth-making industries had developed ahead of England. The spinning of yarn, which in all societies is one of the first raw-material processing activities to be performed as a regular part of the household economy, gradually was commercialized in England as cottagers began to learn the weaving skills of their continental peers and created a domestic market for yarn, a development that gained force in the sixteenth century when the religious persecutions of the Huguenots and the Flemings compelled them to flee with their weaving skills to a welcoming England. By the end of the Tudor age, the English cloth industry was consuming the entire domestic output of wool, the export of which in the best mercantilist tradition was prohibited.

Consistent with that tradition, England was eager to expand export markets for the woolen cloth and worsted industries. And here we can appropriately recall a problem confronted by the first expedition sent out by the East India Company, which was symbolic of a more general problem in the trade relationships between Europe and Asia. Those East Anglian woolen vests, no doubt of the very first quality, that were part of the expedition's outbound cargo did not sell well in Sumatra. Nor would there have been a market for them in India. England's most important export industry, then, did not produce the commodities which could be readily exchanged for the spices and silks of Asia. Pepper could be bought at Calicut with silver or gold but not with woolen cloth. If these commodities were representative of the trade pattern between England and India, the former would lose specie to the latter and violate the mercantilist injunction to maximize the domestic stock of specie. As we shall see, the drain of specie to India was a continuing problem which led the East India Company, less in the period with which we are concerned in this chapter than in the eighteenth and nineteenth centuries, to enter vigorously into the Asian carrying trade and so involve itself more extensively in imperialistic relationships.

In the sixteenth century the growth of the woolen industry in conjunction with the enlargement of the yeomanry and a secular rise in prices occasioned by the inflow of precious metals to Europe from the New World stimulated enclosures. This was not a time of great parliamentary enclosures such as occurred in the latter half of the eighteenth and the first half of the nineteenth centuries. The population–land ratio was still quite low and there were unoccupied fens, wastes, moors, and other land potentially arable or suitable for grazing stock for those ambitious enough or with enough capital to buy or reclaim them. Some of these may have been squatters, interested primarily in bolstering the land base of their subsistence. Others were yeomen and freeholders already producing wool or flax or wheat for a market and, in view of the enhanced profit expectations stimulated by rising prices, anxious to extend the scale of their enterprise. Among the enclosures may have been voluntary reorganizations of the scattered strips of land of the open-field system which were the cause of a good deal of uneconomic movement as well as waste of land in baulk to divide the strips among cultivators. Moreover, ambitious or innovative yeomen or lords undoubtedly found the customs governing the use of open-field strips frustrating and had an incentive to exchange them in order to acquire a large enough holding to make them independent of the communal decisions of the manor. Clapham noted that 'there was something of a campaign' for such reorganizations, but does not venture an estimate of how widespread the campaign or its effects.[17] We can conjecture that voluntary exchanges of land were limited, however, for otherwise the parliamentary enclosures in later centuries would not have been as important as they were to the development of agriculture and to the accelerated growth of the industrial sector.

Whether sanctioned by common law, effected voluntarily, or enforced by parliamentary statute, enclosures increased agricultural productivity without there being any direct change in agricultural techniques. It was not until the eighteenth century that there were significant changes in the kinds of crops planted, methods of planting, cultivation of crops, and so on. But in other sectors of the economy there was the seventeenth century evidence on all sides of pragmatic adaptation of new techniques, less in the production of new than in the use, processing, and transporting of old outputs. Coal exports from Newcastle, so renowned in epigram, increased from 33,000 tons in 1564 to 452,000 in 1634.[18] Throughout the century London received increasing deliveries of coal for local use and for re-export in river carriers. The coastal shipping fleet carrying coal expanded and the English adapted cargo vessels suitable for this purpose that had been developed by the Dutch. 'Single-decked . . . with no forecastle or round-house or guns, and with light simple rigging . . . four to six times as long as wide . . . less fitted for distant, dangerous voyages, [they] could be worked with a very small crew.'[19] First captured from the Dutch during hostilities in the middle of the century (1652–4), the English pressed them into the coastal coal trade, built imitations of their own, and purchased them from the Dutch in violation of the Navigation Acts, a testament to the difficulty of enforcing mercantilist prescriptions on an enthusiastically commercial people.

The growth of the coal industry had forward and backward linkage or inducement effects on demand and supply conditions. Coal was substituted for wood as a source of fuel in households and in firms by ironworkers, salt makers, glass blowers, and brick-makers, among others. Moreover, though the day of the use of coke had not yet arrived in the iron industry, it became apparent that with the demand of government in the roistering Tudor age for cannon and shot increasing, and the supply of charcoal threatened by receding forests, a mineral fuel for firing blast furnaces would be a boon to iron masters. The technical problems of producing coke were not solved in the seventeeth century, but they were on the agenda, as it were, because men in the industry were anticipating fuel shortages. Similarly, the increasing danger of flooding in the mines as they became deeper turned the attention of mechanics and engineers to ways of improving pumps and developing sources of power to activate them. The threat of increasing costs in the mining of coal dramatized the need for a source of power independent of streams and at the end of the seventeenth century there was patented by Thomas Savery (1698) a machine which converted steam into mechanical energy, a distant forebear of James Watt's steam engine.

While the England that was on the verge of entering the Asian world was intensely commercial and pragmatically concerned with the techniques that might break its production bottlenecks, it was not a wealthier society than the countries with which it would compete for the Asian trade. Neither was it clearly richer than India, though this is not a matter we can properly assess until we have had the opportunity to look more closely at India. England, indeed, was a subsistence economy, as were all economies in the world in the seventeeth century, though it no longer was devastated by the famines which had been part of its own history and continued to exact a Malthusian toll in most other countries.[20] Paradoxically, this exacerbated unemployment, vagabondage, and beggary in the sixteenth and seventeenth centuries which gave grave concern to the governing classes and may have accounted for the harsh outlook, the restricted ambience of their empathy in human relationships.[21] The property-owning classes, the landed aristocracy, the gentry, and yeomanry, did not always distinguish between the indigent, on the one hand, and criminals, on the other. And no doubt starving vagrants, for their part, did not readily absorb the normative values associated with the common-law protection of private property.

Tudor England consciously came to grips with these problems in a manner that was vigorously mercantilist. Not yet inhibited by the view that competitive markets were autonomous and self-regulating and that the hand of the state should be invisible in human affairs, it formulated policies that to nineteenth-century liberals appeared to be unreasonably paternalistic, controlling, and destructive of freedom. These authorized local authorities to deal with the problem and enacted tax rates in their support. In consequence they founded workhouses, maintenance houses, and houses of correction for dealing with the indigent who could not care for themselves and for training the unemployed for useful work. They thus had to distinguish between the 'deserving' and 'undeserving' poor, between those whose plight could not reasonably be imputed to improvidence or unwillingness to work and those who were incorrigible. The one, then, fell under the jurisdiction of the Poor Law, a bill passed by Parliament in 1601 which codified the earlier Tudor efforts to deal with unemployment and served as the legal foundation of relief for more than two centuries until amended by parliamentary action early in the nineteenth century. The others were subject to the tender mercies of the criminal law.

Neither the Poor Law nor the sanctions of criminal law could cause the unemployed and indigent to vanish. If the English economy was robust enough to keep them alive, its capital stock was not growing rapidly enough to provide all of them with job opportunities. In the seventeenth century when the English began to colonize North America, the colonies appeared to be a solution to the problem. Labor there was in short supply, while England suffered from a redundant population. The transatlantic imbalances in the demand for and supply of labor did not equilibrate autonomously, because the cost of ocean transportation was high and the capital and skills required to farm successfully in the wilderness were beyond the capability of the unemployed or, for that matter, the typical farm laborer, copyholder, or small yeoman. The labor supply to the colonies was augmented by the system of indenture in which workers in England signed, or put their thumb mark on, a contract which provided for their passage to the New World in return for a term of labor, usually from four to seven years, during which the employer or master supplied their subsistence and after which they received a modest stake for making their own way.[22]

Indentured labor fell somewhere between slave labor and wage labor with respect to the coercion that restricted a worker's freedom of choice. During the term of the indenture the worker was the chattel of the master. 'He could be alienated temporarily . . . so that his services might pay off a debt, or he could be taken by the sheriff for the satisfaction of his master's debts. He could be disposed of by will. . . . He might even be won or lost in a card game.'[23] Unlike a slave, however, an indentured servant, at least formally according to the laws of the North American colonies, could sue in court, could give evidence, and own property like a freeman. In principle, he had legal protection against the failure of a master to perform the conditions of the indenture contract. In fact, the system was readily abused by those not inclined to observe the formal rules. At the very outset when people in England were signed into indenture, the transaction was far from being 'bilaterally voluntary and informed'. Typically they were unemployed vagrants whose knowledge of the conditions of life in Virginia was not likely to be increased by the contracting agent who was primarily interested in delivering warm bodies to a ship captain bound for America. The latter received from the agent along with the indentured worker the relevant documents which had been duly registered in a magistrate's court in England. The captain then sold the worker in an organized market upon his arrival in Virginia. If it had not been for the compulsion of economic necessity, the grim prospect of living from hand to mouth in England, it is unlikely that a worker would have made a mark on a contract. Moreover, having arrived in America they were subject to the contemptuous and harsh treatment that is so often inflicted on individuals who are perceived as being inferior and helpless. So far as their legal rights as indentured servants were concerned, they were no more substantive than the willingness of the magistrates in Virginia to enforce them, a chancy prospect in view of the latter's identification with the plantation owners who were the primary purchasers of indentured servants.

While some observers in England charged that indentured servants headed for the colonies 'were all sadly deceived and imposed upon by false propaganda and lying agents', they were not put off by indenture itself.[24] Though bondmen in the sense of slaves had disappeared in England by the end of the Tudor age, indentures were standard. The Statute of Artificers, enacted by Parliament in 1563, regulated the ancient practices of the craft guilds in indenturing young workers as apprentices to masters. Not until the age of 24 did they become free to marry and to pursue their craft as journeymen. Trevelyan thought that 'on the whole, the relation of master and apprentice . . . served the purposes of society well. For centuries apprenticeship was the school of Englishmen.'[25] Clapham noted, however, that the Act showed 'that legislators still thought of all people who had no property as semi-servile'.[26] Both observations may be valid, but the point here is that as a subsistence society where so many people lived close to the margin of survival, England relied on explicit compulsion to allocate labor, even as have so many other subsistence societies otherwise quite different from England. England was not a stranger in its internal affairs to the uses of compulsion, which may be practiced in an imperial setting with less compunction so long as there is no effective means for those who bear its burden to act upon their grievances.

The England, then, that was about to expand across the oceans in the beginning of the seventeenth century was a vigorous commercial society with a strong agricultural base in which land-owning classes with the support of continually developing common law were establishing their independence of the state. The real test was still before them in the turbulence of Stuart governance and the Cromwellian interregnum later in the century. The sense of private right, however, and its implications for the limits of state power were firmly planted and growing in the English consciousness. To be sure, the idea of an autonomously functioning economic system built on private property and individual choice had not yet been conceived. The state embodied mercantilist beliefs and while its reach may have exceeded its grasp there were not many corners of the economy where its influence was not felt. Queen Elizabeth chartered companies and granted them monopoly trading privileges with Tudor gusto, if not with the same omnibus powers accorded to Portugal and Castile with papal blessing in 1479 in the Treaty of Alçacovas.[27] Yet the initiative for establishing trading companies, as with the East India Company, came from what we would call the private sector. Because individual interest was so firmly rooted in private property, individuals were not reluctant to importune the ministers of the Crown when it served their purposes, even while they were sensitive to the threat from a despotic state.

If the Tudor state was not despotic, it was not democratic. It had no commitment to the achieving and maintaining of the rights of man so forcefully expressed by Thomas Paine at the end of the eighteenth century and acted upon with such portentous consequences in the French Revolution. The state was, indeed, an exclusive association where the monarch, the royal family, the aristocracy, and the gentry engaged in formidable combat as they pursued their public and private interests. Out of these struggles parliamentary and ministerial government would emerge in due time with the Parliament acquiring power at the expense of the Crown and within the Parliament the House of Commons becoming a more critical focus for articulating the political interests of English society than the House of Lords. But the constitution at the time the ships of the East India Company first sailed into Asian waters was extremely narrow. The copyholders, freeholders, and yeomanry, not to mention the unemployed, vagrants, and vagabonds, did not vote for members of the Commons, though their collective voice, especially in London, might be heard in the crowds – mobs to the gentry – that always were part of the English political scene. The mariners in the first voyage who faced the uncertainties of the world east of the Cape of Good Hope and the certain and unspeakable horrors of scurvy did not leave behind them a life of privilege.

India at the time of the initial English connection

When we contemplate the small fleet of East India Company ships, the largest of which was only 600 tons, leaving England for the Indies in 1601, it seems very much as if the one was playing Lilliput to the other's Brobdingnag. India was as vast as England was small and it is appropriate to recall some of its geographical features. Northern Kashmir to Cape Comorin on the southern tip of India measures some 1900 miles and Calcutta in Bengal in the east to Karachi in present-day Pakistan in the west 1200 miles. This vast appendage of Asia, surrounded in the south by the Arabian Sea and the Bay of Bengal, had always been an object of plunder and frequently a terminus for predators and conquerors from the Asian steppes, Afghanistan, Persia, and the Middle East. The Himalayas on the northeastern frontier, of course, were impenetrable, at least with the transportation and communication technology available to these people. In the northwest, however, since time immemorial invaders entered India through the passes of the Hindu Kush mountains and over the plains of the Indus River. At the period with which we are concerned, the most recent invaders had established an imperial presence in northern India where the emperor Akbar held dominion. A descendant of Genghis Khan and Timur (Tamerlane), he was the third occupant of the Mughal imperial throne and had a position in India not dissimilar to that of Kublai Khan in China three centuries earlier. Both were imperialists, as understood by Schumpeter, but by virtue of their occupying societies very much more complex and civilized than the nomadic Mongolian societies to which they traced their origins, their predatory inclinations necessarily were tempered by the need to develop administrative skills.

The Mughals entered India through the geographical gate that had been open to so many previous invaders, but they were inhibited by the internal geography of India from extending their domination to the limits of its natural boundaries. While population could move readily down the Indus river system or the rivers of the Gangetic plain, the southern movement of population was inhibited by the Deccan, a plateau in the Indian peninsula, rising in the north from the Narmada River in the mountain range of the Vindhyas. Bound in the east by the Carnatic, a broad tropical plain bordering the Bay of Bengal, and in the west by a narrow tropical plain running along the Arabian Sea from the Gulf of Cambay north of Bombay to Cape Comorin, the Deccan plateau broke the continuity of Indian geography. It was not penetrated by navigable waters and acted as a physical barrier which helped trigger the monsoons that watered the tropical plains below. The Vindhyas, at its northern edge, separated north India from south India. While Indian geography pulled the center of governmental authority to the north where the dynamic intrusion of peoples from outside India as well as the productive capacity of the Indus and Gangetic plains constituted both the threat to Indian security and the strength to contain it, its internal influence rendered the extension of the control of one region over the other difficult.

These geographical characteristics of India were reinforced by its linguistic, cultural, religious, and social divisions. Many languages were brought to India by invaders. During the period we are concerned with, Persian was the official court language of the Mughal emperors just as French had been the official language of the Norman conquerors of England. Sanskrit was the repository and transmitter of the high culture of Hinduism and Arabic the language of learned Muslim Ulama as well as of those Muslim traders who had settled on the Malabar coast of India. In addition there were many vernaculars with distinct literatures, those in north India being of Aryan and those in the south of Dravidian origin. 'By the later nineteenth century some 179 separate languages and 544 dialects had been identified, . . . grouped into fifteen major literary languages belonging to five or six families, with differences in structure, vocabulary, alphabet and script.'[28] The speakers of Hindustani (Urdu and Hindi) and related tongues in the north could understand the Dravidian languages of Tamil, Telugu, Kannada, or Malayalam even less than the typical Englishman could understand Italian or Spanish.

Language diversity was both cause and effect of cultural diversity. The high cultural tradition referred to above was consciously learned and perpetuated by élitist groups, in Hindu societies the brahman scholars who interpreted the Vedas and the epics that followed them, the *Mahabharata* and the *Ramayana*. It was out of this culture that the belief in reincarnation and the migration of souls with its corollary emphasis on *karma*, the law of moral consequences, emerged. More important in the lives of most Indians were the cultural values of peasant communities where local traditions passed on orally among largely illiterate people established the local gods and the rituals for propitiating them, the ceremonies that marked the rites of passage through birth, marriage, and death, and the customs relating to the organization of social and economic life. The little cultures were as varied as the peasant communities from which they sprang. Cultural fragmentation, then, was both horizontal and vertical. While peasant life may have been infused at far remove by the values of the great cultural traditions, brahmanical communities were not immune to the force of local traditions. The brahmans were not an all-Indian homogeneous class.

Not the least important aspect of cultural fragmentation in India was the variety of religious experience. Two of the world's great religions – Hinduism and Buddhism – originated there and Islam had been imported by Arab traders and Asian imperialists. Though there are conflicting legends about the mission of the apostle St Thomas to India, Christianity was not an important force in Indian life.[29] The Portuguese, of course, were eager to spread the word and while Akbar was pleased to have Jesuit emissaries in his court – less for religious reasons, it should be said, than as competitors for the ulama with whom he was frequently at odds – they made little impression on peasant India.[30] Of lesser world significance, but none the less indicative of the Indian capacity for religious innovation, were Jainism, a variant of Hinduism founded in the sixth century BC and Sikhism, a sixteenth-century outgrowth of an attempt to reconcile Hinduism and Islam. The latter, of course, made communal conflicts and rivalries more intense in Indian life. They are different. Hinduism is:

> Infinitely complicated, luxuriant in its form and ideas and abounding in symbols. The Creator and his creations are one and indivisible; . . . there is no limit to the possible manifestations of the all-pervading spirit, and a new God may therefore turn up at any time or place. The individual matters little, for he, after all, is but one link in an endless chain beginning and ending in a somewhat nebulous merging with the all-pervading spirit. As for equality, it is a concept necessarily foreign to Hinduism, with its highly stratified society. It is important to emphasize the fundamental difference between the psychological foundations of the two religions – Islam, clear cut, individualistic, democratic, simple – Hinduism, abstruse, caring little for the individual, essentially undemocratic and extremely complicated.[31]

More than these metaphysical and philosophical differences were involved in the antagonism between the two religions. Hinduism was and is inextricably bound up with the social life of India, about which we shall have more to say in a moment. It is difficult to know where the one ended and the other began. There was no founding figure who subsequently became canonized and the object of adulation and worship. There was no Christ, Buddha, or Mohammed, no date in history that marked the salvation of mankind. Hinduism thus did not depend upon a well-established church, led by a hierarchy of militant priests. Since it accepted many concepts of God, it tended to be tolerant of other religions and indeed had a remarkable capacity to absorb them. Islam, however, was not one of the absorbed. Militant, aggressive, single-minded in its commitment to Allah, it spread in all directions from the Arabian peninsula, in part because true believers were inspired to convert the infidel and in part because the infidel found the simplicity and directness of the faith attractive. In India, inferior castes often were struck by the contrast between Hindu passive acceptance of the rich variety of statuses in Indian society and the Muslim insistence that all men were the same before Allah. Yet the appeal of Islam appeared to be greatest in the northwest and northeast of India where the caste system was least powerful.

The caste system developed along with Hinduism in the interaction of the Aryan invaders with various people already inhabiting the subcontinent. In classical Hindu legal and social theory society was divided into four great *varna* or classes: brahmans, the priests and scholars; kshatriyas, the rulers and warriors; vaishyas, merchants and agriculturists; and sudras, the menials. The higher three *varna* were twice-born, having undergone a second or intellectual birth upon being invested with the sacred thread. The sudra was only once-born. Those not in one of the four *varna* were the untouchables whom, in the twentieth century, Gandhi called *Harijans*, or sons of God, in his crusade to draw them into Indian society.

It was the rules governing the conduct of the members in each *varna* that made it a caste system with strong bounds and explicit canons of behavior.

> Foremost among such rules are those that safeguard the levels of caste group purity. Its pollution results from contact either with lower caste groups or with objects that are themselves impure.

> Contact with the former is avoided by restrictions on intermarriage and sexual relations with caste groups of less purity, sometimes on personal touch and approach, and on commensal relations, such as eating, smoking, and drinking. Impure materials include things having to do with the dead and with bodily emissions.[32]

Within each caste, councils of elders from highly respected lineages determined how purification should be attained in the event of a member of the caste becoming polluted, their authority carrying with it the power of excommunication.

The caste system with its rigid institutionalization of inequality, buttressed by the belief in the transmigration of souls, which presumably provided the solace of a preferred future incarnation to those of inferior status, was an emanation of the brahman caste, a manifestation of the great cultural tradition of India. In fact, as a social structure India was very much more complex and more heavily influenced by the local cultural traditions that shaped the values of peasant communities. While the four-*varna* hierarchy pervaded all of India, the variations within each, especially in the lower three whose members were likely to be more responsive to local traditions than to the great cultural brahmanic tradition, were great. There were hundreds of subcastes whose rituals and behavioral rules varied from region to region and by linguistic area so that a subcaste formally part of the Vaishya caste in Mysore, for example, might be quite different from a comparable Vaishya subcaste in Bengal. The multiplicity of subcastes thus made the social structure more flexible than the all-India brahmanic ordering would suggest because it permitted the formation of new subcastes when economic or other circumstances disrupted the older order.

Whatever caused the fragmentation of Indian society so palpable in the caste system, religious experience, and linguistic diversity, it seems to have been instrumental in easing its adaptations to the shocks of external invasions. There were many identities in India that gave meaning to life. One's village, subcaste, religion, or language group was more important than a civil relationship to a government far removed from daily routine and likely to be known only as a rapacious tax collector. In the seventeenth century, India as a reified civil presence in the life of the people living in the subcontinent barely existed. While the crew of the fleet that sailed for the Indies from London in 1601 thought of themselves as Englishmen even if only secondarily to their identity as Cornishmen or Devonians, Calicut fishermen at most had only a religious sense of India.

Village life thus endured no matter what happened in India at the 'national' level. The Mughal emperors could come and go, regional princes could struggle amongst themselves in the eternal search for power and security, but the peasant worshipped his gods and lived according to the rules of his caste. It has been argued by modern social scientists that for these reasons India was not susceptible to revolution; it was too absorbed in its own parochialism to be responsive to ideologies calling for the overthrow of oppressive institutions. The pluralism of Hinduism nurtured a tolerance, oddly enough, that defused the temper of the revolutionary and counter-revolutionary alike: 'the caste system made heresy hunting unnecessary. A rebel sect or group in the course of time became a caste.'[33] Whether or not this speculation is valid, it does not bear directly on seventeenth-century India which antedates the revolutionary age with its ideological appeals to individual or class rights and its espousal of utopian solutions to the oppressions of mankind. Tangentially, however, it suggests some interesting and difficult questions for an analysis of imperialism that is focused on its coercive consequences rather than its causes.

The caste system not only is a social system, but an economic system which organizes communities for coping with subsistence and the scarcity of resources. It enjoins a specialization of function and provides the institutional sanctions for supporting the hierarchical relationships it entails. Economic roles are as clear as social status. In the extreme example, untouchables perform dirty jobs such as cleaning latrines. 'Many collect the corpses of dead animals, skin these corpses, eat the carrion, and cure the hides.'[34] Among the castes, the higher the social status, generally speaking, the better the occupation and the material perquisites associated with it, though brahmans often had modest income and political power incommensurate with their social status. As suggested in the first chapter, this sytem is likely to be more effective the more agrarian the economy and the more it relies on the repetition of historically sanctioned behavior. Under these circumstances, the people in inferior positions, in inferior castes, are more likely to have been socialized to an acceptance of their status. Or, to put it another way, they will not have before them much evidence that there are alternative ways of managing their lives. The coercion, then, that is manifest in the organization of castes and occupations may be borne by those who feel its incidence most severely with resignation or equanimity, if not with enthusiasm.

It is difficult enough to know how anyone outside oneself reacts to the restrictions of the present-day world, let alone knowing how a peasant in Bengal in the seventeenth century reacted to the proscriptions and prescriptions of the caste system. So let us suppose, in the sense of Max Weber, that the caste system then was ideal.[35] Individuals accepted their role in the social ordering by internalizing the behavioral norms required of them. If, as untouchables entering streets used by caste Hindus, they 'had to carry brooms to brush away their footprints in the dirt behind them', they acknowledged the inferiority of their status that this implied.[36] Caste Hindus for their part believed that the treatment of untouchables was justified because they were polluted or lacked refinement. Given this kind of decentralized social organization with its attendant economic specialization of function, what difference did it make to the people inside the system if at some remote capital, or seat of 'national' government, a foreign ruler occupied the throne which he had won by force of arms? Did the imperialist emperor in Delhi change the circumstances of the cultivating peasant in Bengal?

These questions are not wholly rhetorical because they ask in what ways and how deeply coercive imperialist relationships penetrate society. If the caste system was a stabilizing force in India, it was because it insulated local communities from destabilizing forces. By the same token, it may have blunted the coercive impact of imperialism. The new emperor, of course, might attempt to take a larger share of the peasants' crops in order to support his armies and administration. On the other hand, he might believe that he could increase the revenue yield by reducing the tax rate and providing peasants with an incentive to increase output. In any event, the taxes and other commands of the emperor would be mediated by the headmen in the local community who were its contact with the outside world. Any changes in the proportion of the crops demanded by the emperor may have been seen by the cultivating peasants as the demands of the local social organization whose norms, we have assumed, had been fully internalized.

We are not arguing that imperialism made no difference to the people being imperialized. Rather we are suggesting that it is necessary to ask who was being imperialized and how they experienced it. It was one thing to be in the path of Genghis Khan's conquering armies who by all accounts laid waste the land and put the conquered peoples to the sword. It was quite another to be part of the realm of his Mughal descendants in India who came to govern rather than to destroy. It is true that the Mughal emperors fought their way to dominance in India and there surely were peasant lands and lives that were lost in the battles. It seems improbable, however, that in the absence of the Mughal invasion, India would have lived in Elysian peace. The evidence suggests rather that there were already in India enough ambitious and contentious princes to satisfy the gods of war in the absence of external invaders.

If we put aside the destruction and killing that is the essence of war, if we assume that the Mughal emperor governed without resort to the use of instruments of violence, how then could imperialism have been experienced? The implication of the ideal caste model is that peasants did not know who the emperor at Delhi was and did not relate their lives to the consequences of his commands. Life was hard, but the social system was contrived in such a way as to make them acquiescent. This leaves open the question of how the intermediaries – headmen, tax farmers, provincial governors, princes, and so on – who formed the chain of governance between the peasant and the emperor viewed the system. Was there some level in this hierarchy where the performance of official duties made the incumbents of the office feel they were oppressive and unjust because they emanated from a foreign presence? If one were high enough in the hierarchy to be close to the emperor, one could be coopted by the politics of imperial power and survival. In Mughal India, although the succession to the throne was fairly stable, occasionally it was Byzantine and sanguinary, not least of all when numerous sons were anxious to succeed to their father. An ambitious son who contemplated the rivalry of his equally ambitious siblings did well to establish a solid base in the realm, which meant seeking the support of princes who could deliver men and resources. But where in the descent down the chain of governance did the style and consequences of imperial rule begin to seem inapposite, wrong, and at odds with a preferred alternative for performing the duties of the state?

This question gets at a puzzling problem of imperialism which was implicit in our asking above 'who was being imperialized?' If you do not believe that you are held in thralldom to a foreign governor, are you being imperialized, if an observer from outside the system determines by objective criteria that the relationship is imperialistic? Preferences, values, norms, one's view of one's place in the social ordering are as relevant to imperialism as demand is to supply in the determination of market prices. The imperialized must see themselves as a group with characteristics that make their governors foreign and not normatively endowed with the perquisites of their office. It is in the differences between 'us and them' that the injustice of imperial rule inheres. The imperialized must have an idea, however tenuous and ill-formed, of an alternative way for doing whatever the foreign oppressor does. It may be nothing more than 'let us be ruled by our own', but without a consciousness of the illegitimacy of a foreign presence, the oppressions that a people experience cannot be distinguished from those that are intrinsic to subsistence and the scarcity of resources. Otherwise put, one must have an identity which transcends the local circumstances of one's daily life so that one can feel outraged by events like Amritsar with which one has neither sensory nor familial connection.

How a wider world enters into the consciousness of individuals is no easy matter to determine. On the one hand, people may see the world of 'them' as workers, slaves, prisoners, or travelers and observe at first hand aspects of the society which differentiate it from their own. It was the report of European travelers in Asia that first made Europeans aware of the differences in the life styles of Asian people and whetted their appetites for the exotic goods that flourished there, as they believed, in such abundance. Marco Polo's account of his twenty-five-year odyssey through Asia gained wide currency in Europe. *The Description of the World* was written at the end of the thirteenth century while he was in a Genoese prison. The first printed edition appeared in Germany at Nuremberg in 1477, but there are known to have been at least 119 written manuscripts in different European languages previously available for the curious and educated reader.[37] When Christopher Columbus sailed for the New World on his first voyage he carried with him a Latin edition of the book.[38] There was no Indian, or for that matter Asian, counterpart of Marco Polo who disappeared into the European peninsula of the Eurasian continent for a third of a lifetime and returned to write about the strange customs and institutions of the natives he encountered. Asians began to learn about Europeans as the travelers to Asia were followed by traders, explorers, soldiers, and missionaries, a learning procedure which is slow, intermittent, and likely to be confined to nodal areas, namely towns, where the intruders from the west congregated. In India in the seventeenth century, the succession of European emissaries was hardly under way and the 'them' that was governing while speaking a different language from the peasants, who often viewed them as conquerors, none the less had more in common with the peasants than the westerners.

On the other hand, individuals may acquire a heightened sense of their uniqueness by consciously learning a history that explained their common origins in the past and projected a collective personality – English, Indian, German, Japanese – setting them apart from others. But this required a guild of historians and writers of history, a literate and reading public, an appropriate past, and an ideological interest in articulating it. In the seventeenth century, except for a small élite, people were illiterate and history was a small craft concerned, where it existed, with chronicling the fortunes of kings. The world had not yet entered into the ideological age which sharpened the sense of nation and class as foci of the welfare of societies as distinct from the advantage of monarch and princes. To the extent that these forces were stirring at all, they were shaping an English in advance of an Indian consciousness. The adventuring spirit that brought the English to India, where Englishmen, far removed from home and ill-informed about the sort of place India was, struggled to survive with little time for those heady concerns that figured prominently in the thinking of nineteenth-century British proconsuls, was the stuff from which the myths and legends of national character were made. At the time the English first encountered India, their perception of 'us and them' was based in an abstract national identity more than a like perception of Indians. By the same token, we may conjecture that the English would have been more aware of the threat of being imperialized than the Indians, though they themselves became the peerless imperialists of the nineteenth century.

The empire the Mughals ruled comprised north India and parts of present-day Afghanistan, Bangladesh, and Pakistan. It extended south to the Deccan where it was bounded very loosely by a frontier stretching from a point between Daman and Bombay on the west to Cuttack in the east at the effluence of the Mahanadi river into the Bay of Bengal. The Mughal emperors had never established permanent suzerainty over the Muslim sultanates and Hindu princes of the Deccan and south India, though not for lack of trying. Akbar, in the tradition, if not the style, of his distant Mongol forebears, believed that 'a monarch should be ever intent on conquest; otherwise his neighbours rise in arms against him. The army should be exercised in warfare, lest from want of training they become self-indulgent.'[39] From the end of the sixteenth century he and his successors exercised these martial proclivities persistently in the Deccan, but whatever temporary successes they achieved in the short run were undermined in the long run by the continued resistance of local princes.

Inside the Mughal empire a system of governance was devised which responded to the limited administrative resources characteristic of any society in a pre-modern era and to the special problems of ruling an alien society. The functions of the Mughal state were overwhelmingly dominated by the need of the emperor to maintain an army for the conduct of its incessant wars, its output of public goods – welfare systems, education, transportation, and public utilities – which loom so large in modern states being non-existent or minuscule. The recruitment of the army was made an integral part of the *mansabdari* system, a hierarchical order in which the emperor appointed officers, *mansabdars*, whose status and pay depended on the number of troops they recruited and commanded in the service of the emperor. *Mansabdars* providing 1000 troops or more constituted the Mughal nobility.[40]

In conferring *mansabs* the emperor created a foreign nobility and also recognized the status of the magnates and princes in the territories he had conquered. The *mansabdari* system, in other words, was used by the emperor to bring in men from outside India, Afghans or Iranians, for example, whom he had reason to trust, and to purchase the loyalty of local leaders who, he had reason to believe, would otherwise be potential sources of opposition. The nobility therefore was not wholly Muslim, approximately 22 per cent of them being Hindu, largely Rajputs and Marathas, from Akbar's to Aurangzeb's reign.[41] Subsequently in his Deccan campaigns, Aurangzeb increased the number of Marathas to whom he awarded *mansabs* in a vain effort to extend imperial governance into the Deccan.

The economic foundations of the *mansabdari* system were designed to forestall opposition to the emperor. Where in England the strength of the nobility inhered in their ownership of land and the constitutional protection they gradually acquired against encroachments and seizures by the Crown, in Mughal India the nobility depended on the state for the emoluments associated with the *mansabdari* rank. They were paid in cash or granted a *jagir*, a form of tax farming. The *jagirdars* collected the land revenue and other taxes in their *jagir* and transmitted a stipulated amount to the emperor, retaining the balance for meeting the costs of collection and providing the income due their status.

However much we may complain today about taxation and the complexity of income tax returns, it is unlikely in the extreme that they have the kind of coercive force that characterized the collection of the land revenue by *jagirdars* in Mughal India. Abu-l Fazl, the chronicler of the reign of Akbar, asserted that 'no moral limits could be set to the fiscal obligations owed by the subject to the rulers: the subject ought to be thankful even if he was made to part with all his possessions by the protector of his life and honour.'[42] The proportion of the peasants' crops taxed varied from regime to regime, perhaps from a lower limit of one-third of gross yield to an upper limit of two-thirds. Aurangzeb taxed 'everything in excess of the minimum needed for the peasant's subsistence'.[43] The *jagirdari* system seems to have been designed to get the most out of the peasant. In the first place, by leaving the tax farmer the residue of the funds or crops after deducting the ruler's share, he was tempted to increase the gross tax on peasants. In the second place, *mansabdars* in possession of a *jagir*, especially if it were a large area, multiplied the intermediaries between themselves and the cultivating peasants by dividing up the *jagir* among their troops, working through *zamindars*, an indigenous class of landlords in Bengal, or by selling the tax-farming privilege in a market. The more intermediaries, each with an incentive to maximize the gross tax yield, the greater was the final burden of taxation on the peasants.

In the third place, and this relates to the paranoia of emperors who were insecure in their tenure, *jagirs* were constantly reassigned so that a *mansabdar* could not expect to remain in a given district for more than three or four years.[44] Just as in feudal Japan during the long years of the Tokugawa seclusion the ruling shogun had devised a system that removed the samurai from the countryside and their fortified castles, so the Mughal emperors tried to prevent the development of an aristocratic opposition based in the occupation of land and alliances with local magnates.[45] But the impermanency of the *jagir* held by the *mansabdar* increased his short-run interest in taking as large a surplus as possible and reduced his long-run interest in increasing the size of gross output.

If the land-revenue system imposed a heavy burden on the peasant, it also restricted the autonomy of the *mansabdar*. Not only could he be shifted from *jagir* to *jagir*, but within each one he had to work with the agents of the emperor in assessing and collecting the land revenue. In other words, the decentralized system of tax farming was overseen by an imperial bureaucracy whose agents, in theory, saw to it that the emperor's mandate was carried out.[46] In fact, the system was loosely administered from bottom to top and at any point in the hierarchy it was common practice for subordinates to give superiors gifts,

> the chief method by which a subject could secure the aid and assistance of the administration, either for his own protection or for the destruction of others, both in accordance with, and in direct opposition to, all the regulations of the state and imperial orders.[47]

Mughal administration, then, was not a Weberian bureaucracy where the rules governing programs and the conduct of bureaucrats were clearly articulated and backed by the force of law. Gifts, tribute, squeeze as it was called in China, or bribes were accepted as the price of cooperation. If one received tribute, one also gave it and it appears to have been a system that was related less to the efficient performance of public functions than to the establishment of precarious and evanescent personal relationships for the achievement of private ends. The demeaning gift, one supposes, could evoke the rage of unrequited love.

Moreover, if the *mansabdar* administered his *jagir* efficiently, was fully alert to the etiquette of the tribute system so that he was able to make the most of it, and thus accumulated wealth, he had no assurance that it belonged to him or that he could will it to the survivors of his choice. 'The *jagirdar* as an individual member of the governing class had no rights or privileges apart from those received from the Emperor.'[48] The emperor could, in principle, confiscate the wealth of his nobles during their lives and received it at death as a matter of right. The privilege did not seem to be exercised ruthlessly for the obvious reason that the emperor needed to retain the loyalty of the noblemen. The state had first claim on a nobleman's wealth, even as the state in modern societies has first claim on the assets of the estate of a deceased. The difference, however, was that the emperor had the right to allocate the balance of the wealth left over after the state had taken its share, the right, no doubt, being exercised judiciously or not depending on the temper of the emperor and his advisers and the peculiar circumstances of the surviving family. What needs to be emphasized is that no rule of law restrained the emperor in these matters; the shariat, Muslim law, did not prevail over the wishes of the emperor.[49]

The autonomy of the aristocracy, then, was sharply restricted by the absence of legal protection of person and property. Indeed, the status of the latter was somewhat obscure and since this bears on the performance of the economy and subsequently became a matter of great concern to the British we need to say something more about it. The problem, which so disturbed the British in the nineteenth century, was that there was no clearly identifiable land-owning class, with proprietary rights confirmed in legal title. The Mughal aristocracy, the *mansabdars*, could not hold their wealth in land because the emperor viewed it as a threat to the security of the throne. The *zamindars* were landlords without a proprietary right to alienate the land from which they collected revenues. Their overlord relationship was with the village rather than the land and in this there seemed to be a hereditary and alienable right. The *zamindari* privilege passed from father to son and there developed a market in which it could be bought and sold.[50]

If the *mansabdars* and the *zamindars* did not own the land, neither did the peasants, at least in the English legal sense. Rather than having a right to the land, they had an obligation to it that was hereditary. They and their descendants were obliged to cultivate the land which they retained so long as they were capable of doing so. If a peasant became permanently disabled or had no children to carry on in his stead, 'the land could be assigned to another, the state having an interest in maintaining the tax base.'[51] Nor could peasants leave the land or refuse to cultivate it, in which case the agents of the emperor would, if possible, seek them out and in the words of an instruction to revenue officials 'coerce and threaten them and visit them with imprisonment and corporal punishment'.[52]

The early European travelers in Mughal India observed that these different classes did not own land and concluded that it belonged to the emperor. François Bernier, who visited India during the early years of Aurangzeb's reign when Mughal power had not yet begun to decline, predicted the demise of the system because the emperor's right in this regard precluded its being founded on clearly delineated rights in private property, a good case of being right for the wrong reasons.[53] These observers no doubt were bemused by the legal and economic categories and norms of their own societies. 'There is no suggestion anywhere that land revenue was in the nature of rent that the peasant had to pay for making use of royal property.'[54] The emperor did not own the land over which he ruled.

Apparently, then, legal entitlements, with their attendant rights and obligations in the use of land, did not exist. How it was occupied and cultivated depended on the customs and traditions of the village which varied with caste, clan, and community. So long as the village met its revenue demand, the emperor, the *mansabdar* in his *jagir*, or the *zamindars* did not care how the peasants organized to meet the obligation. Their contact with the village was through a headman, a role which inhered in the social organization of the village. The headman allocated the tax burden, along with other collective demands, on individuals, family, or caste who paid their share into a 'common financial pool from which the land-revenue, the demands of officials, the repayment of any loan contracted, and expenses for the economic, social, and even spiritual benefit of the village was met.'[55]

Whatever the proportion of the gross output of the villages the emperor was able to secure in the land revenue and other taxes, the taxable capacity of the system hinged on the amount of land controlled and its productivity. The struggle of the Mughal emperors to expand their realm, then, was not simply a consequence of the state being dominated by a warrior class, but of the persistent need for more land to augment the land revenue. Of course, the one went with the other; warriors were no cheaper in Mughal India than they are in the Pentagon. But, 'given high transport–communication costs, the burden of getting and holding territories beyond the core quickly exceeded the revenues derived. Viewed in this way, the warfare and continual political instability were inherent in the system.'[56]

The productivity of the Indian economy during the Mughal era has evoked much heated discussion, in part because there is not much quantitative data on which to base firm judgments. Without measurements of gross national product or the structural characteristics of the economy, one relies on fragmentary evidence or makes inferences from some characteristics of traditional Indian society, the lack of political unity and stability or the rudimentary technology in agriculture and handicrafts. Thus a western economic historian has said of the economy the British acquired in India in the eighteenth century, 'every index of performance suggests the level of technical, economic, and administrative performance of Europe five hundred years earlier.'[57] On the other hand, an Indian economic historian has argued that one cannot speak of an Indian economy during the Mughal era, but rather must assess economic regions, asserting his view that 'highly commercialized coastal regions with their hinterlands, – Gujarat and the west coast, Malabar, Coromandel, the Bengal–Bihar region, – had no less potentialities for growth before 1800 than Japan in the pre-Meiji era.'[58]

Whether one examines the economy of the subcontinent, the Mughal economy, or the regional economy of Gujarat, it is difficult to find in the seventeenth century indicators of economic change as vigorous as those we observed in England. There one could discern the early signs of technological change and economic reorganizations that cumulatively led to the industrial revolution of the later eighteenth century. In agriculture, manufacturing, and trade, there were entrepreneurs of widely varied social backgrounds experimenting with new ways of organizing resources, failing perhaps more than succeeding, but none the less trying. Commercial values had so far permeated England that it would take great pride in being a 'nation of shopkeepers'.[59] In Mughal India the ruling classes had highly developed martial tastes with a concomitant disdain for economic and commercial pursuits. The middle classes were attenuated and submissive without a strong base in property protected in law from the encroachments of the state. The merchants in Surat were no more secure from the arbitrary demands of the emperor or his governor in Gujarat than were the merchants in Ōsaka from the Japanese shogun.[60] There was no tradition of an 'improving' aristocracy with an abiding concern for finding ways of increasing the productivity of the land. The Mughal economy in the seventeenth century may not have been performing at the level of the European economy of 500 years earlier – a judgment that is more rhetorical than substantive – but, as far as one can tell, it was not suffused with signs of a coming economic transformation.

As with most subsistence economics, the Mughal economy was sharply differentiated between the agrarian sector and mercantile centers, the former overwhelmingly greater than the latter. Almost all people in the Mughal empire and in south India lived on the land and were market-oriented only to the extent that they had to monetize part of their output to pay the land revenue. The household economy was self-contained, the food grains produced largely consumed at home. Because the productivity of the agrarian sector was low, these were not sufficiently abundant for building stocks and thus the economy was fragile and susceptible to shocks – a failure in the monsoon, for example – that periodically savaged the society. Throughout the Mughal era regional famines were endemic and exacerbated by poor transportation, which prevented a more salutary matching of the demand for and supply of subsistence goods.[61] Nothing could have been so unrelenting as these Malthusian holocausts. Families did not survive. The weakest members died and parents sold their children or themselves into slavery to avoid starvation.[62]

In contrast to the precarious agrarian economy, the mercantile centers which linked India to the outside world were no less organized or sophisticated than trading communities elsewhere in the Eurasian world. In Surat, the primary port of the Mughal empire in the seventeenth century, banking institutions, money markets, and bills of exchange facilitated commerce and trade. Surat and other mercantile centers in coastal India were as immersed in the market economy as agrarian India was outside it.[63] Of Indian goods passing through Surat none was more important than cotton textiles. They were the counterpart of woolen and worsted manufactures in England and, according to Moreland, their 'aggregate production was one of the great facts of the industrial world in the year 1600.'[64] From Surat buyers purchased the output of household looms in the hinterland of Gujarat and exported it to East Africa, the Middle East, and Malacca and southeast Asia in Indian-built ships. While there were other exports from Surat, opium and pilgrimages to Mecca, for example, these were dwarfed by cotton textiles.

Imports moved through the markets of Surat to the Mughal court and aristocracy. The rulers of north India dazzled visitors with the pageantry of their entourage and the visible and generous use of the precious metals in their clothing, jewelry, and quarters which in a mercantilist age was a sure way of exciting the interests of Europeans. The merchants of Surat ministered to these tastes by importing ivory, coral, amber, silks, velvets, brocades, spices, perfumes, drugs, European wines, horses, African slaves, and, of course, gold and silver. The importation of precious metals was a consequence of the small market in Mughal India for foreign goods relative to the foreign market for Indian goods. The export balance of trade, however, was attributable less to the dynamic development of new markets for Indian output than it was to the limits inherent in the conspicuous consumption of a warrior ruling class in foreign goods.

The mercantile sector thus did not appear to be a growth point in the Mughal economy with links to other potential growth sectors. The Asian trade was ancient: 'the general course of trade had remained substantially unchanged for at any rate more than a thousand years. Gibbon's mordant aphorism that "the objects of oriental traffic were splendid and trifling" is in substance as applicable to the sixteenth as to the second century of our era.'[65]

The sophistication of the mercantile community in Surat was based in the servicing of a well-established Asian trade the linkage effects of which with the Mughal economy were limited by the peculiar nature of Indian market tastes. Rather than being used productively, the export surplus went into hoards or conspicuous display. The Mughal ruling class neither stimulated productivity increases directly through state policy nor indirectly through their use of scarce resources.

In stressing those features of Mughal India in the seventeenth century that may explain the failure in later centuries of the Indian economy to grow as rapidly as the English or other European economies, we do not wish to suggest that at the start of the English–Indian connection India was a disabled giant whose feet of clay could be easily shattered. On the contrary, the Mughal empire was at the height of its power, one of those awe-inspiring states in the history of the world that easily bore the imperial reputation. The system of governance worked. The aristocracy in north India remained loyal to the emperor and exacted a large enough surplus from the peasants in the land revenue to defray the costs of Mughal wars and administration without yet having evoked the flight from the land and armed agrarian resistance that in the end proved so destructive of Mughal rule.[66] Its splendor was appropriately reflected in the Taj Mahal, that extraordinary mausoleum which the emperor Shah Jahan, grandson of Akbar, had built in the years from 1630 to 1648 to commemorate the death of a beloved wife. While we may view it as an example of conspicuous public display that diverted resources from more productive uses, the beholder in 1650, like the tourist in 1950, could not help but brood about the power of a society which could construct magnificence on such a scale.

England and India in the early seventeenth century

It was not until the third expedition sent out by the East India Company that an English ship arrived in India. In August 1608 William Hawkins landed at Surat in the Bay of Cambay. He carried with him a letter in which James I asked the Mughal emperor –

Jahangir had recently come to the throne following the death of Akbar – to grant the Company the privilege of trading in India. That the Company had come to India was a reflection of its weakness in the East Indies, a known source of those spices that were the primary lure for Europeans in Asia. The Dutch exploited the defeat of the Spanish Armada in 1588 and the diminished threat of Spanish sea power to the Cape route to the Indies sooner than the English. Four years before the English, the Dutch, in 1597, organized an expedition to the Indies. Soon they had built a fortified factory at Batavia (Djakarta) from which they could not be dislodged by the British and which became the headquarters of the Dutch imperial system in the Indonesian archipelago. More generously financed than the English, they sent out larger fleets whose ships and crews were superior to those of the Portuguese they dislodged from the European carrying trade.[67]

Though the Portuguese lost out to the Dutch in the East Indies, they were still the paramount European power on the west coast of India when William Hawkins arrived at Surat. With a century-old base at Goa and smaller fortified positions at Díu and Daman on the west and east coastal entrances to the Bay of Cambay, they were strategically located for enforcing monopolistic mercantile objectives. The English had to figure out not only how to establish trading credentials with the Mughal state, but how to contend with the Portuguese who they could be sure would use all their powers of persuasion to poison the minds of Indian authorities against them. That Hawkins entered the Bay of Cambay rather than trying to establish an English presence in Calicut, for example, farther to the south and outside the jurisdiction of the Mughal state, presumably reflected his preference for coping with the unknown problems of seeking trade agreements from the Mughal emperor to the known problems of facing Portuguese naval power off the Calicut coast. European conflicts and power struggles followed the trading companies into Asian waters. England was still at odds with Spain which had entered into a union with Portugal (1580–1640). Portugal therefore was the enemy and remained so until English naval strength asserted itself along the west coast of India and moved the Portuguese to recognize English trading centers in India in a convention signed at Goa in 1635.

However hostile they were to the English, the Portuguese none the less accepted many of the same standards of international conduct. If war was a legitimate means of seeking their ends, so too was negotiation to discover and formalize the mutual interest of sovereigns or their representatives. This understanding did not constrain the behavior of the Mughal emperor. Like the emperor of China, he viewed peoples or states in the external world less as entities with sovereign powers than as potential subjects who ought to pay tribute to him. This required deferential behavior, in extreme cases kowtowing, and gifts from the tributary beyond what was customary in the relationships of the states of Europe. The representatives of the East India Company were thus confronted with a system whose standards they neither understood nor appreciated. Far from being imperialists who could control and coerce the Indians who did not respond to their needs, they were extraordinarily weak. On land away from their ships, they were not much better off than Antaeus when Heracles lifted him off the earth. And Hawkins had arrived, not with a fleet, but in one ship.

The first emissary of the East India Company was indeed harassed in Surat both by the Portuguese and by the Emperor Jahangir's governor or viceroy. Hawkins wrote that 'I could not peep out of the doors for fear of the Portugals, who in troops lay lurking in the by-ways to give me assault to murther me.'[68] And the governor frustrated his attempts to trade by appropriating a large part of his cargo as a gift. When he journeyed to Agra in order to present his credentials to Jahangir, he did not fare much better, though he was taken into the emperor's service and acquired a wife.[69] He came away from Agra without an agreement and the English therefore did not have a legal document conferring the trading privilege on the Company, which to them made their position insecure. Since they lacked the power to impose on Indian society the political and legal order that would facilitate trade, they had no choice but to function within the constraints of the undeniable powerful state that was their host.

While the court in Agra had little interest in trade with the East

India Company and initially looked upon its representatives with some condescension as potential sources of novel and diverting tribute, it began to take the Company more seriously when in 1612 two of its ships defeated a fleet of four Portuguese galleons in an encounter off the west coast of India. Mughal power ended at the coast and with the arrival in Asian waters of superior European maritime and naval forces the state was not able to ensure the security of those Indian Muslins whose journey to Mecca took them across the Arabian Sea to the Gulf of Aden. Less interested in saving souls for Christianity than the Portuguese, the English now in addition seemed to be potentially better protectors of the pilgrimage boats. Jahangir thus granted the Company the right to trade in anticipation of its being able to perform a service beyond his power, but he made no other concessions. It could trade, but had not been granted a right to lease or construct factories in Surat or Agra.

There is little evidence that in these early years the English at Surat were welcomed by local residents angered by the arbitrary and erratic conduct of the emperor at Agra. On the contrary, 'local feeling, which had been for a time in their favour, was now against them, for their active competition injured the trade of the native merchants, while the unruliness of the sailors of the fleets, together with the troubles caused by the hostilities between the Portuguese and the English, estranged the great body of the inhabitants.'[70] The inability of the Company to persuade the Mughal emperor to clarify its status so that it could have some legitimacy in establishing itself in the face of local hostility led it to send to the court an ambassador whose mandate and commanding presence might better impress the emperor with the power and importance of the society he represented. Thus the embassy of Sir Thomas Roe to the Mughal court during the years from 1615 to 1619. We are told that he 'arrived at Surat, in great style, to a salute of forty-eight guns.'[71] The guns, however, were fired by the Company's fleet and notwithstanding the fact that he had been provided with much more sumptuous gifts for the emperor than previous emissaries, he had the same difficulties. The length of his mission attested to that and like Hawkins before him he came away with less than he wanted and what he got came not from Jahangir, but from his son Shah Jahan, the viceroy of Gujarat. In 1618 Roe and Shah Jahan reached an agreement allowing the Company to lease accommodations in Surat. It could neither buy nor construct these so that it had not acquired a right to own property. Moreover, the Company's servants, employees as we would call them now, could not bear arms while on shore.[72]

From these inauspicious beginnings Surat became the headquarters of the East India Company in India during the seventeenth century. Perhaps the Company was not wanted by the court at Agra or by the local inhabitants at Surat, but there was nothing in its conduct that would warrant calling it imperialistic at that time. It was motivated by commercial interests and wished to own land and structures in order to make it easier to pursue them. Neither the Company officials in London nor their servants in India were contemplating the ownership of land as a prelude to the governance of Indians. However much Sir Thomas Roe may have felt put upon by the equivocating treatment of Jahangir, he none the less counseled the Company that 'It hath also been the errour of the Dutch, who seek plantation by the sword. . . . Lett this be received as a rule that if you will profitt seek it at sea and in quiett trade for . . . it is an errour to affect garrisons and land warrs in India.'[73]

Elsewhere in India the attempts of the Company to establish trading bases confirm this view, though the details of the story differ. On the east coast outside the jurisdiction of the Mughal state, the English set up a factory at Musulipatam, the chief port of Golconda, in 1611 and at Armagon in 1626 with the consent of local princes. Just as at Surat in the west, in these locations the Company hoped to expand its trade in cotton piece goods for use in the spice markets of the East Indies. These sites proved to be not wholly satisfactory because local rulers exacted more tribute and imposed more severe restrictions on trade than the Company could profitably absorb. Following the Convention of Goa in 1635 which reduced the tension between the English and the Portuguese, the Company factory at Armagon negotiated in 1639 with the Nayak of Chandragiri, a minor Hindu prince, an agreement conferring on it the ownership of the town of Madraspatam, then close to the Portuguese settlement of San Thomé and the location of present-day Madras. The agreement allowed the Company to build fortifications and to exercise the *zamindari* rights over the territory, in this case the collection of custom duties on goods entering India at this port, in return for the 'payment of a small annual quit-rent.'[74] Thus the Company acquired, as it viewed it, its first proprietary rights in Indian land. By 1640 it had built factories and fortifications which in 1641 as Fort St George became its headquarters on the Coromandel Coast.

Why had the nayak agreed to this arrangement? Was it an exchange in any meaningful sense? Or did the English threaten and bully him into ceding the territory? Can we observe here the first signs of imperialism in the conduct of the English in India? Hardly. The English were no stronger on the east coast of India than they were on the west coast. Or perhaps it is more appropriate to say that they were just as weak. When we speak of the English, we have in mind a handful of men – at the end of the century it has been estimated that there were about 114 European civilians in Madras and somewhat fewer than 300 soldiers – who were only infrequently visited by the ships of the East India Company that took from eight months to a year to reach them from London.[75] They were in no position to bully anyone. The nayak, however, was vulnerable to the attacks of aggressive Muslim kingdoms in the Deccan and may have viewed even as attenuated a force as the British a desirable ally. A descendant of the Hindu rulers of the south Indian Vijayanagar empire which had been destroyed in 1565 in a war with an alliance of Deccan sultanates, he was a victim of anarchic conditions which still prevailed among the kingdoms of south India. The disorders in the interior of the subcontinent thus created the conditions for exchange between the nayak and the representatives of the East India Company. Each one had something to offer the other and after the exchange, given the extraordinary uncertainties facing both parties to the transaction, each one was better off.

In retrospect we know that the nayak did not secure the benefits from the agreement with the English that he might have anticipated. In 1647, Madras was conquered by Mir Jumla, a military leader in the service of the sultan of Golconda. Mir Jumla accepted the presence of the English but rewrote the agreement raising the share of Golconda in the custom duties to one-half. He too entered into an exchange relationship with the English because he apparently believed that they could administer the *zamandari* rights in the interest of Golconda as efficiently as anyone else. The English for their part were fearful that the sultan might wish to have his own officials participate in the collection of custom duties and subsequently in 1658 arranged to 'commute the sultan's share for an annual payment of 380 pagodas. After prolonged disputes the sum was raised in 1672 to 1200 pagodas a year.'[76]

At mid-century, then, the East India Company had established a precarious footing on the west and east coasts of India. It had not yet become established in Bengal, which in the eighteenth century would be the center of British imperial rule, and was still as concerned about competition with the Portuguese and the Dutch as it was with the building of the foundations for trade in India. There was not a single shred of evidence that an observer in 1650 could have cited in support of a prediction that two centuries later England would have more complete dominion over India than the Mughal empire then at the height of its power. The story of the establishment of the English presence in Madras would in the latter part of the eighteenth century be writ large in Bengal and with our telescopic vision of the past we see that in both instances the inability of indigenous rulers to contain conflict and maintain order created opportunities for the participation of the Company in Indian governance. If Bernier predicted the demise of the Mughal empire, it was because its property arrangements offended his European values whose universality he took as a matter of faith. Shah Jahan had eight years to reign and he would be followed by the half-century rule of Aurangzeb. The few Englishmen that served the Company in India were incarcerated in their coastal factories, unknown and unseen by Indian society. The English venture in India was indeed Lilliputian.

Notes

1 Donald F. Lach, *Asia in the Making of Europe*, Chicago, University of Chicago Press, 1965, I, Bk 1, 11.

2 W. H. Moreland, *India at the Death of Akbar – An Economic Study*, London, Macmillan, 1920, 199.

3 Niels Steensgaard, *Carracks, Caravans, and Companies – The Structural Crisis in the European–Asian Trade in the Early Seventeenth Century*, Copenhagen, Studentlitteratur, 1973, 40.

4 After a period of decline in the second half of the fifteenth century, Venice experienced a revival of maritime prosperity in the sixteenth century only to be eclipsed at its close by western European societies which were more enterprising and had better access to the timber and naval stores essential for the construction of ocean-going vessels. Frederic C. Lane, *Venice and History*, Baltimore, Johns Hopkins University Press, 1966, 219–39.

5 Brian Gardner, *The East India Company*, New York, McCall, 1972, 26.

6 The *Mayflower* left England on 16 September and sighted Cape Cod on 19 November 1620.

7 *Richard II*, Act II, Scene 1.

8 Magellan did not complete a circuit of the earth, having been killed in the Philippines in April 1521 during an altercation with the local population.

9 George M. Thomson, *Sir Francis Drake*, London, Futura, 1976, 156.

10 J. M. Keynes, *A Treatise on Money*, London, Macmillan, 1965, II, 156–7.

11 J. H. Elliott, *Imperial Spain, 1469–1716*, New York, St Martin's Press, 1963, 182–3.

12 J. H. Clapham, *A Concise Economic History of Britain – From the Earliest Times to 1750*, Cambridge, Cambridge University Press, 1951, 262–3.

13 The voyages of Vasco da Gama were the stunning pay-off of the systematic efforts of the Portuguese in the fifteenth century to overcome the obstacles to the circumnavigation of Africa. At the beginning of the century European vessels were suitable only for sailing inland seas, navigational technology was not capable of plotting the location of ships out of sight of land, it not yet being known how to determine longitude, and the geography of Asia and Africa was founded more in imagination than in fact. Prince Henry of the royal house of Portugal, known in history as the Navigator, assiduously attacked all these deficiencies in the knowledge and

technology essential for the navigation of the oceans, drawing upon the best sources of knowledge then available in Europe. Cartographers, navigators, astronomers, and others with keen interest in these matters came to the academy that Prince Henry founded at Sagres in the extreme southwestern corner of Portugal on the Atlantic coast. There the caravel was perfected so that it could withstand ocean storms and with its triangular rig sail closer to the wind, thus making the return voyage north against the prevailing winds and currents less hazardous. And there the new knowledge of tides and currents and of the physical and economic characteristics of the West African littoral as well as reports about the indigenous populations brought back by successive expeditions were carefully analyzed and made available to sea captains and the leaders of the expeditions that were to follow. Henry H. Hart, *Sea Road to India*, New York, Macmillan, 1950.

14 Clapham, op. cit., 186.
15 ibid., 189.
16 ibid., 202–3.
17 ibid., 199.
18 ibid., 227.
19 ibid., 235.
20 ibid., 209.
21 The cruel uses to which the Inquisition was put both inside and outside Europe were legion. And even where religious and cultural conflicts were less pronounced, standards of justice were hardly free of brutality. As William A. Robson noted:

> The introduction of torture in the Middle Ages may be traced to the decline of the ordeals and trials by battle, for so long as appeal can be made to the judgment of God, confession is unnecessary. . . . The institution of torture in the modern world was clearly derived from the civil law in ancient Rome. . . . Torture gradually spread from one country to another . . . and all over the Continent it became a juristic maxim that confession is the best evidence, and that all the machinery of law should be directed toward extorting it. *Civilization and the Growth of the Law*, New York, Macmillan, 1935, 135–6.

22 Edmund S. Morgan, *American Slavery, American Freedom – The Ordeal of Colonial Virginia*, New York, Norton, 1975, 108–30; Abbot E. Smith, *Colonists in Bondage – White Servitude and Convict Labor in America, 1607–1776*, Chapel Hill, University of North Carolina Press, 1947, 3–25.

23 Abbot Smith, op. cit., 233.

24 ibid., 56.

25 G. M. Trevelyan, *English Social History*, London, Longmans, Green, 1943, 192.

26 Clapham, op. cit., 213.

27 The Treaty of Alçacovas read in part as follows:

> The Lordship of Guinea belongs to the King of Portugal, and all its regions, lands and markets, together with its gold mines, both those discovered or to be discovered, spoken of or to be spoken of, and including the islands of Madeira, Porto Santo and Deserta, and Açores and Los Flores, and Cape Verde Islands, and all the islands which have been discovered, mentioned or conquered, from the Canaries southward to Guinea – saving only the Canary Islands, which occupied or as yet unoccupied, belong to the Crown of Castile. . . . And if any of the inhabitants of Castile, or any foreigners . . . shall go to trade, hinder, damage . . . without the express licence and consent of the King or Prince of Portugal or their successors, they shall be punished in such manner. Quoted by Christopher Bell, *Portugal and the Quest for the Indies*, London, Constable, 1974, 133.

28 Anil Seal, *The Emergence of Indian Nationalism: Competition and Collaboration in the Later Nineteenth Century*, Cambridge, Cambridge University Press, 1968, 30.

29 Vincent A. Smith, *The Oxford History of India*, Percival Spear (ed.) 3rd edn, Oxford, Clarendon Press, 1967, 145–6.

30 Vincent A. Smith, *Akbar, the Great Mogul, 1542–1605*, Oxford, Clarendon Press, 1919, 155–83.

31 Percival Griffiths, *The British Impact on India*, 2nd edn, Ann Arbor, University of Michigan Press, 1972, 240.

32 Adrian C. Mayer, 'The caste system', in David L. Sills (ed.), *International Encyclopedia of Social Sciences*, New York, Macmillan, 1966, II, 340–1.

33 M. N. Srinivas, *Social Change in Modern India*, Berkeley, University of California Press, 1966, 75.

34 Beatrice P. Lamb, *India, a World in Transition*, 3rd edn, New York, Praeger, 1971, 144.

35 Max Weber, *Economy and Society*, ed. and trans. Guenther Roth and Claus Wittich, Berkeley, University of California Press, 1978, I, 212–54.

36 Barrington Moore Jr, *Injustice – The Social Basis of Obedience and Revolt*,

White Plains, M. E. Sharp, 1978, 59.

37 Henry H. Hart, *Venetian Adventurer*, Stanford, Stanford University Press, 1942, 256.

38 ibid., 262.

39 Vincent Smith, *Akbar*, 346.

40 M. Athar Ali, *The Mughal Nobility under Aurangzeb*, Bombay, Asia Publishing House, 1968, 5.

41 ibid., 30.

42 Irfan Habib, *The Agrarian System of Mughal India, 1556–1707*, Bombay, Asia Publishing House, 1963, 190.

43 ibid., 257.

44 ibid., 260; Ali, op. cit., 78.

45 Edwin O. Reischauer and John K. Fairbank, *East Asia – the Great Tradition*, Boston, Houghton Mifflin, 1958 and 1960, 601–9; John W. Hall, 'Foundations of the modern Japanese daimyo', in John W. Hall and Marius B. Jansen (eds), *Institutional History of Early Modern Japan*, Princeton, Princeton University Press, 1968, 65–77.

46 Ali, op. cit., 89.

47 ibid., 152.

48 Habib, op. cit., 319.

49 Ali, op. cit., 65–7.

50 Habib, op. cit., 154.

51 ibid., 113.

52 ibid., 115.

53 François Bernier, *Travels in the Mogul Empire, 1656–1668*, trans. A. Constable 2nd edn, London, Oxford University Press, 1916, revised by Vincent A. Smith, 200–38.

54 Habib, op. cit., 112.

55 ibid., 127.

56 Morris D. Morris, 'Trends and tendencies in Indian economic history', *Indian Economy in the Nineteenth Century: A Symposium*, Delhi, Indian Economic and Social History Association, 1969, 138.

57 Morris D. Morris, 'Towards a reinterpretation of nineteenth-century Indian economic history', *Journal of Economic History*, 23 (4), 611.

58 T. Raychaudhuri, 'A re-interpretation of nineteenth-century Indian economic history', *Indian Economy in the Nineteeth Century: A Symposium*, 79–80.

59 'To found a great empire for the sole purpose of raising up a people of customers, may at first sight appear a project fit only for a nation of shopkeepers. It is, however, a project altogether unfit for a nation of shopkeepers; but extremely fit for a nation whose government is

influenced by shopkeepers': Adam Smith, *An Inquiry into the Nature and Causes of the Wealth of Nations*, ed. Edwin Cannan, New York, Modern Library, 1937, 579. Samuel Adams is alleged to have used the phrase in an oration at Philadelphia on 1 August 1776. John Bartlett, *Familiar Quotations*, ed. C. Morley, 11th edn, Boston, Little, Brown, 1938, 280, note 1.

60 In 1705 the Shogun Tsunayoshi confiscated the assets of the wealthy and respected Osaka commercial house of Yadoya for 'ostentatious conduct unbecoming to a member of the trading class'. George Sansom, *A History of Japan, 1615–1817*, Stanford, Stanford University Press, 1963, 128–9.

61 W. H. Moreland, *From Akbar to Aurangzeb – A Study in Indian Economic History*, London, Macmillan, 1923, 205–19.

62 ibid., 211–13 for a grim description by a Dutch merchant of the famine of 1630–1 in north India.

63 K. N. Chaudhuri, *The Trading World of Asia and the East India Company, 1660–1760*, London, Cambridge University Press, 1978, 47, 174–5.

64 Moreland, *India at the Death of Akbar*, 179.

65 ibid., 196.

66 For a balanced assessment of the Mughal economy see Irfan Habib, 'Potentialities of capitalistic development in the economy of Mughal India', *Journal of Economic History*, 29 (1), 32–78.

67 M. A. P. Meilink-Roelofsz, *Asian Trade and European Influence in the Indonesian Archipelago between 1500 and 1630*, The Hague, Martinus Nijhoff, 1962, 173–206.

68 Gardner, op. cit., 32.

69 ibid., 33.

70 William Foster (ed.), *The Embassy of Sir Thomas Roe to the Court of the Great Mogul, 1615–1619*, London, Hakluyt Society, Series II, 1899, I, xliii–xliv.

71 Gardner, op. cit., 35.

72 Richard Burn (ed.), *The Cambridge History of India*, New York, Macmillan, 1922, IV, *The Mughal Period*, 166.

73 Quoted by Gardner, op. cit., 38.

74 H. H. Dodwell (ed.), *The Cambridge Shorter History of India*, Delhi, S. Chand, 1964, 404.

75 Percival Spear, *The Nabobs – A Study of the Social Life of the English in Eighteenth-Century India*, London, Oxford University Press, 1963, 11.

76 Dodwell, op. cit., 405.

3

British imperial rule begins: Bengal 1750–1800

The British conquered Bengal in the second half of the eighteenth century. The East India Company thereby was transformed from an enterprise primarily serving and protecting the commercial interests of its presidencies along coastal India and other posts in Asia to a territorial governor exercising the powers of state in association with its mercantile responsibilities. This discrete and abrupt change in the fortunes of the Company marked the start of two hundred years of British imperial rule in India. It also was the occasion for the reorganization and reform of the institutions through which the British gradually strengthened the interests of the home authorities in the administration of Indian affairs.

If imperialism is an unequal relationship, with one country or region expressing and pursuing interests at the expense of another, a shift in the balance of assets in favor of England against India must have occurred in the eighteenth century. This indeed was the case but in the negative sense that the capability of the Mughal emperor to govern north India declined, exacerbating the rivalries of regional Indian princes and providing the Company with the opportunity to enter the competition for power. What happened after Clive's victory at Plassey in 1757 cannot be explained by a surge of British economic and technological strength. To be sure, the industrial revolution in England was soon to reap the productive benefits of those economic propensities that had made Tudor England such a vigorous commercial society and in the seventeenth century had brought the Company into the Asian trading network. The small complement of servants of the

Company in India, however, did not yet have at their command those implements of industrialization and applied science – steam transport, river gunboats, quinine, gatling guns, telegraphic communication, for example – that so dramatically increased the assets of the west in the nineteenth century relative to the east. Nor was there an accession of belief in the right of the British in their own interests to control India and still less in an obligation to bring to Indians the benefits of western civilization.

In 1750, the primary military advantage of the Company lay in its control of the seas, a consequence of its superior deep-water and ocean-going vessels. On land it was scarcely more powerful than it had been in the early years of the Indian connection. Towards the close of the seventeenth century Josiah Child, governor of the East India Company and an admirer of the more forceful, militarized trade policy of the Dutch East India Company, tried to settle the differences between the Company's officials and Mughal authorities in the matter of its commercial status in Bengal by resorting to arms. In the event the troops of the Emperor Aurangzeb drove the British out of Bengal. By the middle of the eighteenth century the strength of the Company's armies had not increased appreciably beyond the time of 'Josiah Child's foolish war with Aurangzeb'.[1] What had changed was the authority and military presence of the Mughal emperor in Bengal; they were in eclipse.

How the tipping of the scales of inequality against India was manifested in the coercion and constraints visited upon Indians is no easy question to answer. A common view holds that the expansion of British rule in Bengal was disastrous. A modern western scholar of the period, for example, has observed that 'it is very unusual to find a Company servant who was prepared to claim before the 1780s that British rule had been anything other than a misfortune for Bengal.'[2] A less retrained Indian historian held the Company culpable for the misery of the famine of 1770: 'Though arising from natural causes, the famine was undoubtedly aggravated by the acute poverty of the people wrought by the early *conquistadores*, whose revenue *janissaries* took a fiendish delight in a rigorous collection of the land-tax even in that year of malaise and mortification.'[3] Adam Smith, who believed that the superior forces of Europeans in the Indies allowed them 'to commit with impunity every sort of injustice in those remote countries', found that the Company servants in Bengal were egregious monopolists, the worst of that species of which *The Wealth of Nations* was such an eloquent and cogent indictment.[4]

Before we can assess these views and the coercive impact of British expansion in Bengal we need a fuller picture of the changes brought about by the British. These changes will reveal the complexity of the interests served by British imperialism at a time when Indian interests were fragmented and difficult to articulate because a transcendent commitment capable of mobilizing individual, caste, and group values had not yet been formed. First, however, we turn to the permissive origin of British imperialism in India, the decline of the Mughal empire.

The decline of the Mughal empire

Had the Mughal empire in the eighteenth century continued to be as strong as it was during the century and a half from Akbar through the reign of Aurangzeb, the East India Company would not have been victorious at Plassey in 1757. Shah Alam would not have granted it the *diwani* – the collection of tax revenues and the administration of justice which also carried responsibility for the *nizamat*, the administration of criminal justice and the maintenance of law and order – for Bengal in 1765 that set the British on their imperial course. The Mughal empire the Company subsequently displaced was hardly a brief historical episode, lasting as it did from the start of Akbar's reign in 1556 to the death of Shah Alam two-and-a-half centuries later in 1806. Its dominion, however, seldom reached south India much as its emperors tried to bring it to heel. Indeed to that purpose they continually engaged in military campaigns which placed a growing burden on the land revenue. Yet they could not develop political institutions capable of penetrating Indian society and engendering extensive support for such demands. One has the impression when reviewing the long years of the Mughal empire that it was a kind of disequilibrium system that could be readily disrupted by random shocks, the idiosyncratic qualities of an emperor, for example, or the defection of a key magnate or prince.

That the Mughal emperors were foreign to India had something to do with their difficulties in securing and maintaining support. It is not a full explanation however. It is salutary to recall that the England which developed such deeply rooted political institutions in the centuries prior to the industrial revolution had been conquered by Normans, a people as foreign to the Anglo-Saxon population as the Mughals were to the Indians. And in a somewhat different sense, it may have been true that in all societies in the eighteenth century and before rulers were foreign to their subjects. Their relationship was only minimally reciprocal, the latter being obliged to pay tribute to the former without receiving in return much more than the equivocal privilege of protected subservience.

As suggested in the last chapter, the Indian social system may have insulated peasant communities from the imperial presence so that the critical backing needed by the emperor came less from village India than from the princes and *zamindars* who were responsible for the collection of the land revenue. Here lay the problem, for the Mughal nobility, created in the *mansabdari* system, were either foreign mercenaries or Indian princes attracted by the emoluments of a *jagir* or service in the imperial court. In either case the probabilities of their institutionalizing Mughal governance in Indian society were small because their uncertain allegiance to the emperors compelled the latter to devise those procedures that would abort the growth of independent centers of power within the empire. The English model, then, of political development based on the conflict of Crown and aristocracy was foreclosed.

Moreover, the Mughal governing classes did not have strong links with the commercial classes. Nor did they have productive economic interests of their own. They were warriors who were disdainful of market behavior except in so far as it was useful for acquiring the adornments of conspicuous display. They were not much interested in technology and the techniques by which the productivity of the resources in their realm might have been increased.[5] The economic basis of governance then inhered in the control of land and the proportion of the gross output that could be appropriated in the land revenue.

In the absence of centripetal forces that might have been given greater scope in a more vigorous commercial society, the aggressive warrior drives of the Mughal ruling class intensified centrifugal factors. The military campaigns of the Mughals inside India, especially against the Deccan, seemed to be never ending, a state of affairs that, however useful for keeping warriors occupied, strained the economic foundations of the state.[6] At the end of the seventeenth century Aurangzeb was already so absorbed in subduing the Maratha princes in the Deccan that he had moved his headquarters there. The longer the campaigns continued, the stronger the Maratha princes seemed to become, the more difficult it became to suborn Indian magnates in the *mansabdari* system, and the less time the emperor had to devote to the governance of his more prosperous realm in the north.

If, as Professor Habib has said, the Marathas were 'the greatest single force responsible for the downfall of the Mughal Empire', it was because their resistance to paying tribute to the emperor revealed the frailty of Mughal governance.[7] Rebellion in the north became more likely, the more apparent it was that the Mughals were not succeeding in the south, quite apart from the fact that the Mughals had to divert their best forces from the north in their long-drawn-out failure in the Deccan. Moreover, the demands of the land-revenue system, onerous in the most benign circumstances, became unendurable in the face of insatiable military needs, leading many peasants to flee the land or to resist the exactions of a no longer omnipotent state.

The decline of Mughal power set in towards the end of the seventeenth century. Aurangzeb himself aggravated the problems of governance by rousing the latent hostility between Hindu and Muslim. Religious tolerance had been an essential part of Akbar's rule, a policy violated by Shah Jahan in the destruction of Hindu temples in the empire. An orthodox Muslim even more austerely committed to Islam than Shah Jahan, Aurangzeb continued the persecution of Hindus throughout his long reign. That too was a problem, for, like Queen Victoria, he wore down the governing potential of his successor, but unlike Victoria his longevity assured a war of succession for the peacock throne.

We do not need to follow closely the declining fortunes of the Mughal empire. In the eighteenth century it disintegrated steadily until it could claim suzerainty over little more than Delhi and its immediate surroundings. As the pale of its rule receded, the anarchic conditions left in its wake invited the aggression of Indian princes and Afghans eager to seize the fabled wealth of Delhi and Agra. The Marathas, now no longer on the defensive against Mughal aggression, invaded north India and by 1738 were in the vicinity of Delhi. There they met the invading power from the northwest in a series of battles ending with their defeat by the Afghans in 1761 at the Battle of Panipat. While the Marathas were thus frustrated in their bid to control Delhi, the Afghans chose to withdraw to their homeland, leaving the Indian contenders for dominion in north India suspiciously at odds with one another. As Percival Spear described the factions following the Battle of Panipat:

> The Sikhs at this time were not more than plundering robber bands, and any strong power could have controlled them. The Rajputs had organized states, the nearest to Delhi being Jaipur, but they were exhausted, slow moving and politically inept. The Marathas to the south were still recovering from Panipat, and were divided amongst themselves. But potentially they were by far the most formidable. The Rohillas were stronger than the Sikhs, and as enterprising, but just as disunited. Oudh was well organized but was too much occupied trying to recover Bengal and warding off the Marathas, to control the Rohillas or to interfere in Delhi. It was the desire of each of these to control Delhi, but each had a deep distrust of all the others.[8]

More formidable than any of these regional Indian powers, at least as we now know in retrospect, was the East India Company. In 1757 at Plassey, in what has been called a transaction rather than a battle, Clive and a small army of the East India Company defeated the larger (but disorganized) troops of the Nawab of Bengal, Siraj-ud-daula, and replaced him with Mir Jafar.[9] The military control of the Ganges delta won at Plassey shortly received imperial legitimacy when Shah Alam granted the *diwani* in Bengal to the Company. Having thus acquired the right to exercise governance in Bengal, the Company became a contender for the control of north India.

The East India Company

The East India Company was a peculiarly English institution, an amalgam of the commercial drive of the middle classes and the developing tradition of constitutional government as both were affected by British expansion in the subcontinent. There never was any doubt about whose interests were being served when, for example, the Portuguese sought out the Cape route to India and established themselves at Goa; they were servants of the king and the commercial and religious values he embodied. In England with its highly developed sense of private property and individual right, the priorities in its imperial role were never so clear. Indeed, the struggle between commercial and state interests accounted for the pragmatic – some might say disorderly – evolution of British imperial institutions. None the less, the Company was evidence of an extraordinary organizational capacity for overcoming natural, economic, and technical obstacles in the penetration of the Asian trading network. Because Asian societies lacked the motivation or the need to enter European commerce, they did not develop the dynamic institutions for organizing, monitoring, and controlling men and resources in the pursuit of private and public purpose half a world away.

By the middle of the eighteenth century the Company had grown from a fugitive venture, whose partners invested in small merchant fleets and a stock of goods in anticipation of earning profits of uncertain magnitude at an equally uncertain time on a return cargo of pepper, spices, and other Asian commodities, to a joint-stock company doing business throughout Asia and paying its proprietors a regular dividend in proportion to their invested capital. It had become a multinational corporation with the home office in London and presidencies, factories (warehouses), and other posts in ports as widely separated as Bantam in Java and

Basra at the head of the Persian Gulf. The Company comprised the proprietors, the Court of Directors, administrative departments, and its servants in India and other Asian posts. As shareholders, the proprietors were entitled to cast up to four votes, depending on the value of their shares, for the directors, of whom there were twenty-four. A candidate for a directorship had to own shares of the Company's stock with a value of at least £2000. Just as the board of directors in a modern corporation selects the management and oversees its performance, so the Court of Directors supervised the Company administration through a number of committees on all of which the chairman and deputy chairman served as ex-officio members. Among these was the Committee of Correspondence which was responsible for the Department of the Examiner of Correspondence.

To the modern mind an examiner of correspondence may sound like a euphemism for a mail sorter who directs letters to departmental secretaries, a title designed to boost morale in the same way that custodian is intended to enhance the self-esteem of janitors. Nothing could be wider of the mark. In an era when communication technology was so rudimentary, the drafting of the dispatches by which the policy of the Company was communicated to its servants in India was an immensely important task. K. N. Chaudhuri notes that it 'acted as a central problem-scanning body in the whole system'.[10] John Stuart Mill (an examiner of correspondence like his father before him) asserted, while testifying before a select committee of the House of Lords in 1852 on the renewal of the Company's charter, that 'the present constitution of the Indian Government . . . seems . . . to have worked very satisfactorily.' He went on to explain that the most important reason for this performance was that

> the whole Government of India is carried on in writing. All the orders given, and all the acts of the executive officers, are reported in writing, and the whole of the original correspondence is sent to the Home Government; so that there is no single act done in India, the whole of the reasons for which are not placed on record. This appears to me a greater security for good

> government than exists in almost any other government in the world, because no other probably has a system of recordation so complete.[11]

With pardonable pride and perhaps a somewhat idealized view of his administrative responsibilities at India House, Mill testified for a lost cause since the Company was soon to disappear in a reorganization of Indian governance following the Sepoy Revolt of 1857. None the less, his observations about the critical importance of correspondence in the management of the Company's affairs in the mid-nineteenth century are not irrelevant to the management of the Company a century earlier when it had not yet acquired territorial power in Bengal.

Prior to Plassey, when the Company was confined largely to the coastal presidencies at Calcutta, Madras, and Bombay, its governmental performance centered on the negotiation of treaties with the Indian princes in whose territories its factories had been set up, the administration of English law for those living within the factories, and the conduct of naval wars occasioned in the eighteenth century primarily by the struggle with the French for the control of the coastal waters of India. Those wars in conjunction with the rivalries of Indian princes led to a Company involvement in Indian affairs that went far beyond anything that could have been observed in the first half of the seventeenth century. P. J. Marshall has noted that 'if an Indian claimant won his throne with European help the price he would have to pay would be a high one: he would become a puppet.'[12] Still the Company was predominantly a trading organization serving the mercantile interests of the proprietors in London; it was trying to maximize the net income from its far-flung operations.

This was no easy task in an enterprise whose success depended so much on conditions that were either beyond its control or difficult to control. A manufacturer employing raw materials and labor services checks and controls them continuously as they are transformed into marketable output. Equally important, the firm can minimize losses by reducing raw-material inventories and laying off workers when profit expectations have not been realized.

Moreover, if purchasing inputs and selling outputs in local or regional markets, it receives information about changes in relative prices rapidly enough for maintaining a viable relationship between current costs and revenues. The East India Company had no such advantages to assist it in its managerial and economic decisions. It invested in locally produced or acquired commodities – woolen cloth, metal ware, gold, or silver – for export to markets 6000 miles or more away which might be reached in optimal weather in six months, but took longer if winds were contrary or did not blow as expected. Warren Hastings observed that Bengal was 'at what may be called a distance of two years from London'.[13] From his careful research of the Company records for the century 1650 to 1750, K. N. Chaudhuri concludes that the minimum round trip for an East Indiaman, including the turn-around time in Indian ports, was sixteen months.[14] Since the English merchant fleets were sailing into a monsoon climate, they were further constrained by the flow of seasonal winds. They could not leave England later than early spring and on the return voyage no later than early December from west India or early January from east India.[15]

The imports of the Company from Asia, the primary source of its revenue, thus arrived in London irregularly within the season for the return of the Indiamen. The sale of the cargoes was not only a measure of the productiveness of investment decisions made a year and a half to two or more years previously, but also the basis for allocating the current investment in outgoing fleets among the Indian presidencies and other market areas in Asia. Demand and supply were singularly disjointed, which is to say that the information necessary for equilibrating them neither reached the home office of the Company continuously nor could be taken as wholly reliable evidence about market conditions in Asia, even in an era when tastes and technology changed extremely slowly. Needless to say, the difficulties of matching supply and demand in markets so far removed exacerbated the problems of financing the investment in England as well as the purchase of commodities in Asia. Without access to credit and money capital the Company could not have survived.

One of the compelling reasons for the organizational features of the Company as they had taken shape by the middle of the eighteenth century was the reduction of uncertainty, the attempt to internalize within its control circumstances that otherwise were beyond it. With the navigational technology then available nothing much could be done about the monsoons. The seasonal fluctuations in prices caused by the infrequent arrival of the India fleets, however, were minimized by the Company's practice of holding auctions four times a year to sell its inventories of Asian goods.[16] The size of the market, moreover, was increased by the re-export trade for which the Company was well served by the merchants and financiers of the Low Countries, France, and central Europe. Commodities that ran afoul of mercantilist sumptuary proscriptions in the home market, for example fine Indian calicoes, could be sold on the continent without the Company having to invest in the offices and the warehouses essential for trade. The Company also maintained a monopoly of the Asian trade in England by being properly attentive to the financial interests of the Crown from which it obtained its charter, minimizing the uncertainties occasioned by domestic rivals and earning the implacable hostility of Adam Smith.[17]

In Asia the opportunities for controlling the conditions that made trade uncertain and risky were a good deal less promising. If the Company could feather its monopoly nest in England, in Asia it faced a host of competitors. The Portuguese arrived in Asian waters a century ahead of the British and the Dutch beat them to the Indonesian spice lode by ten years. Moreover, all the European East Indies companies faced the competition of local traders who had grown with the Asian mercantile system long before the Portuguese rounded the Cape. Typically small enterprises unbeholden to home offices or governing councils of regional presidencies, they had some of the features of the firms hallowed in neoclassical competitive theory. They were flexible and adaptable to local market conditions by virtue of the rapid turnover of their inventory as well as easy access to coastal regions, estuaries, and deltas by the use of small vessels of shallow draft. And even as the European trading companies were vying for Asian markets, private

European traders added to the variety of firms seeking profits in the traffic of the natural wealth of the East Indies.

The goad of competition coupled with the limited market in Asia for indigenous English products led the Company to extend its operations far beyond the trade centered in the Indian presidencies. By the middle of the eighteenth century the carrying or country trade, as it was called, was becoming increasingly important. So long as its trade with India was bilateral, it was compelled to ship in the outbound cargoes more gold and especially silver than was compatible with mercantilist sensibilities. By competing in the country trade and extending its market area, it maximized the commodities it had access to and so increased the value of imports it carried to England for the export of a given value of precious metals. The exigencies of its trade balance with India led to the multilateralism that was little understood in early mercantilist thought.[18] Thus did the opium trade, about which we shall have more to say in the next chapter, develop, for it turned out that the opium extracted from the poppies raised in north India was readily marketable in China. The Company could then exchange opium in China for tea, the drinking of which it had done much to stimulate, and reduce the shipments of silver to China that otherwise would have been used to pay for its tea imports.[19]

Unlike the re-export trade in Europe, the country trade in Asia involved the Company in an extension of the structural foundations of its commerce. This brings us back to the means it used to reduce uncertainty and the coercive side of its mercantile ventures, a behavior that anticipated the imperialist expansion of the Company in India. While paying tribute to the Crown in England, the Company also was liable to tribute demanded of it by the Asian rulers in whose jurisdictions it wanted to do business. The Asian trading system functioned within a congeries of polities, big and small, governed by emperors, princes, viceroys, and satraps whose demands for revenues were no less insistent than European states but appeared to be more arbitrary, more dependent on the whims and idiosyncrasies of rulers than on institutional procedures which might reduce their unpredictable impact. The itinerant pedlars trading in the Middle East and India followed overland and water routes that minimized the cost of tribute. The competition of alternative trade routes placed an upper limit on the costs rulers imposed on merchants – if, that is, they were interested in maximizing tribute over a period of years. Given the nature of the enterprise, the Company preferred – it really had no other choice – to be territorially based with the consent of a local ruler and some agreement about its financial obligation to him. It was this status that it was trying to attain in Surat in those early embassies to the court of the Mughal emperor in Agra.

By the eighteenth century the British had established a post at Calcutta in Bengal, a third presidency to join the older settlements at Madras and Bombay, the latter having displaced Surat as the center of the Company's operations in west India following its acquisition by the British Crown from Portugal in 1661.[20] In the aftermath of Josiah Child's ill-fated war with the emperor Aurangzeb the Company leased in 1691 a seemingly valueless mudflat backed by swamps but adjacent to a deep-water anchorage. The one afforded some protection against the aggression of local rulers in Bengal, the other a harbor for the Company's ships which could not reach the Mughal commercial center at Hugli. In 1696 the settlement was fortified by the construction of Fort William, so named after William III who had been called to the British throne in 1689. In 1698 the Company purchased *zamindari* rights which established its claim for governing Calcutta, the bridgehead from which the Company conquered Bengal.

It might be said that the willingness of the Mughal emperor's viceroy in Bengal to lease the land that became Calcutta was a reflection of a critical inequality in knowledge and understanding of its strategic value. The British were better able to appreciate the importance for commerce and governance of a deep-water harbor than princes whose lives were so much more land-locked. However that may be, the more telling inequality was manifested in the decline of Mughal governing capacity. After the death of Aurangzeb, the Mughal writ rapidly lost its efficacy. In 1717 after protracted negotiations the Company's emissaries persuaded the emperor Farrukhsiyar, in return for an annual payment of Rs 3000, to issue *farmans*, or decrees, which granted the Company free-trade privileges in Bengal and released it from the obligation to pay taxes or customs to local rulers. Farrukhsiyar was not the most distinguished Mughal emperor. *The Oxford History of India*, indeed, dismisses him as 'a good-for-nothing and shameless debauchee'.[21] By exempting the British from making local payments he committed himself to a policy that his more powerful and effective predecessors would not have tolerated. One may doubt that Farrukhsiyar served Mughal interests in the transaction which was not therefore an exchange in the neoclassical sense. This was confirmed in the unwillingness of the governor of Bengal to obey the *farmans*.[22] Presumably he viewed them as an indefensible transfer of benefits from him and his political jurisdiction to the Company.

If locally the *farmans* were not enforced, the Company, especially its servants in India, regarded them as legitimizing their commercial operations in Bengal. Just as it had paid the Crown for monopoly rights to trade in India, so it had paid the emperor for a privilege that was denied to less organized and forceful merchants. What happened thereafter could be seen by the Company as the working out or realization of that privilege, its preeminent manifestation being the acceptance in 1765 by Robert Clive of the *diwani* for Bengal.

By accepting the *diwani* the Company took a giant stride into the cockpit of Indian continental political struggles. It also pointed up how tenuous at those long distances the administrative controls the Company exerted over its servants in India could be. Clive had only recently returned from England to take up for the second time his duties as governor of the presidency of Fort William with the explicit charge to do something about the corruption of the Company's servants in India that so distressed the home authorities. The decision to accept the *diwani* was his; he could not consult the Court of Directors. He was aware of their reluctance to take on more governance than absolutely necessary for performance of the Company's commercial purpose. Yet to have a hand in the ruling of the richest province in India at a time when the disintegrating Mughal empire no longer was able to assert its authority could not have seemed inconsistent with that purpose. In particular, the *diwani* seemed to offer a solution to the continuing problem of the drain of precious metal to India and Asia. In becoming responsible for the collection of revenues in Bengal the Company seemed to have at its command a source for financing its purchase of commodities destined for European markets that rendered the export of silver to India very much less important. Such a prospect would make timid directors bold.

What neither Clive nor the directors could anticipate was its consequences for the organization of the Company and its relationship to the Crown. Since these transformed the Company from a commercial venture to an instrument of imperial governance we must summarize them here. Whether or not the servants of the Company in India were conquistadores, they would have had to have been strong men indeed to resist the opportunities for enrichment that Plassey and the *diwani* afforded them. The latter added governmental responsibilities to the Company's commercial functions the monopoly benefits of which were exploited by its servants who were expected to trade on private account to compensate for their inadequate pay. As collectors of revenue, they were in a position to exact tribute and presents from tax farmers and others seeking to minimize their obligations to the *diwan*. They controlled the salt monopoly. When they traded for themselves inside Bengal they were not subject to the transit dues and other taxes which inhibited the trade of Indian merchants. In consequence, there was a transfer of income from Indians to the servants of the Company without there being an increase in its profitability. The *diwani* initially was a financial disappointment even as the nabobs, the Anglo-Indians who had prospered in the service, returned to England in greater numbers to claim their assets, a *nouveau riche* who perpetuated the illusion of unlimited Indian wealth.[23]

It was the developing combination of the wanton behavior of the Company servants and its declining profitability that prompted its reform and the increased oversight of the Crown. The Regulating Act of 1773 established a governor-general of Bengal with some authority over the governors of Madras and Bombay.

He was to govern with a council of four members initially specified by the Parliament, but subsequently appointed by the Court of Directors. All reports of the governor-general and his council in India were to be reviewed by Westminster within fourteen days of their receipt at India House.

With the conquest of Bengal, the interests brought together in the Company became more diverse. It no longer was attractive only for the dividends it paid regularly to its proprietors in the first half of the eighteenth century. There now seemed to be opportunities in Bengal to strike it rich and men sought access to the Company for its monopoly of Indian employment. The value of its shares increased as did a position in the Court of Directors, each of whom was entitled to distribute patronage.[24] For a family whose sons had limited opportunities at home because they could not succeed to the family estate, did not have the clout to enter the esteemed professions, had little prospect of holding a secure seat in the House of Commons, or were delinquent, a passage to India as a writer for the Company, the first position in its civil employment hierarchy, was an attractive prospect. To be sure, he entered the service at fifteen and the probability was high that he would not survive the first year in India. But at home the nabobs, however disdained, distorted the assessment of the odds. They also acquired seats in the Commons as they exchanged their Indian patrimony for landed estates and met the rigid qualifications of the eighteenth century for membership in that exclusive political forum. So too did directors of the Company; in the Parliament that passed the Regulating Act, thirteen sat in the House of Commons.[25] Conversely, members of Parliament increasingly purchased shares in the Company and took an active part in the meetings of the proprietors. As the imperial role of England took shape in India in the second half of the eighteenth century, at home the Company and Parliament coalesced, with the political role of the former becoming ever more pronounced.

In 1784 Pitt's India Act, which he stated was designed to 'give to the Crown the power of guiding the politics of India, with as little means of corrupt influence as possible', established the structure of the governmental control of Indian affairs that was to last until the

Company disappeared in the aftermath of the Sepoy Revolt and made Parliament the primary arena for venting the conflicts over Indian policy.[26] The Act set up a Board of Control consisting of six privy councilors serving without pay, the president of which was the equivalent to the Secretary of State for Indian Affairs who served in the British Cabinet when the Crown governed India directly after 1858. The Board was responsible for the obviously political functions that had hitherto been the province of the Court of Directors, the administration of the land revenue, diplomatic negotiations, and the conduct of war. The Court retained its control of commercial matters and patronage with these powers no longer inhibited by the veto of the shareholders who in effect became rentiers rather than proprietors. The governor-general's authority in Bengal was strengthened with respect both to his Council and to the subordinate presidencies. The Act declared that 'to pursue schemes of conquest and extension of dominion in India are measures repugnant to the wish, honour and policy of this nation', a salutary reminder that legislative intent and the unfolding of history are not necessarily consonant.[27] The Act also provided for periodic charter reviews which led to successive reductions of the Company's commercial responsibilities until in 1833 its trading rights were divested and it became solely a governing institution.

With the establishment of the Company as a territorial ruler in Bengal and the subsequent reform of its Indian government, it became a more formidable instrument of British imperialism. How did this affect Indians, particularly in Bengal? The outlines of an answer to this question may be gleaned in the policy of the permanent settlement and in the expansion of British trade in Bengal. The former was more deeply institutional than the latter. It altered the rules and conventions governing the use of land and the collection of revenue in Bengal and so had enduring consequences. The scramble for profits in the second half of the eighteenth century by Company servants and private traders was a less enduring phenomenon occasioned by the groping accommodation of the Company to its newly acquired power in Bengal.

The permanent settlement

The idea of a permanently settled tax agreement between governors of the Company and owners of land in Bengal developed gradually in the controversies over this matter among the Company's servants and the directors in the home office. The policy was formally announced in a proclamation by Lord Cornwallis, Governor-General of India, on 22 March 1793:

> The governor general in council accordingly declares to the zemindars, independent talookdars and other actual proprietors of land, with or in behalf of whom a settlement has been concluded under the regulations above-mentioned, that at the expiration of the terms of the settlement, no alteration will be made in the assessment which they have engaged to pay, but that they and their heirs and lawful successors will be allowed to hold their estates for ever.[28]

The definitiveness of the proclamation reflected dissatisfaction with the traditional methods of collecting the revenue, the administrative problems of overlords with small cadres of reliable and loyal officials, and, most critically, extraordinary ignorance of customary tenures and methods of land use.

As the British presence in Bengal expanded, they became more involved in the system of tax farming that, as we saw in the last chapter, had Mughal imprimatur in the granting of *jagirs* to princes and provincial governors in return for their loyalty to and military support of the emperor. A year and a half after Plassey, Clive received a *jagir* worth some £27,000 from the emperor, an emolument negotiated for him by Mir Jafar, the emperor's viceroy in Bengal. This was in addition to local tribute Clive and the Company received for their support of Mir Jafar.[29] In accepting the *diwani* the Company assumed responsibility for a system from which their previous benefits had been the result of following Mughal rules of conduct for the powerful. Thereafter the question of how to formulate rules of their own for the collection of taxes that would maximize the revenues of the Company became an issue of increasing concern to servants in India and the home office. Through the governorships of Clive to Warren Hastings, the latter concluding his tour of duty in 1785, the Company adapted to the traditional system, confirming the tax-farming privileges of *zamindars* and other overlords for varying periods and revenue benefits without concerning themselves unduly with how these agents of the *diwan* made tax arrangements with undertenants, headmen in villages, or ryots.

Whether the famine of 1769–70 was caused by Company abuses of the *diwani* or whether they exacerbated the consequences of a natural disaster, it was a portent – it has been alleged that as much as one-third of the population of Bengal died – that did not reflect credit on the performance of the Company. And from that time one observes the mobilization of ideas and theories by various factions within the Company who addressed the interrelated issues of Company revenues, agricultural productivity, and land tenure. The discussion was a compelling example of the power of theory and ideology in framing a problem and devising a solution to it. By the same token it was an excessively one-sided or unequal play of ideas, for with few exceptions these originated in the experience and thought of the west. This may not be surprising. In the eighteenth century Indian agriculture was organized according to traditional standards and practices which in their very nature were not spelled out analytically. Customary usages had come to serve the purposes of subsistence agriculture in a despotic political order and the not unreasonable argument in their defense was that they had stood the test of time. In the west the industrial economy that was to emerge in the nineteenth century was still submerged in an agrarian society which to percipient observers, however, was undergoing important economic and technical changes. These promised increased agricultural productivity and had already consigned famine in England to history.

As early as 1770 Alexander Dow, an officer in the Company's army in Bengal, was recommending a permanent settlement of the tax obligation on landowners in order to secure the property and status of a class which could provide indigenous leadership in agriculture and support for the Company. In 1776 Philip Francis, known to posterity as the relentless enemy of Warren Hastings both in India and during the interminable impeachment proceedings that Hastings faced on his return to England, began advocating a permanent settlement of the tax revenues on a wealthy landed class in Bengal whom he expected to behave like improving English gentry in the raising of agricultural productivity. Moreover, if a permanent settlement led to the weeding out of inefficient owners, Francis thought that 'a transfer of landed property to monied people, who were able to make improvements, will be in some degree advantageous to Government and to the country.'[30] Thus did he anticipate an expanding role for a market in increasing the efficiency of land utilization when, for example, it had to be sold for tax arrears. By the time Cornwallis arrived in India the idea of permanent settlement had been sufficiently bruited about that he could look to it as a means of reconstructing the *zamindars* of Bengal in the image of the improving English landlords without being overly scrupulous in attributing the idea to his predecessors.[31]

All the proponents of the permanent settlement defended it by reference to western agrarian experience and/or western systematic social thought. If Cornwallis looked to British landowners, Francis looked to the French physiocrats for his understanding of the central role of agriculture in economic development and to the eighteenth-century enlightenment for supporting generalizations unsullied by historical experience.[32] Just as James Mill in the next generation viewed India through the lens of utilitarianism, so Francis saw the world of India through the glasses of the Philosophes. Those in the Company who opposed the permanent settlement, cautioned against doing violence to experience, and urged the gathering of more evidence before changing the revenue system drastically – notably Sir John Shore, ironically enough, the governor-general following the return of Cornwallis to England in 1793 – but they lost out to those whose understanding of the issues was narrowly based on western values.

The influence of western views and theories, moreover, was given powerful reinforcement by the administrative exigencies facing the Company's officers in Bengal. If they continued to rely upon the revenue system as it had evolved during the years of declining Mughal authority, they would have condoned the use of gifts and bribes in the determination of tax and revenue benefits without securing the loyalty of tax farmers who all the while sought to divert income from the Company's treasury. If, however, they wished to settle the land with ownership rights, they lacked the knowledge and personnel to deal with the cultivating peasant or holders of small land tenures – there were simply too many of them. The *zamindars* thus seemed eminently appropriate because in Bengal they were not so numerous and the Company authorities could persuade themselves that by settling with them permanently they at once would secure their loyalty and create a class of progressive agriculturists.

Cornwallis survived the proclamation of the permanent settlement for more than ten years, but was none the wiser about its consequences. The social order and its traditional obligations, rights, and associations were so complex that the superimposing on them of a seemingly straightforward scheme of land ownership with a concomitant contractual stipulation to pay a fixed tax in perpetuity had effects that are still not fully understood. Very little happened in the way the Company anticipated. Prior to 1793 more than 50 percent of the Company's land revenue was paid by twelve great *zamindaris*, the largest held by the Burdwan Raj that accounted for 17 percent.[33] But contrary to the Company's hopes these *zamindars* were not people of entrepreneurial inclination eager to manage their massive estates optimally for increasing agricultural productivity. Rather they were leaders whose social and ceremonial obligations as required by the customs and traditions of their community precluded the development of those calculating and maximizing propensities essential for economic development. The *zamindar*, though prince in his realm, delegated economic functions to his officers, managers, and undertenants. He was not likely to know much more about the arcane methods of estate management, the keeping of accounts, and the assigning of tax liability to undertenants than the servants of the Company.

With respect to the coercive consequences of the permanent settlement, one can no more find a consistent pattern than the

Company's collectors could understand the labyrinthian dimensions of the large estates. It is difficult to discern in Bengal at that time a widely shared interest in opposition to the land and revenue policies of the Company. The proclamation of the permanent settlement in 1793 committed the British to principles of which the *zamindars* approved, but in the administration of the settlement the British turned out to be too assiduous and too insensitive to ancient practices and privileges. By the rules pursuant to the settlement, the Company denied *zamindars* the legal right to 'distrain or sell lands, houses or other real property of their under farmers and ryots, or the taluqdars paying revenue through them'. It also prohibited them from 'confining or inflicting corporal punishment on any defaulting tenant or dependent taluqdar to enforce the payment of arrears of their demands'.[34] With such restrictions on their prerogatives, the great *zamindars* were not inclined to cooperate with the Company's collectors, but rather obstructed, dissembled, and defied them in order to raise the costs of revenue collection and induce a return to more agreeable standards.

What was agreeable to *zamindars*, however, might well have been disagreeable to people in inferior tenures. It is, presumably, the unusual person who enjoys corporal punishment. Moreover, 'the ignorance of zamindars and their indifference to zamindari affairs made them ruinously dependent on their *amla* who, taking advantage of the zamindar's situation, always tried to enrich themselves at the expense of their masters.'[35] The proprietary rights acquired by the *zamindars* carried with them the obligation to pay the agreed taxes to the Company as holder of the *diwani*, the sanction used by the latter being the summary seizure and sale of assets for payment of arrears. A market in land, in contrast to a market in tax-farming privileges, became a more important feature of the Bengali economy and to that extent diminished the role of customary arrangements for accommodating debtors and creditors. The *amla* with his eye on the main chance could contrive to entangle the financial affairs of his *zamindar*, hoping that in the sale of the property for failure to pay taxes he might add to his holdings and enhance his status.

Whoever benefited by the sales of *zamindari* property for tax arrears, by the turn of the nineteenth century the large estates had all passed through the market.[36] In contrast, the smaller *zamindaris* were more likely to remain intact for the reason that their proprietors were more intimately involved with the management of their estates and alert to the defense of their economic interests. It does not follow, however, that the large *zamindars* bore the full burden of the permanent settlement. Historians of the process have noted the intriguing fact that the purchasers of the properties of the old *zamindars* very largely resided in the districts where the large estates were located.[37] This may have been accounted for in part by *amlas* who took advantage of their masters' distress. More importantly, land was purchased by loyal retainers, undertenants, and family of the old *zamindars* so that if the large estates did not remain formally in their possession they managed to retain an interest in them. Furthermore, the outsider with liquid assets – the moneylender from Calcutta, for example – who might have purchased *zamindari* property at auction, had to come to terms with the traditional system if, as absentee owner, he expected to realize the benefits of collecting the land revenue. To do otherwise was to lose the cooperation of all those people in the *zamindari* system whose knowledge of the land and its uses was essential for collection and whose enmity could be manifested in deviously obstructive ways, not excluding falsification or destruction of tax receipts and other critical records of prior performance. The outsider might well be scared off or, if he had purchased the *zamindari* right, induced to sell rather than try to cope with a hostile community.[38]

The coercive impact of the permanent settlement in the short run is no easy matter to determine for, as we have indicated, there was a shifting cast of winners and losers who in the late-eighteenth-century setting did not coalesce in their common hostility to its foreign perpetrators. In the long run the policy arrested the decline of the *zamindars* in Bengal by establishing a stronger administrative foundation for the performance of their obligations. Earlier in the century before the British acquired the *diwani*, the *zamindars* of Bengal had come to rely more on armed retainers as the authority of the Mughal emperors declined and the aggressive behavior of rival magnates became more threatening. This frequently entailed the granting of land free of the revenue demand to retainers in return for their arms and loyalty. The *zamindars* diminished the economic base of their domain, while they exacerbated family feuds in the dissipation of their patrimony. It also was not unusual for *zamindars* to use coercion in the collection of the tax liability of undertenants, to flog and otherwise physically abuse defaulters.[39] In settling the land permanently the British attempted to disarm the *zamindars* and establish alternative methods for resolving disputes and enforcing revenue obligations. This led to the introduction of British standards of law and justice about which we shall have more to say in the next chapter. The British were remarkably successful in substituting administrative–legal controls in raising the land revenue for armed coercion. They also were more relentless in enforcing their demands through these means. Even as the market was extended into the agrarian sector, so was the political–legal integument that made its contractual foundations formidable.

Memories no doubt are short and people do not compare their current state of well-being or misery with what they might have endured in a dimly remembered or unknown past. The renovation of the *zamindari* system in Bengal allowed a class to survive that transmitted the pressure for tax collections internally in its domain through the bewildering network of agents, headmen, chief ryots, and other undertenants, backed now by the most effective administration India had ever experienced. By the end of the eighteenth century the *zamindars* had so far impressed the Company with the difficulties of collecting the tax revenues due them that it revised some of its earlier regulations so that *zamindars* 'were empowered to arrest and detain . . . defaulters if they were suspected' of absconding and were 'at liberty to attach and sell their defaulters' property without waiting for judicial decisions'.[40] In the convoluted evolution of the permanent settlement the British bequeathed to nineteenth-century India an imperial history that became grist for the mill of emerging nationalists who viewed the survival of the *zamindars* as evidence of the subordination of Indian to British interests. What in fact happened in the late eighteenth century, curiously enough, may have been less important for the development of an Indian anti-imperialist consciousness than how these events came to be interpreted.

On any interpretation the permanent settlement thrust the market into customary relationships more abruptly than was consistent with an unburdensome accommodation to its demands. In this respect it was different from the enclosures in England that were taking place at the same time. The initiative for them came from the private sector where improving landowners, responding to the price incentives of expanding agricultural markets, wished to reduce their dependence on communal organization so that they would have greater freedom to experiment with new methods of growing crops or breeding livestock. A meticulous legal procedure was followed for assessing the claims of members in the community for common land and for making awards. If, however, one did not have a deed or some satisfactory documentation of one's claim, it was disallowed. It was not sufficient for a small yeoman, for example, to argue that his father, grandfather, and more distant ancestors had always used the commons and therefore he had a customary right to a share of it. In consequence the average size of farms increased during the enclosures as did farm tenancy and the size of the rural proletariat. So too did agricultural gross product and productivity even while the market for land, labor, and capital grew in the countryside. There, it seems clear, the market had strong behavioral foundations in English society, however much it imposed costs on those who were not in a position to take advantage of it. In both societies the scarcity of resources was an omnipresent fact of life, but in England the coercive consequences of that ineluctable condition were assuaged by institutional conditions that raised agricultural productivity where in India they were exacerbated by more disruptive institutional change.

The scramble for trade and profits in Bengal

The effect of the scramble for trade and profits on Indians is no easier to assess than the effect of the permanent settlement, though, as already pointed out, it was short run as the opportunities for enrichment declined with the reform of the Company. It has been observed of the somewhat less than heroic struggles in which Clive came to dominate the nawabs of Bengal that 'the people at large remained utterly unmoved.'[41] How that marvelously insouciant judgment was reached is hard to say. It is conceivable, however, that it has a kernel of truth for the whole period under review in this chapter. Europeans were an infinitesimal population in Bengal in the eighteenth century. In 1766, the year following the accession of the Company to the *diwani*, there were 232 Europeans residing in Calcutta, the only community where 'the British presence in Bengal was unmistakable.'[42] And even with the increase in the number of men who sought fame and fortune in the Company's service after its change in status there were never enough Englishmen in Bengal to make encounters with the local population anything but a rarity. In fact, the European population was held down by an insalubrious environment which exacted a heavy toll. For the period from 1707 to 1775, 59 percent of all the Company's servants going out to India died there, many of them in their first year. For one decade, 1747 to 1756, the mortality rate for new arrivals was 74 percent, comparable to the loss of 'subalterns on the Western Front in the First World War or the crews of British bombers in the Second'.[43]

For those in the Company's service who survived the hazards to health the opportunities for enrichment came to the men who achieved high position in the revenue administration or who worked in the commercial division and used the Company monopoly to good account in private trade. Neither through the one means nor through the other were the fortunes made as numerous or as great as the notoriety of returning nabobs suggested to the critical English public. The fortune Clive took home after Plassey – Mir Jafar made gifts to him upwards of £200,000 – was not the norm. Moreover, it is not clear when such transfers were made whether the incidence was borne by the local magnate seeking favors from the powerful or by their undertenants on whom the demand for revenue collections then fell more insistently or coercively. And, it should be repeated, gifts or tribute in high places hardly originated with the coming of the British; it was a customary way of establishing and maintaining protection and trade throughout Asia. In any event gifts as a source of enrichment were a wasting asset and by 1781 in the Hastings administration had become relatively unimportant.[44]

Trade was another matter. After Plassey the Company began to realize the benefits of the *farmans* of 1717 with the granting of the *diwani*. Europeans no longer were confined to Calcutta, and performed commercial and administrative functions throughout Bengal, Orissa, and Bihar. The Company's goods moving in this area were not subject to local taxes or tariffs, a privilege enforced by its political–military power and denied Indian merchants. The Company's servants trading on their own account claimed the right to use its seal, or *dastak*, which distinguished its goods from less fortunate competitors and allowed them to pass tariff stations without charge. The advantage conferred upon British merchants may be seen in the schedule of charges imposed by the nawab on different classes of traders: for Muslims $2\frac{1}{4}$ percent on the current prices of goods (in transit), for Armenians $3\frac{1}{2}$ percent, and for Hindus 5 percent of a fixed appraisement of the value of their goods. And in addition to these taxes there were other charges collected by *zamindars* and subsidiary officials along riverine arterial and overland trade routes.[45]

Who then could compete with British traders in view of these cost advantages? And were not local merchants forced out of business by the Company's unambiguous exertion of discriminatory political power in Bengal? That surely happened, but, as so often is the case in the complex story of Anglo-Indian relationships, not necessarily in the simple way suggested by differential tax rates. In the first place, Indian traders had non-tax cost advantages by virtue of their familiarity with local markets, languages, and the regional producers of cotton piece goods, opium, saltpeter, food grains, salt, and other commodities carried in trade. By the same token, English and European merchants were handicapped not only by a relative deficiency in the technical skills for making markets in unfamiliar territory, but by their limited numbers. They did not in the eighteenth century control the production of the goods in which they trafficked. When the interior of Bengal was opened up to the Company servants, there was an increased demand for Indians to perform services they themselves could not perform: *banians*, or brokers, for negotiating title to traded commodities and *gumashtas*, agents or stewards, for keeping track of the affairs of a business firm or a Company servant trading on private account. Moreover, Hindu merchants, who seemed to have borne the brunt of the nawab's charges, might have looked upon the Company's privilege as an opportunity. If they could bribe a Company servant to carry their goods under its seal, they could both be better off so long as the former did not hold out for the full amount of the traditional tax. Although Company policy excluded Asian merchants from British privileges, there is every reason to believe that it was honored in the breach.[46]

If, then, there was a transfer of revenues arising in trade from Indian to European merchants, it did not translate into a proportionate increase in net income. The *banians* and *gumashtas* performing services for the Europeans were a charge against the revenues of the latter. Also by virtue of their relationship with the Europeans they were in a good position to trade on their own account under the cover of the Company's privileges. 'That many Indians were greatly enriched by the British conquest of Bengal is undeniable. Most of the families who were to dominate the rich social and intellectual life of mid-nineteenth century Calcutta trace their origins to the later eighteenth century.'[47]

So far as the producers of the goods traded in Bengal were concerned, their contact continued to be with Indian agents acting for Europeans or for themselves. There is no reason to believe that in the eighteenth century there was any change in the way the latter conducted their business or that they were any less or more willing to exert monopsonistic advantages over producers. Physically coercive methods – flogging, for example – had been used to hold down producers' prices before the Europeans moved into Bengal and there is no compelling reason for thinking that those traditional practices changed, whatever their incidence or burden.[48] The ryots or artisan weavers, however, were not helpless before egregious abuses of monopsony power; the relatively favorable land–population ratios then prevailing in Bengal made movement in search of more benign circumstances not infeasible. In any case, producers were as weighed down as ever by the inexorable forces of subsistence. The expansion of European trading activity in Bengal did not stimulate economic development that might have assuaged that burden. It perhaps caused an increase in poppy production or the weaving of cotton or silk cloth, but, if so, these employments did not generate dynamic change elsewhere in the Bengali economy.

Viewed from the vantage point of the late eighteenth century, neither the permanent settlement nor the scramble for trade and profits in Bengal had yet brought British imperialism as a coercive phenomenon into focus. The coercions that characterized the traditional social and economic systems persisted, now however with a new political overlord which was putting its house in order and, unbeknownst to itself and its fragmented host, getting ready for its most rapid period of imperialist growth in the first half of the nineteenth century. That the coercive impact of the British was unfocused was largely attributable to the weakness of ideological values for giving their presence a pejorative meaning or differentiating their actions from what other overlords had been doing since time immemorial. There is no blinking the fact that the scramble for trade and profits turned on freebooting as much as on the mutually advantageous exchanges of neoclassical economics. Nor can it be denied that while the Company was being reformed, its servants in India, especially those in high office, were the beneficiaries of presents – graft as we call it now. Yet many Indians were pleased to have a share of the booty and were not reluctant to bribe officials in the pursuit of their own interests. One way or another they were willing collaborators, a word that in the eighteenth century, had it been used, did not have the opprobrious meaning it acquired in World War II. The British were but the most recent in a long series of imperial rulers. It would require a good deal more imperial history for imperialism to come to mean in the Indian mind an unwanted and illegitimate foreign presence.

Notes

1 Vincent A. Smith, *The Oxford History of India*, Percival Spear (ed.), 3rd edn, Oxford, Clarendon Press, 1967, 334.

2 P. J. Marshall, *Problems of Empire, Britain and India, 1757–1813*, London, Allen & Unwin, 1968, 18.

3 S. B. Chaudhuri, *Civil Disturbances During the British Rule in India, 1765–1857*, Calcutta, World Press, 1955, 8–9.

4 Adam Smith, *An Inquiry into the Nature and Causes of the Wealth of Nations*, E. Cannan (ed.), New York, Modern Library, 1937, 590, 601.

5 M. Athar Ali, *The Mughal Nobility under Aurangzeb*, Bombay, Asia Publishing House, 1968, 160.

6 ibid., 102–7; Irfan Habib, *The Agrarian System of Mughal India, 1556–1707*, Bombay, Asia Publishing House, 1963, 346–8; Vincent A. Smith, *The Oxford History of India*, 441–2.

7 Habib, op. cit., 346.

8 Percival Spear, *Twilight of the Mughals*, Cambridge, Cambridge University Press, 1951, 6–7.

9 Beatrice P. Lamb, *India – A World in Transition*, 3rd edn, New York, Praeger, 1971, 57.

10 K. N. Chaudhuri, *The Trading World of Asia and the English East India Company, 1660–1760*, London, Cambridge University Press, 1978, 29.

11 Irish University Press Series, *British Parliamentary Papers, 1852–53*, Colonies East India, 15, 301.

12 Marshall, *Problems of Empire* . . ., 18.

13 ibid., 29.

14 K. N. Chaudhuri, op. cit., 74–7.

15 ibid., 72.

16 ibid., 2.

17 Monopolies are not easy to maintain and the Company had its share of competitors. For a brief period from 1698 there was even a rival company chartered by the British government, but the two merged in 1708 as the United Company of Merchants of *England* trading to the East Indies. Later in the eighteenth century Adam Smith was sufficiently incensed by monopoly abuses in the Company that he is thought to have been willing to go to India as a member of a commission to investigate them. The commission never left England. John Rae, *Life of Adam Smith*, London, Macmillan, 1895, 254–6.

18 Thomas Mun (1571–1641) was a notable exception. In defense of the Company's export of silver he argued that critics should not look to

single or bilateral transactions, but to the consequences of all its transactions in the East Indies. William J. Barber, *British Economic Thought and India 1600–1858 – A Study in the History of the Development Economics*, Oxford, Clarendon Press, 1975, 11.

19 K. N. Chaudhuri, op. cit., 385–99.

20 Bombay was included in the dowry from the king of Portugal on the occasion of the marriage of Charles II to Catharine of Braganza. Subsequently he 'granted the island to the East India Company for the trifling sum of ten pounds a year': Vincent A. Smith, *The Oxford History of India*, 334.

21 ibid., 433.

22 H. H. Dodwell (ed.), *The Cambridge Shorter History of India*, Delhi, S. Chand, 1964, 412.

23 Anglo-Indian here refers to the English who went out to India in the service of the Company. In the twentieth century Anglo-Indian came to mean Indians of mixed parentage, a somewhat narrower identification than Eurasian.

24 C. H. Philips, *The East India Company 1784–1834*, Manchester, Manchester University Press 1940, 14–16.

25 Marshall, op. cit., 29.

26 Quoted by Philips, op. cit., 14.

27 Vincent A. Smith, *The Oxford History of India*, 523.

28 Ranajit Guha, *A Rule of Property for Bengal, an Essay on the Idea of Permanent Settlement*, Paris, Mouton, 1963, 11.

29 P. J. Marshall, *East Indian Fortunes, the British in Bengal in the Eighteenth Century*, Oxford, Clarendon Press, 1976, 166.

30 Guha, op. cit., 106.

31 ibid., 126.

32 ibid., 93.

33 Sirajul Islam, *The Permanent Settlement in Bengal: A Study of Its Operation 1790–1819*, Dacca, Bangla Academy, 1979, 5.

34 ibid., 15.

35 ibid., 11.

36 ibid., 163.

37 ibid., 189–90; John R. McLane, 'Revenue farming and the Zamindari system in 18th-century Bengal', in Robert E. Frykenberg (ed.), *Land Tenure and Peasant in South Asia*, New Delhi, Orient Longman, 1977, 29–35.

38 Bernard S. Cohn, 'Structural change in Indian rural society, 1596–1885', in Robert E. Frykenberg (ed.), *Land Control and Social*

Structure in Indian Society, Madison, University of Wisconsin Press, 1969, 89–91; Eric Stokes, *The Peasant and the Raj: Studies in Agrarian Society and Peasant Rebellion in Colonial India*, London, Cambridge University Press, 1978, 71; McLane, op. cit., 32–3.

39 McLane, op. cit., 23–4.
40 Islam, op. cit., 64.
41 Dodwell, op. cit., 431.
42 Marshall, *East Indian Fortunes. . .*, 24.
43 ibid., 254.
44 ibid., 178–9.
45 ibid., 108.
46 ibid., 59.
47 ibid., 267.
48 ibid., 118.

4

England in India: Seringapatam to the Great Revolt 1799–1857

By the middle of the nineteenth century the British empire had approached its geographical limits.[1] From Baluchistan to Burma and from Kashmir to Ceylon the British governed subject populations either directly or indirectly through some 600 princely states of varying sizes and degrees of autonomy. The East India Company, transformed beyond recognition to its founders and shortly to disappear in the aftermath of the Sepoy Revolt of 1857–8, had achieved what eluded the restless imperial energies of the Mughal emperors of the seventeenth and eighteenth centuries. Not only did the British rule the entire subcontinent, but they were beginning to invest in the public goods that reduced the geographical impediments to the formation of an Indian state and nation. Lord Dalhousie, the governor-general of India from 1848 to 1856, enthusiastically addressed himself to the planning of transportation and communication facilities and before the end of his term had the satisfaction of seeing the start of railroad and telegraph construction and the completion of the Grand Trunk Road from Calcutta to Peshwar. Dalhousie's enthusiasm for the accomplishments of western technology was not everywhere reciprocated by his subjects, though he left India 'believing that his successor could look forward to a period of unruffled calm for constructive work'.[2] One year later the imperialist chickens came home to roost and Sir Thomas Roe, had he been able to return from his Valhalla, might have said, 'I told you so.'

The burst of imperial energy in India was paralleled at home by an equally energetic growth of the economy. England led the way into the industrial age with incalculable consequences for itself and the world. If in the eighteenth century the assets of England increased relatively to India because of the decline of Mughal power, in the nineteenth century the gap widened still further because of the economic tilt to the west brought on by the industrial revolution. So diffuse an influence inevitably affected the coercive potential of the imperial relationship and it must be examined at the outset of this chapter.

The industrial revolution and the belief in progress

The industrial revolution from the late eighteenth to the mid-nineteenth century irrevocably altered the structure of the British economy. The economic, technical, and motivational propensities that played such a strong part in England's mercantile expansion in the seventeenth century manifested themselves in mechanical inventions, the development of steam power, agricultural experimentation, and institutional and legal changes, all of which broke one production bottleneck after another and led to the rise of the factory system and the growth of cities, especially in the midlands and Lancashire. The construction of canals, roads, and, later, railways increased the mobility of goods and people, as well as the size of markets and the specialization of function that Adam Smith in the early years of the industrial revolution held to be such a compelling cause of economic growth. And all of these achievements were both cause and effect of the prodigious expansion of coal output and the growth first of the iron and then of the steel industries.

The industrial revolution also changed the structure of the world economy and thus affected the circumstances in which societies interacted. In the mercantile age when the Portuguese, the Dutch, the English, and other Europeans established direct contact with Asian societies, they were seeking the commodities of the Indies already being produced by traditional methods. Commodity exchange was the primary means of obtaining spices and pepper, the Europeans offering for trade precious metals or goods acquired in European or Asian markets. Trade, however, was not always voluntary, especially in the early period when the transactors had seen little of one another, did not speak the same language, had different standards of value in a narrow economic sense, and responded to varying social, cultural, and other behavioral norms. In 1441 when the Portuguese were inching their way down the African coast as they searched for the all-water route to India, they seized ten male and female Africans and took them back to Portugal, thus starting the West African Atlantic slave trade.[3] In 1503, Vasco da Gama captured thirty-eight Calicut fishermen and hung them in his displeasure at the reluctance of the Zamorin of Calicut to grant him trading privileges in its markets.[4] And in the early seventeenth century, the Dutch in their eagerness to enforce a trade monopoly in the spices of the Moluccas exterminated the local population of the Banda Islands and replaced them with Dutch colonists who were supposed to cultivate the nutmeg tree with slave labor bought in Asian markets.[5]

The English perhaps were more circumspect in Asia, but, as we have seen, did not shrink from the opportunity to conquer Bengal in the second half of the eighteenth century. This led to greater involvement in the internal trade of Bengal, though not to the destruction of the Indian producers of the traded commodities. As the industrial revolution transformed the British and western economies, however, the structure of world trade changed to the disadvantage of India. The familiar story of the British textile industry is a good case in point. The imbalances among the branches of that industry were among the bottlenecks that galvanized the entrepreneurial and inventive faculties of English entrepreneurs and mechanics. The inability of cotton spinners to keep pace with the demand of weavers of yarn, for example, reflected the viability of an expanding market in England for printed cotton textile fabrics in the production of which in the early eighteenth century Indian producers had a comparative advantage. Threatened by the manifest enthusiasm of fashionable English society for the calicoes and muslins of India, the woolen textile industry mobilized the whole battery of mercantilist arguments in urging on Parliament more protection. Parliament complied with Acts in 1700 and 1720 which, among other things, forbad 'absolutely the import of printed fabrics from India, Persia, and China. All goods seized in contravention of this edict were to be confiscated, sold by auction and re-exported.'[6] While these acts were designed to restrict the flow of cotton textiles into England, there was no reason to believe that the ingenuity of English and non-English smugglers was in any way diminished by parliamentary statute, which in any case could not reverse the tastes of English consumers. So cautious an economic historian as J. H. Clapham asserted that 'there is reason to think that this restrictive act gave an important, and it may be argued a useful, stimulus to textile printing in Britain.'[7]

In fact it was in the cotton textile industry that mechanical inventions were first adapted and it was here rather than in woolen and worsted manufacturing that the factory system first began to take hold. Cotton textiles were a leading sector of the industrial revolution. Unlike the woolen textile industry, the cotton textile industry had to reach out to those parts of the world whose natural endowment was conducive to the raising of cotton. In the nineteenth century the insatiable demand of English cotton spinners for raw cotton linked the British economy in a deeper relationship than hitherto with suppliers. Exchange no longer merely involved transactions in existing stocks of goods; it compelled reorganization of productive methods. In the United States king cotton did not so much change the social organization of production as, in conjunction with the invention of the cotton gin by Eli Whitney in 1793, give a new lease of life to the system of plantation slavery which was experiencing declining productivity in the raising of tobacco. The mechanization of cotton textile production in England was the occasion, if not the cause, of the perpetuation of an extraordinarily coercive and demeaning system of organizing labor in the southeastern United States.

So far as India was concerned, the impact of the industrialization of cotton textile production in England was felt less in the growing of cotton than it was in the competitive position of Indian producers of cotton goods. Where in the eighteenth century they had no difficulty selling cotton products in England, in the nineteenth century the machine products of Lancashire gradually came to equal and then surpass the quality of Indian goods and could be sold in India more cheaply. Handloom weaving in Indian cottage industry then declined.

We shall return to the Indian textile industry later in this chapter. Its decline in India, however, was a reflection of a general widening of inequalities throughout the world occasioned by the industrial revolution. The west accumulated capital, invented a dazzling array of techniques, and developed political and economic organizations which diminished the assets of the east. It also influenced the ideology that shaped people's attitudes about how this growing strength could be appropriately employed in the contacts of west and east. If we look back at the early years of English involvement in India when the economic and technological inequalities of these vastly different societies were not great, we observe varied attitudes toward India in the English presidencies – curiosity, exasperation, disdain, avariciousness, respect, admiration. One does not get the impression that the British as an outpost of their society in India thought of themselves corporately as being superior. And when English dominion began to extend throughout Bengal in the late eighteenth century,

> there was little idea of reform of manners or the moulding of society. Practices like suttee or widow-burning, hook swinging as an act of religious devotion, infanticide, Hindu widowhood, and Muslim polygamy were deplored as 'heathenish' but regarded as customs of the country which could not be interfered with.[8]

Moreover, Warren Hastings had a scholarly interest in ancient India, encouraged the development of Sanskrit studies, and gave his support to the establishment of the Asiatic Society of Bengal in 1784 which did so much to recover historical India.

Classical economics which was to be such an important ingredient in the nineteenth-century English outlook was beginning to come into its own in the late eighteenth century. Indeed, it was born with the industrial revolution. Adam Smith published *The Wealth of Nations* in 1776, the year following the second patent granted to James Watt. He could hardly worship a new industrialism which was scarcely visible in Great Britain. What he was aware of was the growth of new firms and markets in the interstices of the mercantilist system where 'every man, as long as he does not violate the laws of justice, is left free to pursue his own interest his own way.'[9] Thus would natural liberty harness individual drive and ingenuity in increasing the wealth of nations.

As the industrial revolution gathered momentum in the nineteenth century, there began to develop in England a self-consciousness about it, a belief, at least among those who did not see, or chose to ignore, its dark side, that a way had been found to transcend the ancient curse of subsistence. If the heavenly city of the eighteenth-century philosophers, to borrow the title of Carl Becker's well-known book, was not at hand, many people thought that assiduous labor and accumulation would bring it in view. Based on industrial success, endowed with religious sanction, grounded in utilitarian and classical theory, and, because of these manifold inspirations, contradictory and inconsistent, the improving ethic none the less was a splendid solvent of doubt and an equally splendid call to action.

During the years of high Victorian imperialism its religious manifestation was given a tremendous boost by the opening up of sub-Saharan Africa. On the one hand, there seemed to be dwelling there in primitive tribal groupings an untutored population, bound by superstitious and animistic beliefs and unaware of the salvation that awaited those who gave themselves to the Christian God. On the other hand, the very primitiveness of tribal Africa in juxtaposition to the newly changing industrial world stirred the imagination and spread the illusion of unlimited markets. One recalls Stanley appearing before the manufacturers of Manchester, comforting their philistine souls with accounts of the naked savages waiting to be covered by Manchester cloth. What could be more satisfying than selling them Christian garb while making rewarding profits?

Thirty years before Stanley found Livingstone in Central Africa, Palmerston expressed in the House of Commons the exuberant expectations that the improving capitalist ethic generated:

> Why, Sir . . . it is that the exchange of commodities may be accompanied by the . . . diffusion of knowledge – by the interchange of mutual benefits engendering mutual kind feelings. . . . It is, that commerce may go freely forth, leading civilization with one hand and peace with the other, to render mankind happier, wiser, better.[10]

Perhaps the most eloquent, certainly the most prolix, exponent of the improving ethic was Thomas Babington Macaulay whose service in the governor-general's council in India from 1834 to 1838 gave him the opportunity to apply progressive Whig values in an environment vividly different from that which bred them. The son of an austere evangelical member of the 'Clapham Sect' which had done so much to move English society and government against slavery, he seemed to embody, indeed caricature, the optimism that nineteenth-century capitalism infused in the British outlook. Nowhere was this more apparent than in his famous (or infamous) Minute on Education in which he argued for the support of English language and western education in India so that there could be created a class to act as 'interpreters between us and the millions whom we govern; a class of persons, Indian in blood and colour, but English in taste, in opinion, in morals, and in intellect'.[11] The presumptuousness of this view, as arrogant in its way as the religious views of Pizarro and the Spanish conquistadores of the sixteenth century, should not blind us to the strength it imparted to the believer.

As for economics, there was a difference between the application of its principles in England and India and, for some of its spokesmen, severe doubts about the value of Adam Smith's natural liberty for the peoples of India. There was no lack of faith in progress; the means to that end, however, might require a more visible governing hand in India than in England. James Mill, the eminent disciple of Jeremy Bentham and friend and prodder of David Ricardo, published in 1817 *The History of British India*, a work that so impressed the directors of the East India Company that they made him an examiner of correspondence in its London office.[12] From that position he brought a utilitarian view to the dialogue among the Company's officers, at home and abroad, about its role in performing its various functions. This held that the key to achieving the progress that England was already experiencing lay in the establishment of a strong central government capable of imposing a rule of law in India and collecting a land revenue assessed according to the Ricardian principle of rent.

What may surprise one in this prescription in the light of the ideological commitment to *laissez-faire* we associate with classical economics and utilitarianism was the stress on government. Yet Mill was not really being inconsistent; he simply expressed an optimistic belief that institutional conditions could be manipulated or controlled in order to release constructively the self-regarding drives in India that were so fundamental to the growth of the English economy. Mill was an early harbinger of the development economists in our own day who have addressed themselves with such aplomb to the economic problems of the Third World, confident that their models predict the critical policy variables that may accelerate economic progress. His views were widely disseminated by his son, whose *Principles of Political Economy* was first published in 1848. In the *Principles*, Mill wrote the definitive summation of classical political economy and also reflected on the problems of development in Asia as he had come to appreciate them through his association with the Company.

> In many parts of the world, the people can do nothing for themselves which requires large means and combined action; all such things are left undone, unless done by the state. In these cases, the mode in which the government can most surely demonstrate the sincerity with which it intends the greatest good of its subjects, is by doing the things which are incumbent on it by the helplesness of the public, in such a manner as shall tend not to increase and perpetuate but to correct that helplessness. A good government will give all its aid in such a shape, as to encourage and nurture any rudiments it may find of a spirit of individual exertion. It will be assiduous in removing obstacles and discouragements to voluntary enterprise, and in giving whatever facilities and whatever direction and guidance may be necessary.[13]

This was a far cry from Adam Smith, the position of a man who while weaned on classical economics viewed the colonial world from within the administration responsible for its governance.

Whether the improving ethic had its roots in evangelicalism, classical political economy, or utilitarianism, it instilled in many British proconsuls a quiet sense of superiority. They were not troubled about their right to govern subject peoples who for one reason or another were caught in the imperial net. Leonard Woolf looked back on his years in Ceylon – he was there a half century after the period we are concerned with in this chapter – with astonishment. In his autobiography he commented on his role in supervising a religious pilgrimage and observed that:

> the complete self-confidence of the British imperialist in 1910 was really rather strange. Here was I, an Englishman aged 29, who had collected in the middle of the Ceylon jungle nearly 4000 men, women and children, gathered from all over Ceylon and Southern India. I was responsible administratively for everything connected with the well-being of these people and for the maintenance of law and order. If anything had gone wrong during the pilgrimage I should have been blamed. But we were so firmly convinced that, if one white civil servant was there, nothing could possibly go wrong, that I had no staff and no police. I had the District Medical Officer to look after the health of 4000 people and the village headmen to maintain order among them.[14]

And if the district commissioners of the empire supervised with confidence a pilgrimage, they did not hesitate to carry out the institutional changes that seemed to be required by John Stuart Mill's diagnosis of the Asian economic malaise, however imperfectly they understood their impact on local populations. To these changes we shall return later in this chapter.

Territorial expansion and the Company's armies

At the outset of the century, the Company in India was still not tightly controlled by the Crown. There was opportunity for an aggressive governor-general to play a vigorous imperial role so long as it could be made to appear essential to the purposes of the Company and the British government. Moreover, the rivalries of Indian princes especially when intertwined with England's European conflicts encouraged intervention. These were at a peak as the French Revolution had expanded beyond its national frontiers, exacerbating the enmity of the French and English and raising real or imagined fears among the Company's servants in India that their traditional enemies would like nothing better than to displace them.

Seringapatam was the capital of Mysore, one of the largest princely states in south India whose ruler, Tipu Sultan, known as the Tiger of Mysore, had come under the influence of the French. On 4 May 1799 an army of the East India Company stormed Tipu Sultan's fortified palace in the fourth and last Mysore War. This was the climax of the first military campaign in India of Arthur Wellesley (later the Duke of Wellington) who then was appointed Governor of Seringapatam. The securing of that lucrative post was in no way hurt by the governor-general in Calcutta, Lord Mornington, Wellesley's older brother, and one of the more exuberant imperialists to hold that office during the Company's century of rule. Among the duties of the governor of a captured city was the distribution of the prize money, a euphemism for loot, and Wellesley did not shrink from the task. From a treasure estimated at £1,143,216, General Harris, the senior commanding officer 'got £150,000, the sepoys and Indian surgeons about £5 each and Colonel Wellesley £4,000'.[15] Nor did he neglect his brother, to whom he presented Tipu's musical tiger, a macabre instrument in the shape of a tiger holding with its claws a man,

> presumably a servant of the Company, whose left hand waved helplessly while a shrill, intermittent scream came out of his mouth, to the accompaniment of the tiger's savage growls. A pipe organ inside the tiger and his victim was responsible for this hideous concert, which could be varied by playing eighteen ear-splitting notes on a keyboard in the tiger's belly.[16]

The Company's benefits from its victory over Tipu Sultan were equally concrete and a good deal more pragmatic. About half of Mysore was annexed and the descendants of Tipu Sultan were barred from ruling what remained which was returned to Hindu rajas. The Company had established its dominance in south India where the Madras presidency long survived in uneasy association with its neighbors to the west, sometimes at war and other times in tenuous peace. And just as there can be no doubt that Bengal was won by the sword, there is no doubt that English dominion in south India was achieved by its military strength.

The British in India were now established imperialists. No longer were they seeking commercial goals by negotiating with Indian princes about the conditions for trade. As in the French Mysore War, the governor-general used the pretext of French influence to unleash his army and depose Tipu Sultan by force of arms. The latter may have been a threat to the trade of the Company, but the Company was very much more than an association of merchants. Pitt's India Act had divided the ultimate responsibility for economic and political affairs in London between the Court of Directors and the Board of Control. In India, however, no such division could be made. The governor-general at Calcutta and the governors of the other presidencies were territorial rulers bedeviled with the kinds of problems that face any head of state. Moreover, the governor-generals of India were not men of commerce. General Cornwallis was sent out to India to implement Pitt's reforms. Though not himself a military man, Lord Mornington was bellicose enough and contemptuous of commerce to boot. To him, the directors in London were 'the cheesemongers of Leadenhall Street'.[17]

Once under way, territorial expansion seemed to acquire a momentum of its own. In 1801 the Company annexed the Carnatic and thus filled out the boundaries of the Madras presidency as it was until independence in 1947. With the south more secure, it redirected its military energies to the Deccan where the Marathas threatened all three presidencies. In wars conducted in 1803–5 and 1817–18, the Company at last achieved what the Mughal emperors never could quite accomplish, the subordination of the Marathas, some of whose territories were incorporated in the Bombay presidency. It also subdued the Pindaris, 'vast bodies of masterless soldiery, chiefly horse with many odd guns', that 'had grown from the gradual break-up of Mogul armies, and had continually been reinforced from Afghan tribesmen, Arabs, and any adventurous and lawless lad who liked to hear the lark sing rather than the mouse squeak'.[18] In between these wars, the Company found time in 1814–16 to combat the Gurkhas, a community of Indian warriors who had occupied Nepal from whence they menaced the northern frontier of India. A by-product of these martial enterprises was the acceptance by another warrior community, the Rajputs, of British supremacy. When in 1843 the British conquered Sind in the northwest (now in Pakistan) and after two wars with the Sikhs in 1845–6 and 1848–9 annexed the Punjab in the far north, the territorial bounds of Company rule in India had been reached.

Within these bounds, however, there still remained many quasi-independent princely states that governed about half of the territory of the subcontinent. The standards of governance varied widely between British India and princely India and for a time these differences were tolerated so long as they did not jeopardize the security of the empire. If Indian rajas, for example, did nothing to improve the well-being of their subjects and countenanced those Hindu practices such as *sati* which seemed so barbaric to the English, why should the Company have cared so long as they did not turn their warriors loose on British India? This policy of imperial forbearance fell victim to the ebullient ideology of progress which, as we have seen, gained wide currency in England with the material prodigies wrought by the industrial revolution. When Lord Dalhousie became governor-general in 1848, his utilitarian credo was too much offended by the inefficiency in the princely states to leave them alone. Using as his rationale the absence of direct heirs to the princely throne or gross neglect of governmental responsibilities, Dalhousie annexed territories administratively with the same enthusiasm that Lord Mornington had seized them militarily. From 1848 to 1854 a number of states in the old Maratha Confederacy, the largest of which was Nagpur and one of which, Satara, had been granted by the Company to the descendants of Sivaji, a fabled Maratha ruler and hero of the seventeenth century, came under direct British rule for the first reason. For the second reason, Dalhousie took possession of Oudh in 1856.

If we ask how this half-century of aggressive imperialism was perceived by those enveloped in it, we get back to the problem posed in Chapter 1 about what imperialism is. Lord Mornington behaved in every way like a swaggering imperialist and gloried in it. The directors, however, were unnerved by his insouciant commitment to annexation and in 1805 replaced him by the less adventurous Cornwallis.[19] But did the Indians view the British as imperialist? Not if we have in mind imperialism in the invidious meaning that became current in the western world at the end of the nineteenth century. The British may have been seen as powerful lords, threatening and unfair rulers, or privileged princes, but these characteristics did not distinguish them from Hindu rajas or Muslim sultans. Certainly Indians in Delhi, for example, did not react, or would not have reacted had they known about it, with outrage to the fall of Tipu Sultan, because a consciousness capable of transforming such an event into pan-Indian indignation had not yet been formed.

Had the Indians viewed the British as national antagonists they could not have played so important a part in the armies of the Company which were central to its rule in India. The troops that marched on Seringapatam were largely Indian, sepoys who had enlisted for service in the Company. Some of them were ordered there from regiments stationed in Hyderabad, others came in volunteer battalions from the Bengal army.[20] But by 1799 a tradition of sepoy service was well established. More than forty years before, at the Battle of Plassey, Clive had deployed a battalion of sepoys and thereafter in the Madras and Bombay armies as well as in the Bengal army sepoys comprised the majority of the troops. No commitment to a transcendent political value such as the Indian nation or people prevented these mercenary soldiers from joining an organization whose purpose was to serve the interests of the English in India. By the same token their loyalties were equivocal as they were not bonded with their officers in values that went beyond those that formed in the hierarchical command of army life.

The establishment of command authority in the Company's armies was no mean feat. In the eighteenth century, armies in India were rather ragged, ill-disciplined organizations. Sepoys initially were recruited on an *ad hoc* and decentralized basis as circumstances required, the ranks filling up before a campaign and then diminishing afterwards. They were irregulars rather than regulars. Moreover, European recruits in the Company's armies were of doubtful quality and indeed it is not clear that 'recruit' evokes the right impression of how their services were obtained. Kaye observed of them that 'the refuse of the streets was swept up and shovelled at once into ships. Embarked as rabble, they were expected to land as soldiers.'[21] They came from a number of western European countries and they hardly formed a coherent body of troops identified with the Company's purposes, good or bad. Like the sepoys, they were mercenaries with their eye on the main chance.

The British officers who commanded these troops came from the middle and upper classes, men whose prospects may not have been bright at home either because their social status denied them preferment or because their inferior position in the family precluded their inheriting estates and title. In India their service was likely to be soured by the superior position of royal officers, who, like Colonel Wellesley, took precedence over them at the same rank whenever they were in the same command. In addition, royal officers had benefits denied Company officers who came to be especially covetous of their economic circumstances. In consequence, a conflict between the interest of the Company in holding down costs and a disgruntled officer class was never far below the surface. Indeed, in the haphazard development of the Company's armies in the eighteenth century there was a mutinous tradition among the officers for pressing demands on the Company, an example that was not lost upon the sepoys.

In 1796 on the eve of the Company's great surge of territorial expansion it promulgated reforms that were intended to cope with these problems of command. The autonomy of regiments in the older service gave way to greater centralized organization with staff officers acquiring command authority at the expense of regimental officers. Battalion size and structure were standardized. A training program for cadets scheduled for duty in the Company's armies, stressing Indian languages and disciplines related to military operations, was established in England. In order to abort the economic source of discontent, the reforms standardized promotion procedures, set out the schedules of pay in rank, including the allowances for service away from the home base, and specified the pension rights of the troops. Moreover, they provided for regular furloughs with pay and inaugurated a system for awarding campaign medals for meritorious service, the wearing of which, presumably, would not have been prudent had an Indian national consciousness been extant. Nor did they neglect the sanctions that armies could impose for refusal to obey orders. The Articles of War of the royal army were published in both Hindustani and Nagari and they were to be read periodically to the sepoys.[22] A system of courts martial was set up to review the cases of those charged with violation of the Articles of War and to sentence those adjudged guilty.

Two years before these reforms were proclaimed there were 82,000 sepoys in the Indian armies. By 1856 there were 214,000.[23] These numbers are not large relative to a total population which in 1800 has been variously estimated from 100 million to 192 million.[24] But for an analysis of imperialism they were a critical subset of the population because they were placed in one of the few institutionalized relationships in the subcontinent between Indians and Englishmen. The sepoys came from relatively higher classes than did European privates and non-commissioned officers whom we have seen were likely to be 'recruited' in city streets. A large proportion – perhaps as much as a half – of the Bengal army was recruited among high-caste Hindu brahmans and Rajputs in Oudh.[25] Most of these were the sons of peasants and landowners who were people of substance in their villages. We are not concerned here with a rabble, an assemblage of anomic, purposeless individuals. The high-caste Indians who enlisted in the Company's armies were attracted by the benefits of the service and these were viewed as a supplement to the subsistence their families earned in the villages. While the evidence is fragmentary, it suggests that the sepoys did not receive more rupees per month than in comparable alternative occupations, but rather were paid more regularly.[26] Furthermore, the pensions for which they qualified after fifteen years' service, and at a higher rate after forty years, were then unique. And it may not have been unimportant that the sepoys were given precedence in civil suits before the Company's courts, a privilege that landowners found advantageous in an era when the various land settlements forced upon them by the Company generated an extraordinary amount of litigation.[27] That the service was indeed attractive may be gleaned from the fact that, particularly with the Bengal army, there was little difficulty in recruiting sepoys. This responsibility fell on Indians already in the armies who were pleased to bring into the service friends and family when new levies were needed, especially if, as sometimes was the case, a bounty was offered for each new recruit.[28]

Notwithstanding the attractions of service in the Company's armies, they were a gathering place for Indian disaffection from British governance, much as Marx thought the rise of the industrial factory was a center of discontent of the industrial workers with capitalism. However strong the caste divisions that the sepoys brought with them to the armies, they could not shatter grievances that were common to all of them. The sources of these grievances were both diffuse and concrete. A sense of unease and insecurity about their own way of life pervaded the Indians as they became more conscious of the life style and values of Europeans. The differences separating them became greater as industrialization made the intrusion of one upon the other more pronounced. In the eighteenth century when the English were isolated from European society they were more inclined to accommodate to Indian values and it was not uncommon for them to acquire Indian families. In the armies the social distance between European officers and sepoys was not yet heightened by the seeming omnipotence of the English and their threat to impose their way of life on the troops. When the technological revolution in transportation and communication reduced the distance between Great Britain and India, the British presence became more clearly defined. English women came to India in growing numbers as wives or sisters of Company servants in search of husbands. As the nineteenth century advanced into the Victorian age, the English family, with its social and religious values, its standards of dress, entertainment, and commensality, and its sense of proper deference of inferiors to superiors, was recreated in the midst of Indian society, at once raising barriers between the races and making Indians fearful of the intent of those whose interests they served.

These diffuse sources of discontent were made pointed by economic complaints and the insensitivity of the British to the religious commitments of Hindu and Muslim troops. When it broke out in open mutiny, one or the other or both were the precipitating cause. In Vellore in the Carnatic in 1806, sepoys in the Madras army rebelled, seizing and killing the European garrison in the fort, because British officers, eager to Europeanize the appearance of their troops, ordered them to shave their beards, remove caste markings, and on parade wear a round leather hat made from the skin of the unclean pig or the sacred cow. When the anticipated support from the followers of the family of Tipu Sultan did not materialize, the mutiny was repressed. A court martial sentenced to death by hanging the mutineers alleged to have been responsible for the killing of the Europeans and dismissed the rest from the Company's service.[29]

In 1824 in Barrackpore in West Bengal, some divisions in the Bengal army scheduled for duty in Burma during the first Burmese War (1824–6) refused orders. The troops were apprehensive about serving outside India in a campaign where the casualty and death rates were extremely high and to which they might be transported by boat across the Bay of Bengal in violation of caste prescriptions. The land route to Rangoon by Chittagong and the Arakan coast on the east side of the Bay of Bengal required bullocks to carry the military and field gear of the sepoys, a logistic problem that was exacerbated by a disagreement about whether the Company or the sepoys should bear the cost of the necessary bullocks. The former asserted that the regular allowance for sepoys serving away from the home base was adequate for this purpose, the latter that the high price of bullocks occasioned by the army's demand reduced their pay for hazardous service abroad. When these difficulties could not be resolved and at a regimental assembly the sepoys would not ground their arms on order, a European regiment fired artillery loaded with grape-shot on the recalcitrant troops. A few were killed, most of them fled, and about eighty were taken prisoner. In the court martial forty-one of these prisoners were sentenced to death, of whom twelve were executed the following day, the balance having their sentences commuted to various terms of hard labor in chains.[30]

Conquest was not cheap and the Company found that with each one its costs placed severe strain on the land revenues, leading it to fret about ways of lessening the burden of its armies. The allowance, at issue in the Burmese War, also became a bone of contention in the Sind War of 1843. Again regiments of the Bengal army, which was called upon to garrison Sind after the Bombay army had conquered it, were in the eye of the storm. In this case the difficulty arose over the definition of the sepoys' service as it related to the value of the allowance for duty away from home, which was greater outside than inside British territory. The Madras troops received the extra allowance normally granted for fighting in a foreign campaign, but after incorporating Sind into its territories the Company would not allow the Bengal regiment the extra allowance for garrison duty in the newly conquered territory. The difficulty was complicated by the considerable sympathy that many officers had for the sepoys' view in the matter, but when the latter asked to be discharged if they could not be paid the extra allowance for service in Sind, their officers informed them that they were not empowered to release them. In the end the offending sepoys in the disaffected regiment were arrested and court-martialed, six of them being sentenced to death and twenty-five being given prison terms of varying length and conditions.[31]

The limited resources of the Company were a compelling factor in military administration, for the matter of the allowance recurred in the Sikh wars of 1845–6 and 1848–9 and in the same way. Sepoys would not accept their pay because they had been denied the extra allowance they thought due them for service in foreign territories that through conquest had become British. Just as in Sind, the mutinies were repressed and the inevitable court martial passed judgment on the alleged ringleaders. What did distinguish the first mutiny in the Sikh wars was the administration of military justice. Four sepoys were sentenced to fourteen years hard labor, a sentence that subsequently was changed to death at the insistence of General Sir Charles Napier who, in his turn, commuted the sentence to transportation for life so that they would 'in external exile expiate their crimes' and 'for ever separated from their country and their relations, in a strange land beyond the seas, linger out their miserable lives'.[32]

There were other manifestations of sepoy disaffection in the years before the Great Revolt. In 1845 in Patna, the capital of Bihar, a wealthy landowner tried to subvert the loyalties of a sepoy infantry regiment whose ranks already were unnerved by the rumor that the British were going to Christianize them, a rumor that gained credibility when it was learned that a magistrate in Patna wished to gather census data about the caste, community, and employment of the local population.[33] The signs were there, but those who saw them failed to take steps to allay the anxieties of the sepoys. For the most part, however, they were ignored. Indeed the arrogance of British officers compounded in their command role by a belief in the inferiority of Indians gave them the illusion that the bond between them was very much greater than the pay for which the latter served. As an early historian of the Sepoy Rebellion noted,

> The fidelity of the Native Army of India was an established article of faith. . . . Commanded by officers whom he trusted and loved, though of another colour and another creed, there was nothing, it was said, which he would not endure. . . . History for a hundred years had sparkled with examples of his noble fidelity; and there were few who did not believe, in spite of transitory aberrations, that he would be true to the last line of the chapter.[34]

The suspension of disbelief of British officers in the command of Hindu and Muslim troops was rudely broken in the Sepoy Rebellion and we will take up that disaster in the next chapter. In the half century preceding it, the Company's armies were an incubator of hostility to British governance, initially manifested in economic inequities and apprehensions about violations of religious belief but then transmitted to the larger society as a more general sense of the injustice and frustrations of foreign rule. The history of the sepoys was for subsequent generations a seminal influence in the formation of an Indian anti-imperialism, as opposed to localized hostility to oppressive rulers.

If the grievances of the sepoys passed into the larger society, it was because the latter had grievances of its own. Territorial annexation fostered these not so much because of the occupation of old provinces by new rulers – this, after all, was an old story in India – but because of the conscientious commitment of the new rulers to efficient administration of governmental authority. This was the distinguishing characteristic of British imperialism. While Britain's performance in the ancient imperial game of territorial annexation ranked with the best, its more enduring influence derived from the application to India of policies, programs, and institutions that originated in British practice, but none the less were deemed appropriate for a dramatically different society. The British did not always understand what that influence was, and it is paradoxical that the most efficient government that had yet ruled India began to crystallize Indian interests and preferences so that it came to be seen as an unwanted foreign oppressor. In no other phase of government was this so clear as in the administration of the land revenue and land settlement.

The land revenue and land settlement

When the Company acquired the *diwani* in Bengal and became a viceroy in the system of Mughal governance, it seemed to have at hand a resource that bid fair to reduce the costs of its imperialist involvement. No longer did its financial performance depend wholly – or so it seemed – on the relative prices of commodity transactions for European markets and the Asian carrying trade and of the services essential for maintaining its Asian establishments. The cost of the Bengal army, for example, could be charged against the land revenue raised there. Not only were the enlisted ranks staffed largely with Indians, but their pay, as well as the pay of European officers and enlisted men, could originate in the gross product of Bengal. And just as the Mughal emperor, or any prince in India, could anticipate greater revenue with the acquisition of more land, so too the Company could hope that territorial annexations would bring their own reward.

In proclaiming the permanent settlement in Bengal, Cornwallis had superimposed the institution of proprietary rights in land on a traditional society for which the notion of private property as it had emerged in the English common law had no meaning. If, however, the British were puzzled by the evanescent character of property rights in Indian custom, they became no more diffident in the nineteenth century about injecting their own theories into the settlement of the land revenues in their new territories. Even before the publication of *Principles of Political Economy and Taxation* in 1817, Ricardo's version of classical economics, especially its rendering of the theory of rent, had become a compelling influence in public discourse. It will be recalled that when pushed to its logical extreme, it predicted the approach of the stationary state. In the face of population pressures which extended the extensive and intensive margins of cultivation, rents would rise at the expense of profits as the cost of subsistence and money wages rose. The villains of the piece were the landlords who engrossed the product in higher rents while making no contribution of their own to the growth of output. By depressing the profits of capitalists they undermined the foundations of economic growth. It is curious that a society whose economy was growing so vigorously and which was so committed to private property would none the less conceive so subversive a theory. For rent, in this version of classical economics, was a surplus which could be taxed without diminishing gross product since it reflected the varying, God-given, natural conditions of the soil.

The radical implications of this doctrine were not lost on later generations, not least of all John Stuart Mill who was a bridge between the market-oriented utilitarians of the first part of the century and the state-oriented Fabian socialists of the last part of the century. In India, however, the radical force of the theory was felt simultaneously with its birth. James Mill's *History of British India* was an expression of his extraordinary faith in the relevance of utilitarianism and Ricardian economics for transplanting in India the fruits of western progress as well as an indictment of the permanent settlement. What was required were clearly codified laws and a settlement with cultivating peasants whose taxes – rents, in principle – were to be assessed according to the differential fertility of the soil. There would be no intermediate holders between the state and peasants who would be motivated to apply capital to the improvement of the land because the increments to output would be protected in the settlement and not engrossed by an idle landlord class. The older Mill was no shrinking violet as he surveyed the needs of India from the bastion of western capitalism. He was wholly unmoved by the pragmatic problems that confronted Cornwallis; the *zamindars* were a parasitic, idle class and to have settled permanently with them was a sure way of aborting economic growth and the Company's land revenue.[35]

Before going on to outline the other kinds of settlements made in India during the first half of the nineteenth century, we wish to reassert the one-sidedness or inequality of these ideas in the relationship of England and India. In the administration of the new territories, the British might have continued to govern in the tradition of Warren Hastings. Appreciative of and sensitive to the institutions and history of Indian cultures, he wished to rule through them with the intrusion of alien British norms kept to a minimum. The Company had replaced the nawab of Bengal, but, in his view, it was entirely inappropriate to tamper with customs and methods of governance which had been fashioned in an ancient and sophisticated civilization and had withstood innumerable imperial occupations. In the reform of the Company, which was in part brought on by the tolerance of Hastings for practices which may have seemed less corrupt to him in India than they did to Pitt's government in England, the British turned away from India, as it were, and looked to their own norms for the proper standards of Indian rule.

These norms were much influenced by the ascendant ideas of classical economics and utilitarianism, which were both cause and effect of the economic and political changes that were transforming Great Britain. Not many societies, if any, have had as pragmatic an association of intellectual discourse and politics, and the ideas of Adam Smith, David Ricardo, Jeremy Bentham, and their followers were sharpened in the open forums of Parliament and in the controversies generated by the quarterly reviews for which England was famous. These involved not only intramural doctrinal differences, but value conflicts with social thought in the tradition of Edmund Burke and other conservative philosophers. The point is that there was an extraordinary range of ideas in England that could be brought to bear on the economic and political problems which had been thrust up by the industrial revolution. These were the ideas through which the problems of a non-growing, traditional society in the process of changing imperial masters were viewed. Even those protagonists of the preservation of Indian institutions and values were likely to find the premises of their argument in English conservative rationalization of customs and practices that had survived time and usage.

The Indian view of themselves, if represented at all in the English dialogue on the management of Indian territories, was derived at third or fourth hand or was assumed to be adequately reflected in the universal categories – the pleasure–pain calculus in utilitarianism, for example – that informed their diagnosis of the problem. The exclusion of Indian perceptions from British deliberations perhaps does not need to be explained in an imperialist setting. This is what imperialism is all about – the imposition of one set of values, norms, practices, and policies which are foreign to those who must live with them. Yet the one-sided dominance of British ideas gave its imperialism its peculiar form. I am not suggesting that English thought and belief were better than Indian. Rather they had a greater capacity to penetrate Indian society than Indian values to penetrate English society. If the English brought to India the idea of economic growth and then proceeded to make land settlements that tried to release the process in agriculture, they introduced an idea that eventually found a more congenial home than the policies it inspired. Today many Indian economists are inclined to condemn British imperial policy precisely on the grounds that it aborted continuing economic growth in the nineteenth century or prevented it from getting under way.[36]

The land settlements thus were an emanation of English economic, political, and legal ideas seasoned by the pragmatic difficulties of carrying them out. In South India the Bengal Settlement was resisted by the Company's servants. Sir Thomas Munro settled with the individual peasant or ryot – the ryotwari system – in the Madras presidency not because he sympathized with the utilitarian outlook of James Mill but because he believed 'the peasant embodied the pastoral values of an uncorrupted society, whose traditional simple way of life it was the duty of the Government to preserve,' and because the pattern of land holding and social customs did not interfere with such a settlement to the extent that they would have in Bengal.[37]

While Munro's settlement influenced subsequent settlements in the Bombay presidency where land was held in conditions similar to south India, in the North-Western Provinces, to the west and north of Bengal, the initial settlement, but not in perpetuity, was with a class of superior holders similar to the *zamindars* in Bengal, the *taluqdars*. As the Company's officers became more familiar with the territory, they saw the coparcenary joint village, in which 'land was the possession of a unified group of cultivators bound together by ties of common ancestry' and where 'each member of the community usually held certain fields . . . from which he drew his own subsistence', as the foundation of the agricultural economy.[38] In 1822 they started to make the land surveys necessary for a settlement with the villages, which were then carried out over a period of more than thirty years.

After the Company annexed the Punjab in 1849 following the second Sikh War, the Company applied the formula that was guiding the settlements in the North-Western Provinces and settled with villages that formerly were inferior to magnates of the stature of *taluqdars* and *zamindars*. This was accomplished over the resistance of commissioners who were not yet persuaded that utilitarian theory should prevail in its councils over sensitivity to the values of the local élites, the differing viewpoints having their most dramatic airing in the intra-familial quarrel of Henry and John Lawrence, two of the more famous Indian proconsuls.[39] Similarly in Oudh after it was annexed in 1856, the Company settled with village communities, disregarding, as far as it could, the claims of *taluqdars* who had acquired wealth and power in the wake of the declining Mughal empire. In this case there was no equivocation as it was enthusiastically ordered by the governor-general, Lord Dalhousie, 'without so much as a cursory investigation of the actual nature of land tenure in the province'.[40]

On the eve of the Sepoy Revolt the Company over a period of more than fifty years had been entering into land settlements with different individuals and groups according to prevailing English norms about how land ought to be held and to English views of the pivotal and potentially productive landholders throughout British India. From Cornwallis to Dalhousie these criteria varied, but reflected with greater intensity towards the middle of the nineteenth century the values that were riding high in the industrial revolution. What were the consequences for Indians of these attempts to inject into the countryside the English institution of private property with its attendant rights and obligations? How did they respond to these institutional changes? Did they become better off or worse off? If the latter, did they lay the blame for their deteriorating condition at the feet of foreign English interlopers? Or did all of this leave village India untouched as once again it accommodated itself with minimal strain to still another imperial rule? If we cannot answer these questions with any precision, we can at least raise issues that may get us a little closer to what we have already referred to as the underside of imperialism.

Perhaps the first thing to note is that whatever kind of settlement was made, permanent in Bengal or for terms in the other presidencies, with superior holders or with cultivating peasants or villages, the land revenue assessment was high. This may have reflected a carry-over from previous regimes which were not reluctant to squeeze out of the land, and hence the peasant, as large a surplus as was practicable. More importantly, to the extent that settlement officers were influenced by Ricardian rent theory they were inclined to set tax rates that left the property owner only with that part of gross product representing the cost of labor and capital, taking the balance as revenue which, it was assumed, would not affect his productive effort. Moreover, since the assessment procedure was only a crude approximation of the differential natural fertility of the land and since the fixedness of the assessment rate – in perpetuity or for long term – was held to be the feature in the British administration of the land revenue that made it less capricious than previous systems, settlement officers were biased towards high rates. The burden of a high rate on land of uncertain fertility could be reduced by the skillful and assiduous application of labor to it, increasing agricultural productivity, one of the prime objectives of the land revenue system.

If the assessment rates were high, the costs of non-compliance were equally high. Since the land settlement devolved upon the holder a property right which was alienable, in the event of failure to pay the land revenue from current output he had to borrow or be forced by the government to sell some part of the assets that had been settled upon him in order to meet the obligation. In either case the market influenced more vigorously his life's chances than hitherto. In Mughal India, a village headman might have had to sell part of the village crop in order to pay the tax obligation in rupees, but if there were a crop failure the customary relationship between village and *zamindar* or *jagirdar* was sufficiently flexible and the idea of property so diffuse or alien that the obligation might have been deferred or some suitable substitute devised. On the other hand, the superior holder might have descended upon the village with his armed retainers and seized what crops he could. The settlements, then, hardly exorcized the specter of force that always is the companion of scarcity; rather it substituted market for non-market coercion on those occasions when revenue claims, for whatever reason, were not paid as required.

It is not easy to assess the impact of these changes and to decide who were the winners and the losers. One thing can be said unequivocally, however; the settlements were imposed on Indians from above by foreigners with an imperfect understanding and erratic sympathy for the complexities of Indian agrarian organization. People prefer to be ruled by governors with whom they identify for non-economic reasons – racial, national, religious – perhaps even at the cost of lower income. In India, cumulative forces shaped the Indian consciousness of British rule. So long as the Company was confined to the coastal presidencies, the British were viewed by those who came in contact with them as another tribe, another community, another piece in the gaudy patchwork of the subcontinent. As that community pursued inexorably the course of annexation in the first half of the nineteenth century and in its governance reached into the social substance of Indian communities, the differences between them were seen as more threatening. As the British presence became more pronounced and stereotyped, it broadcast the seeds of an Indian consciousness which having germinated and grown to maturity could not tolerate British governance on any conditions. In the first half of the nineteenth century the imperialist expansion of the British was so rapid because an Indian consciousness did not exist, but it was in policies such as the land settlements that the ground was being prepared for its growth.

In Bengal the settlements precipitated a century of litigation, a Byzantine struggle on the part of the *zamindars* to retain their status, and a splitting up of the larger *zamindari* estates into many smaller ones. But in those parts of India where the Company settled with cultivating peasants it was not much more successful in achieving its expectations. In south India the ryotwari system was not só much out of step with traditional land holding patterns as the permanent settlement in Bengal, but the force of tradition, the web of personal involvement as in Bengal, dominated the efforts of the Company to administer it. 'The British district collector . . . could never really discover, much less cope with, what was going on beneath him within the agrarian order. In consequence, his words did not carry the weight of authority. He was the chief executive over the district administration on behalf of the imperial power in little more than name.'[41]

Imperial officials made ineffectual by the little-understood workings of a traditional community may not have been beloved by the persons inside it, but they may not have seemed unduly threatening. The settlement in Oudh had a deeply unsettling effect on the communities affected. In by-passing the *taluqdars* and settling with the village communities, the Company's officers presumably felt that by dealing directly with inferior and more numerous holders, who may have had reason to be unhappy with their subordinate position to the grasping *taluqdar*, they were gaining their support and strengthening their capacity to govern. In any event the policy was energetically pursued until early in 1857 when Henry Lawrence, whose antipathy to it had not prevailed over his brother's views in the Punjab, became chief commissioner. By that time the damage had been done. In no part of north India was the civilian response to the rebellion of the sepoys more strongly sympathetic. The Company had not only incurred the enmity of the *taluqdars*, but had raised the apprehensions of peasants by abruptly withdrawing them from an older, often explicitly coercive, but familiar system of revenue collection, and confronting them with unrelenting proponents of efficiency and improvement. One cannot suppose that the peasants in Oudh were any less ingenious than the peasants in south India in the canny manipulation of the social environment to protect their traditional prerogatives. That environment, however, was more rudely disrupted in Oudh by the derogation of the authority of the *taluqdars*. The known devil was preferred to the unknown devil and a pervasive sense of unease became a congenial host for the growth of hostility to British rule.

English law and legal institutions

The land settlements were egregious imperialist policies. They imposed on Indian communities standards of property ownership that would not have developed in the absence of the foreign sponsor. They also created a need for the legal institutions that could deal with the disputes arising from the definition and application of property rights. During the century of the

Company's rule there was a continuing infusion of English law and legal institutions into the Indian legal order to facilitate the resolution of these and other problems.

The British law sense, strongly based in their own struggle to establish the rights of private property, had become more austere as the improving ethic replaced the spirit of tolerance in the passage from the eighteenth to the nineteenth century. There was much in India to offend it. Not only were there built into the Hindu social order inequalities of legal status that were the antithesis of the common law ideal, but there were practices tolerated in varying degrees – *sati*, thuggery, female infanticide, slavery, human sacrifice – that were disturbing to English moral sensibilities. Moreover, the sanctions in criminal law and the methods used to extort confessions seemed fiendishly cruel to Englishmen whose own criminal law in the late eighteenth and early nineteenth centuries, though hardly benign, had shed its harsher medieval features.

Unlike England, where ecclesiastical courts and canon law had all but disappeared in the legal system, India, formally at least, based its law in sacred religious texts. For Hindus the divinely inspired Vedas and the *Dharmashastras*, the oldest of which was the Code of Manu written between 200 BC and AD 100, contained the rules of right conduct. For Muslims the Koran, the teachings of Mohammed, and their exegeses by learned ulamas were the source of legal norms. The 'function of the state was to enforce the law but not to make it, since the law was already complete, enshrined in the sacred texts and in immemorial custom.'[42] Throughout India the resort to these religious standards of law varied with the community. In Mughal states, Muslim law was applied in criminal cases and in civil matters – marriage, divorce, inheritance – Hindus and Muslims were subject to the laws of their own religion. Wherever Hindu states existed independently of the Mughal empire, legal norms in principle were derived from sacred Hindu texts for both criminal and civil proceedings.

Everywhere in India, however, law was heavily seasoned by the customs of the community. Procedures were not highly institutionalized with the formal rules and rituals of the modern court. Rather than being presided over by a somberly gowned or bewigged judge sitting behind an elevated and weighty bench that symbolized the detachment of the judiciary, the typical legal proceeding in India was likely to be conducted by a village headman or a committee, a *panchayat*, consisting of local men of status. Plaintiffs and defendants could conduct their own cases and the esteemed members of the village called upon to pass judgment were not bound by the rules of evidence and conduct in common law trial courts. Indeed the legitimacy of the proceedings inhered in the special knowledge of the community they were privy to; justice could be separated neither from the particularistic traditions and beliefs of the peasants nor from their characteristic social relationships.

The quality of justice in such a system must have varied tremendously. Individuals differed in their capacity to plead their own cases, presiding officers, dependent on an oral tradition, carried in their minds an erratic record of previous decisions in similar cases, and the community itself could be variously tyrannical where individuals had deviated from its norms. But given those norms it probably produced a rough measure of justice that was plausible and acceptable to the peasants who lived with it. As superior authorities became involved in the administration of law, either through appeals from the decisions of headmen or the enforcement of the policies of the state, the quality of justice deteriorated. The village community became a less critical factor in assuaging the harshness of Hindu or Muslim law which did little to moderate the oppressive behaviour of superior authorities. There was, in short, no body of law that applied to rulers and ruled alike.

Until the Company accepted the *diwani*, its servants had had relatively little contact with these legal systems. Inside the presidency towns at Bombay, Calcutta, and Madras, Europeans in residence were subject to English law, which in civil disputes and felonies was administered by the Company's own magistrates. In the early years of its Indian tenure the occasions for Europeans and Indians to be on opposite sides of a judicable issue were limited by the restrictions on movements of Europeans away from the coastal presidencies. Thereafter the situation changed markedly, for the collection of the land revenue obliged the privileged holder to enforce the agreements reached with those holding collecting rights. As viceroy of Bengal for the Mughal emperor, the Company had reduced the survey costs of collecting the land revenue by settling with the *zamindars*, but it thereby increased the enforcement costs.

As Bengal and the subordinate presidencies coped with the peculiar problems of their respective settlements, there emerged in India hybrid legal systems with English institutions grafted into the traditional Muslim and Hindu orders. These systems varied among the presidencies but they all were constructed on a foundation of district officials – collectors or magistrates – who were responsible for collecting the revenue and hearing complaints and appellate processes which allowed aggrieved parties to carry their case to higher authority. Above the collector was a district court from which decisions could be appealed to a superior court in the presidency town. At the outset of its rule the Company did little more than administer Hindu and Muslim justice in civil and criminal matters, applying English law where these lacked relevant legal norms. By the end of the eighteenth century the district courts were presided over by English officials with the assistance of Muslim and Hindu scholars who advised them on issues of civil and criminal law pertinent to the proceedings of the court. As in Mughal India, the criminal court applied Muslim law to everyone and the civil court applied Muslim or Hindu law depending on the community from which the litigants came.

It is not difficult to appreciate that this system worked with maximum frustration for the presiding English judges, whatever the quality of justice the courts administered. They were not fluent in Indian languages nor familiar with the sources of Indian law. They were at the mercy of their Hindu and Muslim assistants. There was then an almost inevitable tendency for the courts to become more anglicized. As early as Warren Hastings' regime the Company employed learned Indian scholars to prepare digests of Hindu and Muslim laws which were translated into English.[43] Moreover, the governors and their councils, which acted as the superior courts, injected into substantive law English legal standards when these were thought to be lacking or inadequate in Indian law. As the English became more censorious of Indian customs, they were less reluctant to change the law. Concomitant with the increasing importance of digests and records of court proceedings was the increasing emphasis on the procedural niceties of English common law. By Cornwallis's day, Bleak House had made its appearance in the Company's courts.[44] It had become more difficult for litigants to conduct their own pleadings; the essential condition for the formation of a professional bar had been realized.

Whether the courts were more important in the legal system as in Bengal, the commissioners as in the Punjab, or the collectors as in the Madras presidency, their jurisdiction was as anomalous as the basis of the Company's rule. The Company argued, when it was convenient to its purposes, that its position in Bengal rested on a legal grant from the emperor in Delhi to collect the land revenue and that its courts derived their authority from that source rather than from the charters of the British Crown. That the Company in Bengal acknowledged two masters so that it might play one against the other was scarcely palatable to the British government. Consequently, in the Regulating Act the home government asserted its sovereignty over the Indian legal system by creating a Supreme Court in Bengal and subsequently established similar courts in the subordinate presidencies. Empowered to hear civil, criminal, admiralty, and ecclesiastical cases, its authority extended to all British subjects in Bengal, Bihar, and Orissa and it was to be presided over by four justices appointed by the Crown with at least five years' experience as barristers.

Almost from the beginning of the Company's rule, therefore, there was overlapping jurisdiction between the Company's courts and the Crown courts and conflict between the purposes they served. While the former evolved in the administrative context of the difficulties of land settlements and the collection of land revenue, the latter were created as a bastion of English law and legal standards. The one was primarily concerned with enforcing the unfamiliar obligations of property ownership, the other was 'avowedly established for the purpose of controlling the actions of the Company's servants and preventing the exercise of oppression against the natives of the country'.[45] The Supreme Court was the conduit for the transfer to India of English common law standards. It was both the symbol and custodian of the rule of law.

There was nothing tidy about the evolution of this hybrid system. Indian law and usages, Company statutes and rulings, and English statutes and common law lived together in unstable equilibrium through the decisions of the courts with the last growing at the expense of the others. In the nineteenth century when the tide of utilitarianism was running strong in the affairs of India, law reform became a panacea among the Indian modernizers. The Charter Act of 1833, which greatly strengthened the legislative authority of the governor-general relative to the governors of the subordinate presidencies, provided for the addition to his council of a new member, subsequently known as the law member. Macaulay was the first appointee to the position and was made chairman of a commission mandated by the Act to make recommendations about ways to reduce the conflicts of law that plagued the overlapping court systems. Macaulay's Herculean labors led to the codification of criminal law, the first of a number of legal codes that eventually were enacted after the Crown assumed the government of India in 1858. Thus in the last years before direct rule, the Company was already responding to the strongly held views in the home government that all Indians of whatever community ought to be subject to the same laws.[46]

And how was all this viewed from below by the subject peoples for whom the rule of law was supposed to bring the benefits of western civilization? Thomas Metcalf asserts that 'one of the most widely detested of all British institutions in India was the system of judicial procedure. If not among the major causes of the Mutiny, the complexity and corruption of the courts certainly helped pave the way for rebellion.'[47] He does not tell us by whom it was detested and several pages on notes that 'the courts, in Indian eyes, were above all a check on arbitrary rule and a guarantee of civil liberty.'[48] The only thing that was unambiguous in the development of the legal system in India was that it was imposed by the British without systematic consultation with the people it affected.

The preferences of the servants of the Company and members of the home government counted for everything, those of Indians for nothing. At best the latter entered into the decisions influencing the evolution of the legal system only in so far as the former empathetically incorporated Indian values. In its operation, however, the legal system was often determining winners and losers in civil conflicts and disputes that came before it as a consequence of the enactment of substantive law, the permanent settlements for example. One cannot conclude that adversary legal proceedings made 50 percent of those involved happy and 50 percent unhappy, but surely there were a considerable number of people who did not detest the system, especially as its workings came to be understood. What we do not know is how much is a 'considerable number' any more than we know the extent of 'widely detested'.

Moreover, there is the ineluctably difficult problem of the time when one views the impact of the legal system on those caught up in it. Attitudes, values, and preferences may change as people become accustomed to a new institution and learn how it may be used to their advantage. The courts in Bengal in the first twenty years after the permanent settlement may have appeared more bewildering to *zamindars*, for example, than they did thirty years later when with the assistance of a newly developing Indian bar, as defendants or plaintiffs, they could marshall the mysterious procedures of the common law. Were they then more likely to accept the standards of the rule of law? Or only if they were winners? And if they were losers, did they long for the days when the issues at conflict were resolved in the scuffles of armed retainers? The continuing development of the law and legal tradition in India suggests that while English governors and judges may not have been beloved, the institutions of governance which they fashioned were not uncongenial to Indians.

Again, consider *sati*, in the English view a criminal matter which however had sanction in Hindu family tradition, especially among the brahman castes. The English never accepted it as a quaint custom hallowed in Indian usage, but they were reluctant to interfere in the Hindu personal, familial realm. It was not until

1829 during the governor-generalship of Lord William Bentinck, in whom the improving ethic ran deep and strong, that *sati* was made a criminal offence in Bengal. How was this change in the criminal law received? The power of belief is extraordinary and undoubtedly there were some women, fully accepting of brahmarical values, who were outraged at this presumptuous interference with ancient practice. To them it must have seemed better to follow one's husband to the next incarnation by mounting the funeral pyre than to continue in the present one. But it strains credulity to assert that most, or even many, women were so subordinate, so unconcerned about their physical self, that they would spontaneously submit to self-immolation on the death of their husbands. Among brahmans, the prohibition of *sati* was received with little enthusiasm, though their attitude in 1829 was different from what it became in the ensuing half century. For the norms of the rule of law did penetrate the brahmanical castes, from whom the Indian bar and bench were most likely to be drawn, and in consequence their views of appropriate familial conduct changed. In fact, under the influence of western values more generally, some unconventional Hindus urged the government of India to ban *sati* before it could bring itself to make the change.[49]

The legal system that evolved in the course of the Company's rule, while upsetting to customary practices in local communities, laid a foundation for the growth of the Indian nation. On the one hand, in fostering an Indian bar, whose members had to know English in order to have access to the courts, it created an all-Indian community which transcended the particularistic interests of caste and religion. On the other, the legal system created a public forum where issues could be adjudicated outside the small, parochial world of peasant communities and stimulated the emergence of national standards of law.[50] It is for this reason that the time when one views the legal system is so important. During the century of the Company's rule, these 'modernizing' influences were not so apparent as they were to become in the century of the Crown's rule that followed. Whatever the English intended, when they imposed the rule of law in India, they set in motion indigenous forces that in good time formed the Indian nation that no longer tolerated English governance.

Economic imperialism

We have deferred an explicit discussion of economic imperialism, not because it is unimportant, but because it can be dealt with more intelligibly in the framework of the political and legal orders that the British imposed on Indian society. Whether or not territorial annexation in the first half of the nineteenth century was motivated by economic forces it extended the sway of British authority and its power to mold the environment affecting the utilization of scarce resources. Moreover, the fact of scarcity entails the use of coercion in social and political organization. Economic imperialism may not be unequivocally distinct in its coercive impact from what would have prevailed in the absence of the foreign intruder. This is all the more true of the British in India. We are not dealing with the Assyrians, those fine exemplars of Joseph Schumpeter's imperialists. Nor are we concerned with Spanish conquistadores, who did not scruple to enslave infidel populations to mine their gold and silver. The British in India carried with them in varying degrees a commercial outlook that sanctioned markets and exchange as the appropriate way for organizing economic activity. Economic imperialism, therefore, must be observed in the extension of markets associated with British rule and the reaction of Indians to them.

The relevant markets were for goods, labor, and capital, though in the nineteenth century prior to the Sepoy Revolt the last was less important than the first two. The Company paid little attention to infrastructure investment until the governor-generaliship of Lord Dalhousie in the decade immediately preceding the rebellion, and private investment was dominated by the structure of demand occasioned by the industrialization of the British economy. This expanded the market for primary output that was grown or mined in tropical and subtropical regions: cotton, sugar, tea, indigo, jute, tin, and so on. However India might have been governed, therefore, whether by the Company, a vigorous Mughal emperor, or a Maratha prince who had succeeded in conquering Delhi, the world economy exterior to India was articulating a demand for goods that could not be produced, or could be produced only in inadequate quantities, in the middle latitudes of the northern hemisphere. The Company, of course, in the performance of its commercial function was anxious to accommodate the Indian economy to the world economy or, more specifically, to the market needs of the British economy. Had there been a vigorous Mughal emperor still ruling in Delhi, it is reasonable to assume that his relationship with the Company would have remained much as it was in the early eighteenth century. He would neither have served the expansionist interests of the British economy nor always have resisted the initiatives of the Company's servants to extend commercial contacts. In any event it is unlikely in the extreme that, given the warrior traditions of Mughal society, he would have brought to his governance of India the knowledge and motivation to turn to its advantage the structural changes in demand and supply that were transforming the world economy. Still less, if we may continue this conjecture further, would a conquering Maratha prince have been able to administer the state in this fashion. Unlike Japan, India in the eighteenth century was not developing an indigenous administrative class whose energies and skills could be directed to the expression and realization of Indian national interests. These speculations are prompted by the charge already referred to that the burden of British imperialism lay in the aborted economic growth that otherwise would have occurred if the Company had not come to dominate the subcontinent. This charge we shall return to later.

What were the consequences of the extension of markets during the Company's rule in the first half of the nineteenth century? We have already seen that the market was used to recruit sepoys for the Company's armies and that it created an unaccustomed mobility in the transfer of the ownership of land, particularly in Bengal. With the one the market offered an opportunity that could or could not be taken up according to one's needs and inclinations, with the other the market facilitated transfers of property that made some people worse off and others better off. In neither case were many Indians involved, though the new thrust of the market was disproportionately felt in the Bengal presidency. Neither the sepoys nor *zamindars* constituted a large proportion of the population.[51]

Perhaps of more quantitative significance were the effects

of the growth in the demand for sugar which raised the demand for plantation labor in the production of sugar cane. Prior to the nineteenth century much of this labor would have been supplied through slavery. In 1807, however, the British Parliament had passed a statute declaring the slave trade illegal and later in 1834 a statute making slavery itself illegal in its colonial possessions. With British squadrons patrolling the west and east coasts of Africa, the supply of new slave labor was cut off at its source. Plantation owners then turned to indentured labor to recruit workers in India for service in British Guiana, Trinidad, Jamaica, Fiji, and Mauritius. The inducing of a Bengali or Bihari peasant to indenture himself for five years as a plantation laborer in a part of the empire a half a world away required a complex organization of peasant recruiters, agents, factotums, managers of collecting depots, shipping masters, doctors, and government officials, all of whom were imperfectly informed about the market and many of whom had little interest in the peasant. The latter indeed was the most imperfectly informed of all and a five-year indenture to Jamaica more often than not turned out to be transportation for life.

The full force of the indentured labour system was not felt until the years following the Sepoy Revolt. During the preceding quarter century it evolved amidst the conflicts of the plantation owners, the anti-slavery movement, and the governments in Westminster and Calcutta, the latter of which was moving somewhat equivocally against the slavery that still existed in India in contravention of the Parliamentary Act of 1834. As the abuses of the system in recruitment, in the passage to the plantations, and on the plantations came to light, it was feared by abolitionists that formal slavery had been abolished only to be replaced by something that was little different. As Hugh Tinker described the work of the touts, called *arkatia*, who assisted licensed recruiters, they made great good use of their special knowledge of Indian communities and the ignorance of the peasants.

> Usually the arkatia worked within a local radius; he relied upon his local knowledge and local contacts. He knew who was in trouble, who had fallen out with his family, who was in disgrace,

> who was wild or wanton. If a big man wanted to get rid of a troublemaker, the arkatia was in contact. If the police were making things hot for anyone, he was in the know. Seldom – hardly ever – did the arkatia venture into the village to seek out his prey: this was too dangerous. The village folk would surely beat him if he showed his face within their walls. So he waited for his opportunity when the possible emigrant would stray outside. He would then tell a story calculated to appeal to the individual prospect. To the most timorous and ignorant he would say that the government wanted people to be gardeners, somewhere in the vicinity of Calcutta. The place lay up a river, so it would be necessary to go there by boat; but it was not far away, and the work was easy. . . . To more robust souls he would truly say that they were wanted to work in *Mirich* or in *Damra*: but he would give an inflated account of the wages and other advantages to be provided.[52]

Whether willingly or unwillingly caught up in the recruitment network, peasants were subject to high rates of mortality in the passage to the sugar plantations. During 1856–7 the average mortality rate on twelve ships carrying indentured labor to the West Indies from Calcutta was 17.27 percent, 707 deaths among 4094 men, women, and children.[53] Once on the plantation the indentured servant suffered the abuses – long hours, inadequate housing, starvation diets, brutal enforcement of the indenture conditions – that so often are visited upon people who have been systematically deprived of recourse or alternatives to their exploited state.[54]

It may be objected that if the abuses of the indentured labor system that developed in the wake of slavery made Indians worse off than they would have been had they remained in India, these should not be attributed to the extension of markets but rather to their attenuation. The man who died on board ship *en route* to Trinidad had no market opportunities to escape the festering, diseased conditions into which he was packed any more than he would have had he survived to work out his indenture at his destination. It certainly was true that so far as the Indian laborer was concerned, the market worked intermittently and with discriminatory force. Until he put his thumb print to the contract, his options in theory were open, though in the fact the combination of his ignorance and the circumstances pushing him out of his home community scarcely made these viable. In this respect the differences between the Bengali peasant in the nineteenth century bound for Trinidad and the English vagrant in the seventeenth century bound for Virginia are unimportant. But markets were imperfect in varying degrees and the organization of the labor migration to the sugar plantations could not have been effected without them. The enslaving alternative had long since been foreclosed and while the emigrants' opportunities were severely restricted, the system that sought them out and transported them to the plantation owners was a creature of the market. Recruiters were paid for finding workers and merchant ships for transporting them to the plantations were built, victualed, and staffed by profit-maximizing criteria. It is not a persuasive argument that a more mobile and competitive market would have obviated the occasions in which one person could coerce and demean another.

If the growth in the world demand for sugar had coercive repercussions in the organization of the labor supply to produce it, these were dispersed throughout the British empire outside of India. This did not make them any more palatable, but it rendered them a less sharp, less insistent, less observable ingredient in the amalgam of British imperialism in India. In this respect the market for sugar was less aggravating than the market for indigo. A plant whose properties were known in both ancient Egypt and India, indigo produced a highly durable blue dye used in the finishing of textiles. Early in the eighteenth century the Company tried to expand the indigo trade in India, but had not been able to compete successfully with plantation output in the West Indies. With the expansion of the cotton textile industry in England during the industrial revolution the demand for dyes increased. As Company rule extended in Bengal, it became possible for Europeans to enter directly into the management and supervision of indigo production, the technical characteristics of which required continuous attention to cultivation and exacting care for the timing of the harvest. Moreover, the interest in producing indigo was heightened by its suitability, in its processed form of pressed cakes or molds, for the remittance trade, a market by which Europeans resident in India transmitted funds to Europe. When in the Charter Act of 1833 the Company was separated from its commercial functions and British territory in India opened to settlement by Europeans, indigo production, which already was a major agricultural enterprise, increased in lower Bengal. In the thirty years before the Sepoy Revolt, the exports of indigo grew to become second only to opium.[55]

The European indigo planters either leased land from *zamindars* or bought land which, the government of India had ruled, was legal in British territory. While there was sometimes friction between these foreign intruders and the *zamindars*, who may have felt that their leaseholders were not properly appreciative of the social and behavioral obligations of the agrarian order, and in any case did not ask to have the foreign interloper in their midst, the more enduring and serious conflict was with the peasants or ryots, on whose labor indigo production depended. The source of conflict inhered in the monopsonistic relationship between planter and cultivator, an exploitative setting which is familiar to any student of labor movements. The peasant was confronted by a landowner or leaseholder with specific production interests which differed from his. The relative price of rice and indigo made the cultivation of the former the more profitable output for the peasant, for the reasons that he could meet his subsistence needs directly and would not be subject to the adverse terms of trade between rice and indigo that were made all the more unattractive by the monopsonistic purchase by the planter of the cultivator's services. The latter were spelled out in some detail in the contract into which the peasant entered with the planter. He was required to plant, cultivate, and harvest indigo in a specified area of the land he undertook to work. The planter supplied the peasants with seeds at a contracted price, at the harvest bought the indigo at a contracted price, and kept the records of their financial status. It was an arrangement not dissimilar to sharecropping or the advancement of wages in kind through a company store in an isolated mining community. Just like the sharecropper or the miner, the indigo ryot seldom knew what his financial position was and might find after the harvest that he had little more than the rupees needed to cover the seed cost. Moreover, the contract was enforced by the police or by the planters' own retainers and towards the end of the period the planters were bringing pressure on the government of India to enact a criminally enforceable contract law.[56] They thus anticipated that the rule of law could be used to discipline disaffected indigo cultivators.

Unlike the peasants indentured to work on the sugar plantations, the indigo cultivators were concentrated, the industry being almost wholly located in lower Bengal. Their grievances were reinforced as they became aware that they were not the consequence of a few grasping indigo planters, but rather were the burden of the system for organizing indigo production. Where coalminers in Galbraithian fashion organized monopolies of their own to offset the monopsony power of the coal owners, the indigo cultivators learned to use the Company's courts to bring charges against planters where they were deemed to have violated contract obligations and organized social boycotts against peasants who would not cooperate in the struggle against the planters.[57] In the immediate aftermath of the Sepoy Revolt there were disturbances in lower Bengal that became known as the Blue Mutiny. This source of peasant discontent was removed by the long-run decline of the indigo industry as a consequence in 1856 of the synthesizing of the first aniline dye and the prodigious growth of the German dyestuff industry in the second half of the nineteenth century.[58] Even before this technological change, the exports of indigo from India were beginning to fall off.

The growth and decline of the indigo industry in the nineteenth century was an ephemeral occurrence in the history of economic imperialism in India. The European planters imposed costs on the peasants, though these were not unequivocally a net increase over the costs they bore prior to the expansion of the industry. Even as producers of rice, for example, they raised little more than subsistence and if they were not held in financial bondage to a European planter, they may have been similarly indebted to a local money lender. Poverty took its toll whatever was being produced. If the occurrence was ephemeral, however, its history endured in the Indian consciousness and played a greater part subsequently in the formation of an anti-imperial outlook in India than did the migration of indentured workers to the sugar plantations. The very fact that the planters were a foreign presence made them culpable in the minds of a developing Bengali and Indian intelligentsia for conduct that was more easily excused or ignored when all the principals were Indian.

Neither the migration of Indians to other colonies in the British empire nor the discontent of indigo cultivators in lower Bengal has received as much attention in accounts of the economic impact of Great Britain on India as the competition of the cotton goods of Lancashire. The decline of the Indian handloom weaver, which we noted earlier in this chapter, was caused in most general terms by the fact that the price elasticity of demand in Indian and Asian markets for English cotton piece goods in the nineteenth century was high so that they were a desirable substitute for Indian output. The technical changes that transformed the methods of production in England also raised the quality of the goods produced. When their price fell with the reduction of the costs of transportation in the passage from England to the east, Asian consumers substituted Lancashire cotton piece goods for the products of Indian cottage handloom weavers. In inducing a decline in India's most ancient and highly regarded industry, Indian and Asian consumers were acting like consumers anywhere confronted by a structure of prices for goods of varying characteristics and quality; they maximized their familial interest.

Had there been in India in the nineteenth century a government of Indians who were intent on serving an Indian interest, what should it have done? One answer to the question is that Indian industry should have been protected against what has been called the free-trade imperialism of Great Britain.[59] If prohibitive duties had been imposed on the importation of Lancashire cotton goods in order to protect Indian manufacturers, the latter might have retained their eighteenth-century preeminence, but at the cost of reducing the real income of the Indian consumers of cotton fabrics.

Moreover, protection would not have prevented the loss of Asian and European markets to the English textile industry. More generally, one may imagine a government, perhaps like the United States in the period following the Civil War, imposing tariffs in order to protect modernizing industries in the short run so that they might learn in the long run to stand on their own feet. As we have already asserted, however, there was no indigenous Indian governing class in the first half of the nineteenth century waiting in the wings with a conception of an Indian national interest and still less with ideas of how one might develop and modernize industry.[60] Nor would it have been possible for an Indian government to administer a Japanese-type seclusion from the external world, an alternative that worked best when the external world cared little for what happened inside the secluded country.[61]

As a manifestation of economic imperialism, the decline of the Indian cottage textile industry stands in sharp contrast to the migration of indentured labor. The losses experienced by spinners and handloom weavers can be balanced against the gains of the Indian consumers of English cotton textiles. Quite apart from the question of how much Indian cottage industry declined and therefore the extent to which Indian textile workers against their wishes were deprived of their traditional livelihood, the market revealed strong preferences for British goods. There were two sides to the coin of free-trade imperialism. For the suffering of the Bengali peasant inveigled and coerced into the long trip to the West Indies there was little benefit experienced elsewhere in the Indian economy. The exporting of labor to the plantations of Jamaica enhanced the profits of plantation owners and the sweetness of the European and American cuisine. India had fewer bodies to burn or bury.

In much greater measure than the indigo cultivators the decline in the economic status of the Indian textile workers became a symbol of imperialist oppression. Where indigo production had been increased under the supervision of European planters and against the interests of the cultivating peasants, textile production had been the greatest industry in India built on the skills of Indian spinners, weavers, and merchants. As we noted in Chapter 2, it was the weavers of Gujurat and Madras whose assiduous labors accounted for the import balance of specie that was so central to the life style of the Mughal ruling classes. The displacement of the spinners, and to a lesser extent the weavers, by the technological changes in western textile industries came to be seen as the wasting of a basic Indian resource and the destruction of a uniquely Indian community. The full force of this view, however, was not felt until very much later than the period with which we are now concerned when Mohandas Ghandi had become a national leader and was exalting home-spun cloth, village India, and the simple life. Where the history of the British handloom weaver was, as E. P. Thompson put it, 'haunted by the legend of better days', the history of the Indian textile workers was haunted by the British imperial presence which made traditional Indian values more precious.[62]

Unlike indentured plantation labor, indigo, and cotton textiles, the development of the opium trade did not reflect the structural impact of European industrialization on supply and demand in world markets. It turned rather on the peculiar trade relationships between the East India Company and China as influenced by the financial needs of the Company. While the history of the opium trade may belong more properly to the imperialist role of Great Britain in China, the initiative in the organization of trade came from India. That the opium trade was an unambiguous case of economic imperialism is not in doubt. It is hard to find clearer examples of foreign merchants, supported formally and informally by their governments, forcing trade on an unwilling state. Chinese rulers did not want opium imported, though the history of the trade revealed among Chinese merchants and users a keen interest in the drug. Not only was it noxious and debilitating, but it threatened a drain of gold and silver and attracted an excess of foreign traders who were little appreciated by Chinese officials. Indeed, at the turn of the nineteenth century they were legally confined to Macao in southeast China, a barren peninsula on an estuary of the Canton River that the Portuguese leased from the emperor, and to Canton itself where there were physical restrictions on the location and size of factories and limitations on the movement of merchants and the Chinese with whom they might transact business.[63]

In this era the Chinese state was more inward-dwelling and suspicious of foreign contacts and exchange than it had been five centuries earlier at the time Marco Polo and his uncle served Genghis Khan. As a Mongol emperor, he necessarily brought to the affairs of China an interest in and knowledge of the world outside. The Ching dynasty, however, by the nineteenth century had absorbed the traditional Chinese view of the external world as barbarian whose representatives could only enter their realm as supplicants bearing the tribute that exemplified their inferior status. As for foreign commerce and trade, the emperor Ch'ien Lung in a letter to George III of England made clear that China did not need them:

> Your merchants, and those of all the European Kingdoms who trade to China, have been used for a time immemorial, to repair for that purpose to Canton. The productions of our Empire are manifold, and in great abundance; nor do we stand in the least Need of the Produce of other Countries.[64]

The English, as well as other western merchants trading in the Far East, had a quite different view of these matters, and they were less willing than they had been in the seventeenth century, when they were trying to validate in the Mughal emperor's court their trading credentials in India, to accept the rules of proper behavior that followed from the Chinese view of the world. The Anglo-Chinese War of 1839–42 was precipitated by the attempt of the Chinese to enforce a long-standing prohibition against the traffic in opium, but more generally it was caused by the insistence of the British that they be allowed to trade in China on something like the terms that prevailed elsewhere in the world economy. In the Treaty of Nanking concluding the war, China ceded Hong Kong to the British and opened four cities in addition to Canton to British trade and residence, under conditions that restricted Chinese sovereignty and formally started the century of western domination of coastal China.

The interest of the Company in the opium trade grew with its long-standing financial problem of maintaining the profitability of its commercial operations while it performed its governing duties, and its capacity to remit profits to its owners in England. As we have seen, India did not offer a ready market for British goods when the Company's traders first entered into the Asian mercantile economy and from the start the carrying trade was an important source of revenue. If, however, there were an import balance of trade on current account between England and India, the loss of specie from one to the other manifested the difficulty of effecting the remittance of funds which required a transfer of resources from India to England. Had there been a rapidly expanding market in India for British goods the problem would have taken care of itself. Traders receiving rupees for commodities sold might have exported them as specie or purchased Indian commodities for sale in British or European markets or exchanged them for bills of exchange in sterling issued by the Company. The value of the Company's bills of exchange, the willingness of people to hold them in anticipation of receiving pounds in London, depended on the underlying real trade they were financing. At a time when Europe was so distant from India and communication and transportation so slow and uncertain, there were risks no matter how one tried to remit funds. No commodity was free of disaster at sea and a Company servant who invested in an outbound cargo as a way of exchanging rupees for pounds waited, prior to the nineteenth century, for a year before he learned the rate at which the exchange was finally consummated.

If the Company in possession of the *diwani* in Bengal could have administered the land revenue so that it received taxes in excess of the expenses of collection and the other costs of governance, it could have applied the surplus to the purchase of Indian goods for subsequent sale in European markets. It thus seemed that the Company's need to import specie to buy Indian goods was obviated even while the commodity foundations of its sterling bills of exchange were strengthened. But, of course, this expectation was frustrated by the increase in the Company's expenditures brought on by the imperialist wars of expansion which were so central to its rule in the first half of the nineteenth century.

Whatever scruples the Company had about trading in a commodity with the destructive effects of opium were overcome by these financial exigencies. In the nineteenth century the production of opium in British India was a monopoly of the Company centered in Patna in north India on the Ganges River where the climatic conditions for raising the poppy were optimal. Cultivating peasants were induced to grow the poppy by being offered advances at a price fixed by the state. Unlike the peasants raising indigo who were forced to forgo the growing of rice, the peasants raising the poppy seem to have responded to a market incentive, even though monopolistic, which was changed from time to time when the Company wished to alter the production of opium. These changes were affected through contractors who had been authorized by the Company to deal in opium. It does not seem, then, that at this point in the organization of the industry there was anything peculiarly coercive or imperialistic in the way the British conducted themselves. Opium previously had been produced in Mughal India as a state monopoly and the Company did not force a change in the production function. They did not enslave peasants in order to expand output; the peasants responded willingly enough to price incentives.

After the delivery of the juice of the poppy to the contractors and further refining which took up to six months, the drug was sold at auction in Calcutta to private merchants who distributed it in Asian markets. The Company was only involved with marketing it in India. Its profits came from the difference between the price it paid the cultivating peasants and the price it received at the Calcutta auction, this being enhanced by its monopsonistic relationship with the cultivating peasant. The auction prices, however, were influenced by a supply of opium not directly under the control of the Company which came from princely states in the Malwa region of Central India. This part of the opium supply had to pass through British territory to Bombay where it was sold and carried by ship to Calcutta and the Company imposed transit dues on its passage as an indirect control. Early in the nineteenth century the Company's revenues from opium were second only to the land revenue.[65]

More important than the revenue the opium trade generated inside India was the part it played in reducing the Company's negative balance of trade from its Asian operations occasioned especially by the English taste for tea which came on so strongly in the eighteenth century. It was the demand for Indian opium in China which largely offset the English demand for Chinese tea. The opium bought by merchants at the Calcutta auction was carried to Canton in non-Company ships licensed by the Company which also carried for the legitimate Chinese market the other great staple of the China trade, Indian cotton. Opium entered China through illicit exchanges with smugglers and with the connivance of the Chinese officials charged with the responsibility of controlling the trade but traditionally responsive to bribes or 'squeeze'. In the twenty years prior to the Anglo-Chinese war, the bribery rate considered appropriate by the commanders of the Chinese fleet patrolling harbor waters outside of Canton seems to have been one dollar per chest, a charge that with little doubt was passed on to the ultimate consumer.[66] The market was sufficiently attractive in fact to have brought to Chinese waters an international community of European, Asian, and American traders, not least of all respected Boston commercial houses which used the newly developed clipper ships in the highly profitable tea and opium trade.

The Company formally had a monopoly of the India–China trade until it was abolished in the Charter Act of 1833, but where smuggling and bribery were so central to exchange it was clearly ineffective. On the Indian side of the market its advantage lay in the control of the production of opium of high quality and in its licensing system. Moreover, as a well-established Asian trading company, it was in a position to finance the China trade by issuing sterling bills of exchange to any trader from whatever part of the world and however he had come by Chinese funds. The Company's representatives in China acquired either silver or currency for bills of exchange which then were applied to the purchase of a legitimate outbound cargo of tea. The need to ship specie to China for buying tea was obviated while the Company's earnings benefited from the provision of financial services to merchants in the country trade.

The growth of the markets we have been discussing did not have a wide impact on India during the first half of the nineteenth century. The opium trade and the market for indentured labour had their primary effect outside India. The indigo trade and the expanding imports of English cotton textiles adversely affected a small proportion of the Indian population. The overwhelming majority of Indians were isolated in their village communities beyond involvement in British-induced market changes. These market developments were vignettes in the history of economic imperialism that at the time did not reinforce one another in the Indian consciousness. The reasons for this are twofold. In the first place, neither an Indian nation nor Indian awareness yet informed the minds of Indians so that they could view these disparate markets as related in some way to an anti-Indian purpose. However exploited the indigo workers and deeply felt their grievances, their reactions were parochially conditioned by local circumstances in lower Bengal. In the second place, there was as yet no theory or explanation of the economic consequences of British rule that could transform the coercive experiences of individual Indians into socially significant experiences capable of enraging those who were not directly affected. Theories of imperialism were beginning to stir in the imaginations of western observers, but these awaited the mature expression that was stimulated by the maturing of western imperialism in the last part of the nineteenth century in the scramble for sub-Saharan Africa. In the first half of the nineteenth century the ideas from the west that influenced Indian leaders were more likely to be drawn from the utilitarian and liberal outlook which viewed the British presence in India as a progressive force.

It is in the half century between the Great Revolt and World War I that the idea of economic imperialism begins to permeate an Indian intelligentsia along with growing aspirations for self-rule and independence of British imperial governance. That period also marked the apogee of British imperialism in India for reasons that we shall make clear in the next chapter.

Notes

1 Quetta on the northwestern frontier was occupied in 1876 and in 1886, following the third Burmese war, upper Burma was annexed by British India.

2 Percival Spear, *India, a Modern History*, 2nd edn, Ann Arbor, University of Michigan Press, 1972, 268.

3 Henry H. Hart, *Sea Road to the Indies*, New York, Macmillan, 1950, 13.

4 ibid., 230.

5 M. A. P. Meilink-Roelofsz, *Asian Trade and European Influence in the Indonesian Archipelago between 1500 and 1630*, The Hague, Martinus Nijhoff, 1962, 219.

6 Paul Mantoux, *The Industrial Revolution in the Eighteenth Century*, trans. Marjorie Vernon, 2nd edn, London, Jonathan Cape, 1952, 204.

7 J. H. Clapham, *A Concise Economic History of Britain – from the Earliest Times to 1750*, Cambridge, Cambridge University Press, 1951, 239.

8 Spear, op. cit., 213. In *The Nabobs – A Study of the Social Life of the English in Eighteenth-Century India*, London, Oxford University Press, 1963, Spear observed that 'Europeans and Indians disapproved of each other's social systems, but they had not yet the tolerant pity which comes of a sense of inborn superiority,' (p. 129).

9 Adam Smith, *An Inquiry into the Nature and Causes of the Wealth of Nations*, E. Cannan (ed.), New York, Modern Library, 1937, 651.

10 Quoted by Ronald Robinson and John Gallagher, *Africa and the Victorians, the Official Mind of Imperialism*, London, Macmillan, 1961, 2.

11 John Clive, *Macaulay, the Shaping of the Historian*, New York, Knopf, 1973, 376.

12 James Mill, *The History of British India*, 4th edn, London, J. Madden, 1840, 8 vols. For those who have neither the stomach nor the endurance for eight volumes of Mill's earnest prose there is a fine abridgement: James Mill, *The History of British India*, abridged by William Thomas, Chicago, University of Chicago Press, 1975.

13 John S. Mill, *Principles of Political Economy*, 5th edn, New York, Appleton, 1883, II, 602–3.

14 Leonard Woolf, *Growing, an Autobiography of the Years 1904–1911*, London, Hogarth Press, 1961, 230.

15 Elizabeth Longford, *Wellington, the Years of the Sword*, London, Panther, 1971, 102.

16 ibid., 102–3. Tipu's Tiger is now housed in the Victoria and Albert Museum in London. It may be seen in its glass case but not heard.

17 Spear, *India, a Modern History*, 221.

18 G. F. MacMunn, *The Armies of India*, London, Adam & Charles Black, 1911, 17.

19 Cornwallis died three months after taking up his duties and was replaced by Sir George Barlow, one of the few governor-generals who came to the office after long service with the Company in India.

20 Amiya Barat, *The Bengal Native Infantry, its Organization and Discipline, 1796–1852*, Calcutta, K. L. Mukhopadhyay, 1962, 189.

21 John W. Kaye, *Lives of Indian Officers*, London, Strachan, 1867, I, 109.

22 Barat, op. cit., 156.

23 Stephen P. Cohen, *The Indian Army, its Contribution to the Development of a Nation*, Berkeley, University of California Press, 1971, 32. MacMunn, op. cit., 35, noted that in 1857 there were 311,538 troops in the armies of India, including 39,500 Europeans. Whichever estimate is closer to the actual size of the armies, it was not a large subset of the Indian population.

24 *Indian Economy in the Nineteenth Century: A Symposium*, Delhi, Indian Economic and Social History Association, 1969, 149–50.

25 Barat, op. cit., 123.

26 ibid., 134–44.

27 ibid., 150. The court privilege was withdrawn in 1815, but reinstated in 1852 when the Bengal army experienced a higher than normal desertion rate.

28 ibid., 126.

29 John W. Kaye, *A History of the Sepoy War in India, 1857–1858*, London, W.H. Allen, 1877, I, 218–45.

30 ibid., 266–70; Barat, op. cit., 201–21.

31 Barat, op. cit. 237–66.

32 Quoted by Barat, 276.

33 Kaye, *A History of the Sepoy War. . . .*, 303–5.

34 ibid., 202–3.

35 James Mill, *The History of British India*, abridged edn, 493.

36 B. Chandra, 'Reinterpretation of nineteenth century Indian economic history', *Indian Economy in the Nineteenth Century: A Symposium*, 35–75. and T. Raychaudhuri, 'A re-interpretation of nineteenth century Indian economic history', ibid, 77–100.

37 Thomas R. Metcalf, *The Aftermath of Revolt, 1857–1870*, Princeton, Princeton University Press, 1964, 38.

38 ibid., 39.

39 ibid., 43–4.

40 ibid., 45.

41 Robert E. Frykenberg, 'Village strength in south India', in R. E. Frykenberg (ed.), *Land Control and Social Structure in Indian Society*, Madison, University of Wisconsin Press, 1969, 243.

42 Donald E. Smith, *India as a Secular State*, Princeton, Princeton University Press, 1963, 265.

43 ibid., 274–5.

44 'It came to be a saying that with luck a decision might be reached in the life-time of the grandson of an original suitor. In fact Cornwallis had confounded law and law-courts with justice': H. H. Dodwell (ed.), *The Cambridge Shorter History of India*, Delhi, S. Chand, 1964, 498.

45 Courtney Ilbert, *The Government of India*, Oxford, Clarendon Press, 1922, 53.

46 This view was very much less firm in matters of personal or family law.

47 Metcalf, op. cit., 249.

48 ibid., 253.

49 Particularly notable in this regard were the Bengali brahman reformer Rammohun Roy (1772–1833) and Dwarkanath Tagore (1794–1846), entrepreneurial magnate of the great Bengali family of that name: Blair B. Kling, *Partner in Empire, Dwarkanath Tagore and the Age of Enterprise in Eastern India*, Berkeley, University of California Press, 1976, 20–3.

50 Marc Galanter, 'The displacement of traditional law in modern India', *Journal of Social Issues*, 24 (4), 65–91.

51 According to the data already cited on population and sepoys, the latter comprised between 0.1 and 0.2 percent of the former.

52 Hugh Tinker, *A New System of Slavery, the Export of India's Labour Overseas, 1830–1920*, London, Oxford University Press, 1974, 122.

53 ibid., 163.

54 According to Hugh Tinker, the suicide rate among Indian indentured servants in Natal was 640 per million and in Fiji 780 per million, where in Madras it was 46 per million and in the United Provinces 54 per million: ibid., 201.

55 Blair B. Kling, *The Blue Mutiny, the Indigo Disturbances in Bengal, 1857–1862*, Philadelphia, University of Pennsylvania Press, 1966, 25.

56 ibid., 125–46.

57 ibid., 172–95.

58 David Landes, 'Technological change and development in western

Europe, 1750–1914', in *The Cambridge Economic History of Europe*, Cambridge, Cambridge University Press, 1970, VI, Pt 1, 502–3.

59 Bernard Simmel, *The Rise of Free Trade Imperialism*, Cambridge, Cambridge University Press, 1970.

60 While there was a small, but active entrepreneurial Indian community in the first half of the nineteenth century in Bengal, it neither received support from the British nor infused other communities in the surrounding provinces with its industrial and commercial ambitions. Blair B. Kling, *Partner in Empire*, 252–3.

61 The Japanese 250-year seclusion from the outside world prior to the establishment of the consular relationship with the United States in 1854 was possible because the expanding west was little interested in Japan, its energies being absorbed in what were thought to be greater commercial opportunities elsewhere in Asia.

62 E. P. Thompson, *The Making of the English Working Class*, London, Victor Gollancz, 1963, 269.

63 Hsin-pao Chang, *Commissioner Lin and the Opium War*, Cambridge, Mass., Harvard University Press, 1964, 1–9.

64 Hosea B. Morse, *The Chronicles of the East India Company Trading to China*, Oxford, Clarendon Press, 1926, II, 188.

65 David Edward Owen, *British Opium Policy in China and India*, New Haven, Yale University Press, 1934, 80–112; Rhoads Murphey, *The Outsiders*, Ann Arbor, University of Michigan Press, 1977, 80–98.

66 Owen, op. cit., 113–45.

5

England in India: the Great Revolt to World War I 1857–1914

If one were to graph the course of British imperialism in India against some measure of its acknowledged strength, the curve would reach a maximum sometime in the half century before World War I, perhaps in the years from 1899 to 1905 during the viceroyalty of Lord Curzon. In that period the British were self-confidently imperialistic and had perfected the institutions of imperial rule. Every bit as important as objective indicators of state power, India was taking shape in the minds of an Indian élite as an oppressed society. In the first half of the century the curve would have risen sharply, reflecting the annexations and the extension of direct British rule and continued to rise after the rebellion as a developing Indian consciousness began to convert the British presence into an unwanted intrusion. The rebellion itself revealed the naked power underlying British imperialist rule even as it precipitated an Indian self-awareness that in the long run undermined the capacity of the British to rule India.

The Great Revolt 1857–9

The facts of the Great Revolt are not in dispute. It was triggered by sepoys in the Company's Bengal army who were apprehensive about what they thought were attempts by the British to attack and demean their religious beliefs. As we saw in the last chapter, there already had been a scattering of mutinies occasioned by economizing in the Company's armies and by the insensitivity of some British officers to Indian values. When the rumor got about that the new Enfield rifles with which the sepoys were being armed in 1857 used cartridges that were greased with the fat of cows and pigs, Hindus as well as Muslims were alarmed at the possibility of being polluted. The assault on religious belief and the intent to Christianize the Indian armies appeared inexorable.

The initial outbreak occurred in Meerut in north India in May 1857 and spread to Delhi and other military posts in the North-Western Provinces and Oudh. At the height of the rebellion the British military forces in those territories were reduced to besieged garrisons in Lucknow and Kanput (Cawnpore) and a detachment of troops holding a ridge outside of Delhi. Bengal remained loyal as did the Punjab. Nor did the disaffection of the sepoys in the Bengal army spread to the Bombay and Madras armies. Moreover, most of the princely states remained firm in their support of the Company. What made the rebellion more than a military jacquerie was its support among the civilian population in north India, particularly those magnates in Oudh, the *taluqdars*, who had lost their prerogatives or had been threatened by the precipitous policy of the Company in making land settlements with the peasants. When the *taluqdars* joined the rebellion, so did many peasants who, whatever their stake in the land settlements, looked to them as local leaders.

The rebellion was crushed in 1858 as the British brought additional troops to India whose reoccupation of the north was facilitated by the inability of the sepoys to organize and coordinate their command, by their being 'so wrapped up in their own individual grievances that the British were able to defeat them one at a time'.[1] The reprisals inflicted upon the sepoys and civilians were appalling. Summary executions were widespread with British soldiers paying scant heed to whether the victims were rebels. For a brief moment the British seemed bent on racial extermination and in the Punjab John Nicholson suggested that a bill be proposed allowing the 'flaying alive, impalement, or burning of the murderers of the women and children at Delhi. The idea of simply hanging the perpetrators of such atrocities is maddening.'[2] The fury of the British in victory was a measure of their disillusionment, not simply with Indian subjects who turned out to be less pliant than supposed, but with themselves for misreading the strength of their command in India. It also reflected the fear of a tiny minority in the midst of a vast, unknowable, and racially different host that it would be consumed, that its imperial mission was doomed to failure. By the same token it extinguished the spirit of reform that periodically animated Company policy in the years following the permanent settlement as its servants no longer were so confident that Indian society could be regenerated through western wisdom and administrative skills. Thereafter British policy in India was designed less to fulfill the purposes of a trustee charged with the responsibility of guiding its ward to maturity than to increase the efficiency with which a foreign ruler governed a subject people.

For the peoples of India the Great Revolt did not shatter illusions, except perhaps the illusion of British invincibility, much as the Japanese sweep through the Pacific after Pearl Harbor revealed the hollowness of European power in the Far East. They were, after all, subject peoples who, however benign the intent of British imperial rule, experienced its consequences in a different frame of reference. The Great Revolt spoke for itself; it revealed Indian preferences that had been hidden from British view both by the separateness of the British and Indian communities and by the former being prisoners of their own preconceptions. Clearly the rebelling sepoys and civilians of north India did not like British rule. It is also clear that at the time most Indian communities did not support the rebellion. In 1857 the grievances of sepoys in the Bengal army failed to rouse their empathy. This was attributable in part to the fragmentation of Indian society. It also reflected the interests of some communities and their concern about what would happen to them if the Company's rule were overthrown. Rightly or wrongly, the Sikhs of the Punjab feared that a victorious rebellion would restore Muslim power in Delhi, a prospect they did not relish. In Bengal the *zamindars* did not hesitate to profess their loyalty to the British Raj because if it were defeated they were unsure that the benefits acquired in the permanent settlement would continue.[3] Moreover, they anticipated, as an educated minority, that they were the intended heirs of

British rule.

One needs, however, to separate the specific events – the mutinies, the sieges, the forced marches, the summary executions, the looting – that comprised the Great Revolt from its history and interpretation which had consequences independently of whether they were accurate or plausible. When General Dyer ordered his troops to fire on the assembly at Amritsar he had the events of 1857 in the back of his mind. He viewed it as part of a pattern of insurrection which justified a demonstration of the overwhelming power of the Raj. Like most British proconsuls he was haunted by his understanding of the rebellion and was all the more sensitive to its possible recurrence. In England and India the history of the Great Revolt was put to different uses. British historians initially were inclined to render it in a light that justified the role of British rule in India, emphasizing the misguided and misperceived grievances of the sepoys and minimizing the extent of the disaffection of the civilian population. Indians writing under the influence of the nationalist movement viewed the Rebellion as the first installment of the continuing struggle of Indian peoples for independence from England. Subsequently many historians in both England and India have interpreted it as a revolt against the reforms the British introduced into India, a last stand of conservative, traditional, backward-looking communities against the threats to its privileges, a position not dissimilar to the one expressed by Marx in his dispatches to the *New York Daily Tribune* at the time the events were unfolding in India.[4]

However the Great Revolt is interpreted, it was a break in the continuity of British governance in India. Thereafter, there was little pretense that imperial rule was anything but imperialist, a bearing that was pointedly symbolized by an Act of Parliament in 1876 which made Queen Victoria Empress of India. This is not to say that with Crown rule, British standards of administration in India deteriorated. On the contrary they became more efficient, if more impersonal. What was lacking was the belief in and hope for Indian transformation that had animated much of the Company's rule. The arrogance of a superior, but exportable civilization now gave way to the arrogance of inherent superiority.

Crown rule in India

The passing of the East India Company was less a matter of substance than form. In England, by the Government of India Act of 1858, the Board of Control was replaced by the Secretary of State for India, who had Cabinet status and was advised by a council composed of men with experience in Indian affairs. The Court of Directors limped on for another fourteen years, holding meetings in quarters provided for it by the government until 1874 when the Company charter ran out.[5] In India, the governor-general became governor-general and viceroy, was appointed by the Crown, and was directly responsible to the Cabinet through the Secretary of State for India. Initially the administration of the presidencies and the other districts of direct British rule continued as they had under the Company.

Throughout India on 1 November 1858 the Queen's proclamation of Crown rule, issued in eighteen languages, was read at many different locations. Romesh Dutt, an economic historian of British India and an early Indian nationalist leader, recalled the occasion with unabashed enthusiasm:

> It was one of the happiest days of my boyhood when I heard this Proclamation read by the highest English official in one of the district towns of Bengal on November 1, 1858, on which day it was read in all district towns in India. Hindus and Mussulmans had gathered there, and hailed the Proclamation with shouts of joy.[6]

The shouts of joy, if indeed there were shouts of joy, may have been occasioned by the conditions in the proclamation for the amnesty of the rebellious sepoys which were a good deal milder than might have been expected from the ruthless manner of their repression; or by the promise of equal opportunity for Indians in the service of Her Majesty.[7] Or perhaps it was thought that the demise of the Company was a rebuke for the grievances it had visited upon Indians which now would be remedied by the queen. Some Indians may well have felt that the Company was too much conecerned with the commercial interests of its shareholders to be able to govern India in the interests of Indians. They may really have believed what *The Oxford History of India* asserted a century later:

> The government as a whole was now consciously looking forward to a modernized India, not unconsciously harking back to a Mughal tranquility, and the people became aware, as they had not been before, that their welfare was the concern of the rulers over the water. The royal courts and the royal law had once been the terror of the Bengali; the person and declaration of the new queen were to become the focus of Indian loyalty and the fountain of Indian hope.[8]

It cannot be denied that the British government in Westminster had an interest in the welfare of Indian society, but it was an interest that was mediated through Great Britain's role as a world power and its immediate obligations to its constituents in the British Isles. Crown rule, if anything, made these latter interests a more compelling factor in the governance of India. At a time when the British economy was already caught up in its most vigorous domestic and international expansion and when the political spokesmen of the entrepreneurial classes responsible for it were becoming increasingly articulate, there was little reason to believe that Indian welfare was of direct, primary concern to British policy-makers. India's welfare was derivative from the welfare of England. What was good for England was good for India. While the British government in India undoubtedly weighted Indian interests more heavily than the British government in Westminster, the difficulty, as Mr Dutt ruefully observed many years after hearing those shouts of joy, was that neither one included an 'independent deliberative body, representing the people of India and safeguarding their interest and their welfare'.[9]

An overriding concern of the British in India after 1858 was the consolidation and securing of their rule so that this keystone in the imperial system would not again be shaken by rebellion. To this end they strengthened their authority and efficiency in maintaining order and raising revenues and sought support among Indians who, they had reason to believe, might be possible sources of disaffection. Particularly important with respect to the former, the government of India addressed the problem of reforming the Bengal army whose disproportionate recruitment of brahmans in Oudh, it was held, led to the rebellion.[10] The proportion of Europeans in the armies was raised and Indians no longer were recruited for artillery battalions which had been used to good advantage against the British. In the years immediately following 1858 when the British had not yet regained confidence in the Indian armies they inclined to a policy of mixing communities in the ranks and being responsive to their religious sensibilities. Later as the armies became less important in maintaining domestic order and increasingly an instrument of British and Indian foreign policy, greater emphasis was placed on recruiting sepoys among the so-called martial races, Gurkhas, Sikhs, Punjabis, Pathans, and Jats. By the end of the century the three presidency armies of the East India Company had disappeared in a unified Indian command.

If the Indian army became a more effective instrument of British rule, the administrations in India became a more austere, professional service. The worst features of the patronage system had already been remedied and in 1853 competitive examinations for places in the Indian civil service were first held in England.[11] The covenanted civil service positions, the higher offices in Indian judicial and revenue administration, were thus filled with more attention to ability and less to pedigree.[12] Moreover, Macaulay's Minute on Education was beginning to pay off. Universities offering a western curriculum were established in the three presidency towns during the rebellion and there was a growth in private colleges founded in part with the support of subventions from the Indian government. The number of English-speaking Indians, especially among the Hindu communities, who were capable of performing clerical and other subordinate jobs and viewed them as an opportunity, increased and formed part of an emerging all-Indian middle class. Furthermore, the codification of Indian law, which had got under way during Macaulay's term as Law Commissioner in the governor-generalship of Sir Charles Metcalfe in 1835, accelerated following the assumption of authority in India by the Crown with the enactment of the Code of Civil Procedure (1859), the Penal Code (1860), the Code of Criminal Procedure (1861), the Indian Succession Act (1865), and the Indian Contract Act (1872).[13] However much the law courts in Bengal may have been a source of irritation and frustration to the Indians who came before them, the continuing transmission of western procedural and, to a lesser extent, substantive law to India expanded the Indian legal profession whose members became particularly articulate and sensitive spokesmen for Indian society.

Railroad construction, which had already got under way during the days of Lord Dalhousie's ebullient support for internal improvements, now acquired added administrative significance. An India knit together by railroads could be penetrated more readily by the Indian armies. On the eve of the Great Revolt there were 200 miles of track; in 1869 there were 4255 miles which by 1880 had doubled to 8494. In the next twenty-five years the rail network expanded more than three times so that by 1905 there were 28,054 miles of track.[14] We shall return to the matter of railroads when we again take up economic imperialism, for they were not viewed in the same light by Indian nationalists as they were by British–Indian administrators.

So far as the potential sources of disaffection were concerned, the government of India brought the princes of India more securely into the governing process and attempted to alleviate the economic oppression of Indian peasants. Prior to the rebellion, the princes lived with the uncertainty of the doctrines of lapse and of gross neglect of government. Lord Dalhousie had taken advantage of both in extending the territories of India under the direct rule of the Company. When there was a governor-general of improving propensities and a censorious view of the manner in which the princes ruled their realms they were especially subject to extinction. The British now asserted their sovereignty over all of India and no longer maintained the fiction that there were enclaves in their midst whose rulers were independent except in matters of foreign policy and Indian security. In return for the loss of their nominal independence the princes were made 'subordinate partners' to the British Raj and honored as Indian proconsuls.[15] If it were now thought essential to improve the efficiency of princely rule, this was effected through the British resident assigned to the court, presumably in cooperation with the prince, rather than by coopting his territories into British India.

While the *zamindars* of Bengal had remained loyal to the Company because of their vested interest in the permanent settlement, many peasants in the presidency had become tenants-at-will, subject to rack-renting that was enforced by the courts the Company introduced into Bengal. They were neither generating the agricultural improvements promised in some versions of classical economics nor receiving assistance from the *zamindars* who engrossed the surplus as collectors of the land revenue for the Company. They also were the most numerous members of the populated province of India. In order to improve the status of tenants in Bengal the government passed the Bengal Rent Act in 1859 which granted peasants occupancy rights when they had held a tenancy for twelve years and then limited the rights of owners to raise rents. It spoke well for the *zamindars'* eye for the main chance that there were widespread refusals to renew the leases of those peasants who had cultivated a piece of land for close to twelve years. The benefits conferred by the Act were confined largely to the wealthier tenants, leaving the poorer undertenants with little control over the product of their labor. This is a matter to which we shall return.

Perhaps the most significant change following the repression of the rebellion had less to do with the disappearance of the Company and its replacement with direct Crown rule than with the changing world context in which the British viewed India. In the first half of the nineteenth century England had a monopoly of industrial development – free-trade imperialism inhered in this advantage England had over potential rivals – but in the second half of the century its leading position was no longer secure against countries, particularly Germany and the United States, that had responded so energetically to the industrialization impulses that had emanated from England. Moreover, the formation of Germany following the Franco-Prussian War of 1870 added a new dimension to the political rivalry of the nations of Europe. Strategically located in central Europe with easy access across the north European plain to the countries east and west of it and with an opening to the oceans from the North Sea, its potential impact on its neighbors, for good or ill, was profound, especially as it put its locational advantage to such good use in industrialization. On the eastern fringe of Europe, in part because of the growing strength of Prussia and then Germany, Russia's colonizing interest in Siberia grew apace in the nineteenth century reaching a climax in 1892–1905 with the construction of the Trans-Siberian railway. There was then in the interior of the Eurasian continent a movement of Russian peoples east which had its counterpart in North America in the movement of American peoples west. Neither one was devoid of the violent dispossession of indigenous populations that we associate with imperialism. And while the forces of economic growth and external expansion were permeating the northern hemisphere, the technology of transportation and communication was shrinking the globe and enhancing the geopolitical outlook of the chancelleries of the world. India came in instantaneous touch with England when a marine telegraph cable was laid in 1865 and with the development of steamships and the opening of the Suez canal in 1869 the all-water passage from England to Calcutta was reduced by two weeks.[16]

In the early years of Great Britain's involvement in India the rivalry of European states was keen, but it was centered in Asia in the struggle to secure bases from which to carry on the East Indies trade. Because of the slow pace of transportation and communication, the decisions affecting the outcome of these rivalries were made by the men immediately involved, responding to the exigencies of the moment and, as they understood or chose to interpret them, the policies of the merchants and monarchs they were representing. The direction and control of events in the capitals of Europe were minimal. In the later nineteenth century, empire became a more explicit political force, if not more amenable to control, because the capacity of central governments for involvement grew along with the industrial revolution. And conversely the autonomy of empire officials tended to decline. Even in the unlikely event that they did place the welfare of the indigenous colonial peoples above the interests of the metropolis, they had less power to do much about it.

In India, the changing ambience of empire affairs manifested itself in an outward turn of British policy, notably a concern for the security of the northwestern frontier in the face of Russian expansion in Turkestan and for the control of the Suez canal. In discussing theories of imperialism, we noted the seminal role of the canal in the scramble for Africa as European powers competed in an imperial game of political oligopoly. England came to dominate Egypt and rule the African territories surrounding the headwaters of the Nile while the other parts of sub-Saharan Africa that had not already succumbed to European states were divided among Germany, France, Belgium and Great Britain. It may be argued that the Suez canal compelled England to take a strong position in Egypt in order to safeguard its lifeline to India. The Turkish sultan to whom Egypt was formally subject could not control the competing European interests that were drawn there by its strategic location. Neither could the Khedive of Egypt, his viceregent. Moreover, because of the decline of the Turkish empire, Istanbul no longer was a reliable barrier against the expansion of Russian power in the eastern Mediterranean which therefore required a strong British presence in Egypt. Furthermore, the Khedive Ismail was so prodigal and inefficient in support of his household and modernizing projects, including the Suez canal, that his European, mostly English and French, creditors insisted that there be stronger financial management of Egypt.[17] Through their intervention with the sultan he was deposed in 1879 and replaced by his son Tawfiq. Subsequently in 1882 when Colonel Arabi, a nationalist in the Egyptian army, raised the standard of revolt against the Khedive and his European advisors, the British crushed it and occupied Egypt.[18]

This chapter of British imperial history affected Indians through the resources they were required to provide in support of policies formulated in England by statesmen who were motivated primarily by the threat to their security from other European states. If the apprehension about Russian expansion toward the northwest frontier of India had a somewhat closer relationship to Indian welfare, it had the same manifestation, the diversion of resources for policies about which Indians were not consulted. To be more concrete, the Indian Army was used in the Afghan War of 1878–80, the Egyptian expedition of 1882, the Sudan expedition of 1884–5, and the Egyptian expedition of 1896, the costs thus incurred being borne largely by India.[19] It had become an enforcing agent of British imperialism and, under direct Crown rule, India had become an administrative center for the management of British imperial affairs in Asia.

The economics of British imperialism as seen by Indian nationalists

In the years between the Great Revolt and World War I, economic imperialism became an Indian grievance. In the first half of the nineteenth century, the exploitation of indigo ryots in Bengal, the transportation of indentured workers to the plantations of Mauritius and the West Indies, and the decline of handicraft manufacture in cotton textiles were local manifestations of economic coercion that were not yet seen as part of a pattern of British domination in India. They were events in the struggle for survival in a subsistence economy whose potential for forming and aggravating an Indian consciousness was still to be developed. None of them abated following the rebellion, though indigo markets declined relatively. Household manufacturing of cotton textile fabrics continued to suffer as the construction of railroads lowered the cost of marketing Manchester cloth in the interior of India while the government of India lowered the duties on its importation so that for a time it was admitted almost without charge.[20] And the export of indentured labor reached a peak in the period as demands for Indian labor in Africa augmented the continuing demand of the sugar colonies.

Moreover, new centers of economic oppression formed as the structure of the Indian labor force continued to change in response to the changing demands of the world market. In Assam, tea plantations first established in 1851 expanded rapidly so that by the turn of the century there were more than a half-million indentured workers there, recruited largely in Bengal, and suffering in much the same way as their peers in the sugar plantations, but as a more visible, concentrated irritant to Indian sensibilities.[21] There also took place the early stirring of an industrial labor force with somewhat less than 450,000 workers in cotton mills, jute mills, and coal mines by 1905, who were experiencing the long hours and hazardous working conditions that always bedevil incipient industrial firms.[22]

Gradually there emerged an analysis of these, as well as traditional agrarian, problems which related them to the economic malaise of India – caused, it was held, by the imperial policies of Great Britain. The leaders of an English-speaking Indian middle class, the product of the educational policies first established by the Company and continued by the Crown, discussed, probed, and publicized Indian poverty, the persistence of famines under the British Raj, the fiscal burden of Indian government, and the drain of resources from India to England as the economic consequences of British rule. In creating a framework with which to view the struggles of workers and peasants for subsistence, they raised many issues debated today in the economics of development. They also evolved an economics of imperialism which in contrast to the theories of imperialism of the early twentieth century was grounded at first hand in the experience of the imperialized. And it was intensely nationalist, unsullied by the ideological values that informed the Marxian outlook.

The time when Indians became interested in the economics of British imperialism may be set around 1867 when Dadabhai Naoroji put forward the idea of the drain in a speech in London before the East India Association on 'England's Debt to India'. Subsequently in 1870 and 1871, also in London, he delivered seminal papers on 'The Wants and Means of India', in which he estimated the per-capita gross output of India, and 'On the Commerce of India'.[23] A Parsi from Bombay, born in 1825, who took a college degree in mathematics and went to England in 1855 to open up an Indian commercial house, Naoroji set the tone for much of the discussion of these problems by developing their quantitative dimensions, hoping thereby to persuade the British of the validity of his arguments about the causes of Indian poverty.

When Naoroji spoke before the East India Association in 1867, the German edition of the first volume of *Capital* was in press and the first English translation of it would not appear for another nineteen years. The theories of imperialism derived from Marx's analysis were still another generation off. Far from their having influenced the early Indian writers on economic imperialism, the influence may have worked in the opposite direction. H. M. Hyndman, a British socialist of Marxist inclination who had become concerned about the economic plight of India, published in 1878 an article entitled 'The Bankruptcy of India' in which he relied heavily on the statistical data contained in a collection of Dadabhai Naoroji's papers published as the *Poverty of India*.[24] At that time Hyndman still believed in an enlightened imperialism and charged the British with not living up to their responsibilities to the Indian people. So too did Naoroji. As late as 1901 he wrote that:

> True British rule will vastly benefit both Britain and India. My whole object in all my writings is to impress upon the British people, that instead of a disastrous explosion of the British Indian Empire, as must be the result of the present dishonourable unBritish system of government, there is a great and glorious future for Britain and India to an extent unconceivable at present, if the British people will awaken to their duty, will be true to their British instincts of fair play and justice, and will insist upon the 'faithful and conscientious fulfillment' of all their great and solemn promises and pledges.[25]

Three years later Naoroji publicly and unequivocally asserted his commitment to Indian self-government, a measure of the force of his theory of the source of Indian poverty on his political outlook. That his view was not widely accepted then by the Indian nationalist leaders was a measure of the continuing power of British values and political ideals as well as of the still weak influence of western theories of imperialism. Their belief in British justice and disinterested rule was from the outset strengthened by their English allies who, like Hyndman, were outraged by what they thought was British irresponsibility in India.[26] A separation was thus made between the economic condition of India, on the one hand, and the appropriate way of organizing the political community, on the other. The two were not linked in a deterministic bond as they came to be in Marxian theory. In contrast to the self-confident assertions of so many nationalist leaders during the decolonization of the Third World following World War II, the nineteenth-century Indian nationalist leaders appeared to be tentative and ambivalent in their political remedies for British imperialism.[27]

However slowly the commitment to self-government evolved, the economics of imperialism, which in the end undermined the faith of the nationalist leaders in disinterested British rule in India, came on steadily. Its importance lay in its normative power in persuading Indian leaders that if the British had not been in India, the economic hardships of Indian society could have been distributed in a less burdensome way. Whether or not the analyses were correct, they raised the critical issues that had to be addressed if one were to assess the economic impact of British rule. Generally, the charges laid on the British Raj were that its policies, subordinate to the industrial interests of the British economy, aborted the development of the industrial sectors of the Indian economy, encouraged the growth of industrial raw materials and food grains for export, and imposed revenue demands on the Indian economy for imperial, non-Indian purposes, all of which impoverished the economy and exacerbated the chronic famine problem even while it led to a growing drain of goods and resources from India to England. In this there was no vision of an international specialization of function pursuant to the principle of comparative advantage that shed benefits on all parties entering into exchange relationships. India and England were not better off because of their involvement. Rather England's gain was India's loss.

So far as the detailed defense of these charges was concerned, the Indian nationalists found no lack of evidence in the management of Indian affairs, some of which we have already mentioned. The financial problems of the government of India, difficult in any circumstances, became more pressing because of the Great Revolt and it was tempted to manipulate for revenue purposes tariff rates which already had been reduced under the influence of the ascendant belief in free trade. In the latter half of the century the changing structure of tariff rates seemed to respond more to the interest of the textile manufacturers in Lancashire than to the depressed manufacturing interest in India, the former always being alert to the use of duties for protection against its cloth and yarns and anxious even for revenue tariffs to be removed. At the end of the century in 1894 the government of India removed the tariffs on the importation of cotton yarn and 'reduced the import duty on woven goods from 5 per cent to $3\frac{1}{2}$ per cent on all woven goods produced by Indian mills'.[28] It could hardly escape notice that financial policy discriminated against the higher stages of production in the Indian cotton textile industry.

Moreover, the railroads, whose construction and operation were a fiscal burden on India up to the twentieth century because of required subsidies and financial guarantees, stimulated the expansion of primary outputs by integrating the hinterlands of the presidencies more closely with their seaports so that they could be transported at lower costs to world markets. If the railroads played a part in creating the Indian nation, they were not laid down with the intent of stimulating the industrial development of the Indian economy. It must be said, however, that even if the government of India had intended railroads for that purpose, it was not clear where they should have been built. Industrial development was a nebulous goal, an aspiration more than a concrete blueprint for the future of India, with little market pull to compete with the much better-known capacity of the Indian economy to expand primary output.

A more telling criticsm of the government's railroad policy was that rail expansion was too rapid, imposing greater revenue burdens on Indian society than necessary and holding back the rate of growth of public investment in irrigation projects, the rate of return for which was positive where it was negative for railroad investment.[29] By the first decade of the twentieth century, cumulative government expenditures on the railroads were nine times greater than on irrigation canals.[30] With railroad construction and operation subsidized, a market was created for steel and engineering output which benefited English industry more than relatively greater investment in irrigation would have. In the English view, this pattern of public investment was justified not only as a means for facilitating the flow of primary output into world markets, but as a way of combatting the endemic scourge of famine. Famine seldom devastated all of India. Rather it struck particular locales and regions, while elsewhere there was a surplus of food grains. Famine could best be overcome by improving the transportation system so that the surpluses could be moved to remedy local shortages. Industrial Europe would exorcize, in this view, the specter of famine in agrarian India.

Famines in India have always been precipitated by the failure of the seasonal monsoons, or to a lesser extent by an excess of unseasonal rain. Average rainfall varies widely throughout India and in any location the variance of rainfall from year to year is great. Famines occurred most often in regions which experienced an average annual rainfall between 15 and 60 inches, the tendency being for them to be more severe and less frequent in parts of the country that received rain in the upper range of those limits and thus could normally support a large population.[31] In the years between the Great Revolt and World War I, no part of India was untouched by famines whose irregular incidence bore more heavily on the northern provinces. Between 1860 and 1879 some eight famines were recorded one of which from 1876 to 1878 had the dismal distinction of taking the lives of more than 5 million Indians in British territories.[32] For the next fifteen years they subsided, there being no case where local shortages threatened the overall supply of food grains.[33] From 1896 to 1908, however, India suffered three major famines before they again subsided.

However committed the British were to *laissez-faire*, they could not ignore these persistent catastrophes as for a time they had tried to leave the destructive force of the 'great hunger' in Ireland in the late 1840s to the equilibrating mechanism of the market.[34] A famine commission was appointed in 1880 to devise systematic procedures for governments to follow in famine emergencies that would try to deal more fundamentally with their causes than the *ad hoc* relief measures that had hitherto tried to stem the flood of starvation.[35] A Famine Code was promulgated in 1883 for the guidance of the provinces in the use of the resources available to them and later in 1901 was expanded as a result of the deliberations of another commission appointed following the succession of severe famines that closed out the nineteenth century. Some of its provisions concerned the priorities in the use of the new transport capacity, especially railroads, that had been built during the second part of the century. Since the famines at the end of the century had led to only 750,000 deaths which were concentrated largely in central India where transportation was least developed, the government of India felt that it was beginning to master these grim reapers of subsistence populations. As *The Oxford History* put it, 'The Famine Code could not prevent famine, but succeeded in converting the terrible famines of food into more tolerable famines of work.'[36]

In the view of the Indian critics of British imperial policy, the railroads were part of the problem. To the extent that famines could have been relieved by work, which is to say that they were primarily a failure of the market to distribute income to peasants and workers so that they could buy subsistence goods, the railroads inhibited the growth of job opportunities by stimulating primary output and holding back industrial development. But, they contended, the trouble ran deeper. The railroads were indirectly responsible for reducing the supply of subsistence foods for the Indian population. On the one hand, the priority of public investment for railroads rather than canals inhibited the development of the infrastructure, to use a word that has gained currency in the literature of economic development, which could have increased the productivity of land and foodstuffs. In an arid natural environment with uncertain rainfall, the husbanding of water resources required 'large means and combined action' in John Stuart Mill's phrase. Only the government could construct irrigation canals and coordinate their use so that water could be more evenly distributed to peasants than it was in nature's dispensation. On the other hand, the railroads encouraged the raising of industrial raw materials at the expense of food grains and stimulated the export of the latter even during times of extreme scarcity and famine. During the great famine from 1876 to 1878 'while there was an all-round scarcity in the country and the prices were four times the normal price . . . the exports [of food grain] not only continued but even showed an increase.'[37]

Moreover, the sluggish performance of the Indian economy and its susceptibility to famine not only were not alleviated by the public expenditures of the Indian government, but, it was contended, their fiscal burden rendered them more obdurate. The army, the railroads, and the civil administration of the government of India employed Europeans in the top positions whose salaries were far out of line with the remuneration Indians would have received for comparable employment. The exigencies of taxation were thus occasioned by the government being bound by the opportunity costs in Europe of attracting to India military officers and covenanted civil servants. These men wished to maintain a western standard of living during their years there and in the anticipated home retirement that followed the long service in the subcontinent. However efficient they may have been, they were an oppressive charge on a society with subsistence income.

While the British were inclined to point to the low absolute level of taxation in India, the nationalists looked to the more sensitive indicator of per-capita taxation as a proportion of per-capita income. In Naoroji's aphoristic statement, 'while a ton may not be any burden to an elephant, a few pounds may crush a child.'[38] On the basis of inadequate and incomplete data supplemented by bold assumptions regarding agricultural productivity, he had estimated the income per capita for India during 1867–8 at 40 shillings, though he thought it was actually closer to 30 shillings.[39] At the same time, again using equally fragmentary evidence, he tried to measure the cost of subsistence per head which turned out to be greater, even when he used the food and clothing allowance mandated for prisoners in the jails of British India.[40] Throughout the whole period between the Great Revolt and World War I, the land revenue was the most important fiscal instrument, the assidous collection of which, if we are willing to give credence to Naoroji's heroic quantitative estimates, may well have appropriated more than those economic rents that were the fair game of Ricardian theories of land settlements in India. In any event, the nationalist leaders asserted that the tax burden was too high and that the failure of the Indian government to extend a permanent settlement to the provinces other than Bengal led to periodic enhancement of taxes and rural indebtedness which inhibited the development of a vigorous agricultural sector. The government of India was depressing subsistence income for the servicing of non-Indian interests.

Much of what we have said thus far about the economics of imperialism may be summed up in the statement that the British in India caused the internal allocation of resources to lower the Indian net product below what it would have been in their absence. The external analogue to this assertion is that the loss of income was transferred to England. The drain, alternatively called trade with no equivalent returns, remittance of surplus, the annual tribute, or unrequited exports, was the most comprehensive charge brought against the English and the one to which they were most sensitive. This was hardly surprising, for the British, while imperialists, thought that their rule was just in the sense that India benefited from the high standards of administration and the maintenance of order which they brought to the subcontinent. The theorists of the drain, however, argued that there was no exchange of benefits in the relationship of England and India. Rather England was doing in the guise of superior administration what the Company had done so blatantly after assuming the *diwani* in 1765 – appropriating India's surplus output.

The drain was such an important part of the economics of imperialism that Indians fashioned in the latter nineteenth century that we need to consider the historical circumstances in which an annual tribute or unrequited exports may be plausible. An unambiguous instance, already referred to in Chapter 2, may be called the conquistadore model. With superior military and transportation technology at their command, the Spanish conquered the Inca and enslaved local populations in the mining of precious metals which they regularly shipped in convoy to Cadiz and Seville. In a mercantilist age that placed great store in the accumulation by the state of gold and silver, their loss was viewed as a drain which was to be obviated to the extent that its administrative and colonial capacity allowed. While mercantilist theorists placed little weight on the preferences of colonial peoples, it could not have been difficult to see that Castile's gain was the Andean Indian's loss. In this case gold may be considered a surrogate for commodities. If the conquistadores had compelled slaves to weave highly valued fabrics for transport to Spain, the outcome would have been the same. For weaving them, the latter would have received less than the value of their marginal product, a surplus thus being transferred to the Spanish which formed the commodity stock that was transported to Castile without there being a commodity flow in the reverse direction to the Indians. Clearly the key factor here was the open use of coercion by Spaniards in the organization of resources in Peru.

Consider, however, mercantilist practice in the quite different circumstances of North America during the colonial era. The proponents of mercantilism in England were no less enthusiastic about accumulating stocks of precious metals than they were in Spain. The colonies along the North Atlantic coast, however, did not contain them in their natural environment and they were populated initially by freeholders and indentured servants from England. In this case the strategy of the metropolis was to try to rig the terms of trade so that it would have an export balance of trade to the colonies which would impose on the latter an import balance on current account, thus requiring them to transmit to the former gold in fulfillment of their commercial obligations. As we know, this came to be an onerous burden on the colonists because their freedom of action in monetary matters was restricted as it was in manufacturing, not to mention the taxes the British government imposed on them as their share of the costs of the Seven Years' War from 1756 to 1763. And they had to hustle in their external trade to acquire the means of payment. The Yankee sea captain was working the appalling Middle Passage in the lucrative triangular trade linking New England, West Africa, and the West Indies before he entered the China trade.

But was there a drain from the colonies to England, an unrequited transfer of exports? The answer is no. If we put aside mercantilist preconceptions of wealth and examine trade in non-precious commodities, the colonists had an import balance which meant that they were receiving more real goods than they were sending out. Moreover, they were acquiring the means of payment in the carrying trade. They were not digging gold out of the ground or monetizing the precious artifacts of ancient monuments, tombs, or temples. Moreover, though the British, especially after 1753, imposed galling policies on the colonists who did not feel that their interests had been properly consulted, their ability to use force in the organization of economic relationships in North America was circumscribed. The colonies were self-governing even if within the constraints of the British imperial system and, while far from being democratic organizations, the colonial assemblies were none the less articulate spokesmen of the colonial interest. They were indeed a part of Greater Britain, as Charles W. Dilke later came to view the British empire in the nineteenth century, and the colonists either had or felt they were entitled to the rights of Englishmen.

Now consider the British in India in the nineteenth century before the rebellion. Let us suppose that they administered the land revenue in such a way that the Company in India received a surplus which was used to purchase indigo. The indigo was then shipped to England where it was sold for sterling, the proceeds being used to pay dividends to shareholders of the Company, the pensions of retired Company servants and so on. India's external balance of payments, in consequence of these transactions, showed at the margin an export surplus on current account. There was no offsetting importation of goods from England. This would appear to constitute a drain unless one is prepared to argue that direct rule by the Company so improved the administration of the services collateral to the collection of the land revenue that they represented the *quid pro quo* for the export of indigo, an importation of good government.

But suppose that the budget of the Company were balanced and that it applied the land revenue to the expenses of civil administration and to the maintenance of the Company's armies with no funds allocated to commercial accounts, what then? Was the impact of the Company's governance wholly internal without there being a drain of resources to England? If both the civil and military administrations had been staffed by personnel whose commitment was to India, then there need not have been an external drain. Resources would have been drawn into the Company's sector – sepoys, for example, would have been employed by its armies rather than serving Indian magnates – and the distribution of income would have changed with the changing incidence of taxation and the changing pattern of its expenditures. So far as the balance of payments was concerned, there might have been an increase in imports as the Company purchased armaments and other equipment in England and Europe that could not be produced in India, though these might have been offset by a decline in the consumption of foreign luxury commodities by wealthy Indians. It would have been extraordinary, however, with these restrictive assumptions if exports had increased.

The Company, of course, was managed by Europeans and the officers of its armies were Europeans, all of whom wished to transmit to England some of their pay. This was not a simple matter since international money markets were not yet organized so that currencies could be readily exchanged for one another at great distance. A Company servant who wished to remit rupees to England might have purchased diamonds and entrusted them to a supercargo on one of the Company's ships with instructions to sell them in England and deposit the proceeds in a bank, after having deducted the appropriate commission. Or he might have purchased indigo as a medium of remission. If this were the accepted method of exchanging rupees for pounds, then the domestic Indian economy would have experienced a net increase in the demand for indigo. In the agrarian sector there would have been a reallocation of resources from the raising of rice, say, to the raising of indigo. While there would have been no decline in aggregate expenditures, the output of food grains would have decreased and the output of industrial raw materials increased. By the same token the export surplus on current account in India's balance of payments would have risen. Had all of the Company's servants been Indians, domestic expenditures would have been directed more towards subsistence and consumption goods and less towards indigo, reducing the size of the export balance of trade. In this example, the drain was a consequence of foreign rulers being resident in India, its manifestation, however, in contrast to the previous example working with less force and through more volatile private expenditures. In both cases resources were exported without any equivalent return except in the equivocal sense indicated above.

Let us finally make one more supposition, namely that money markets and markets for commercial paper became sufficiently developed that funds could be transmitted from India to England without first being embodied in a commodity asset. What then happened to the drain where the conditions of imperial rule remained the same as in the above examples? Now rather than purchasing indigo in the Indian market, European Company servants purchased sterling bills of exchange that were acceptable in England. The imperial relationship between India and England was such that there was a net demand for remittance from the former to the latter. That is to say, there was not a remittance demand in England for rupees to offset the remittance demand in India for sterling. Looking at this item on the international balance of payments in isolation, it generated a demand for sterling in excess of the supply. If the exchange rate were not to fall, India had to acquire sterling in some other balance of payment account. Again we return to the export of commodities, but not necessarily to indigo. In order to facilitate these remittances, India had to export industrial raw materials, food grains, or other commodities so that sterling would be available in sufficient supply to make the sterling bills of exchange drawn in India negotiable in London and other money markets. The importation of capital, of course, in the short run might have increased the supply of pounds, but such capital was earmarked for specific uses and in the long run added interest payments that had to be transmitted to England.

In fact, the remittances of British civil and military servants were only part of the problem which was exacerbated by what was known as the home charges, namely the obligations incurred by the government of India in England in the maintenance of the imperial establishment. These included a variety of charges among them (following the demise of Company rule) the costs of the office of the Secretary of State for India, interest on the Indian public debt as well as the debt incurred to guarantee the railroads, the cost of military supplies shipped to India, the cost of troops transported to India, and the pensions of civil and military personnel retired in England. These were public remittances on current account for which there was no equivalent commodity return and, at best, an ambiguous service benefit.[41] They thus increased the burden on India's export of commodities.

It will be recalled that Mughal India always had an export balance of trade, a reflection of the strength of its household textile industry and the coastal commercial centers which facilitated the flow of its output to Asian and European markets on the one hand, and, on the other, of the skewed income distribution which restricted imports largely to items of conspicuous consumption favored by the ruling classes. The balance was made up by the importation of precious metals which went into hoards, ornamentation, and the money supply. This did not constitute a drain, in the view of the Indian nationalists, because the economic relationship of India with Asia and Europe was not distorted by the presence in India of rulers whose purpose was defined by a foreign sovereign. While the Mughal emperors traced their ancestry to the Great Mongol Khans, they had become residents of India. They had no interest in transferring resources to the steppes of Asia. However oppressive their rule may have been, however grim the relentless force of a subsistence economy, however conspicuous the consumption of the ruling classes, the structure of demand and the organization of resources in response to it were, in the circumstances, natural. The export surplus of manufactured textile goods and the importation of precious metals reflected the pull of Indian technology and Indian tastes.

The intrusion of British rule distorted the natural economic order in India by subordinating it to the needs of the expanding

British economy. The export surplus of commodities that persisted in India during the half century before World War I was a consequence of the expansion of primary output that accompanied the forced decline of manufacturing. This was unnatural and stood in sharp contrast to what had happened in the white colonies of the British empire. Naoroji observed about investment in India that

> It is the exhaustion caused by the drain that disables us from building our own railroads, etc., from our own means. If we did not suffer the exhaustion we do, and even if we found it to our benefit to borrow from England, the case would be one of a healthy natural business, and the interest then remitted would have nothing to be deplored in it, as in the case of other countries, which, being young, or with undeveloped resources, and without means of their own, borrow from others and increase their own wealth thereby, as Australia, Canada, the United States, or any other native-ruled country that so borrows.[42]

In India, Naoroji and the nationalist critics argued, the export surplus was never put to good account in stimulating Indian development. Rather than being evidence of healthy economic growth as it was in the United States, in the half century before World War I it was a measure of aborted growth, an index of the extent to which British rule distorted the allocation of resources in India in serving the imperial and economic interests of England.

The Indian view assessed

In assessing the Indian view of the economics of British imperialism, one may distinguish its empirical validity from its normative force. While there were many issues raised that were in principle susceptible to quantification – the decline in manufacturing, the agrarianization of the labor force, the impoverishment of the economy, the increasing burden of the drain – the available data were less than adequate and their interpretation sufficiently loose that few people found their values overwhelmed by incontrovertible evidence. As we have already suggested, the controversies over economic imperialism were low key and not laced with the ideological animus against capitalism that characterized Marxian debates in these matters. The value that sustained their relevance in India was nationalism, the belief that there was an Indian interest not being well served by the imperial connection. The number of Indians who participated in these controversies was very small and there was not yet a mass following to which they could turn for support.[43] The Indian National Congress, which became the bearer of the Indian national consciousness and held its first congress in 1885, was an important forum for airing grievances about economic imperialism, but initially represented an infinitesimal proportion of the Indian population. None the less, the development of the Congress, the articulation of an economics of British imperialism, and the formation of the Indian nation were intertwined, interdependent forces which in the end undermined the foundations of British imperial rule. Perhaps it may be said that Dadabhai Naoroji performed for India in the economic realm a similar function to Alexander Hamilton in the United States and Friedrich List in Germany.[44] Hamilton was a vigorous advocate of industrialization as a means of breaking colonial economic dependency and giving substance to recently acquired political independence and List was an equally fervent advocate of a customs union in Germany to stimulate industrial development and political unification. Naoroji too made economics work for independence.

If, however, the economics of British imperialism can be viewed as a critical element in the forming of the Indian commitment to independence, it also can be assessed as economics. In this respect the argument that British imperialism was impoverishing the Indian economy as manifested especially in an external drain of unrequited exports had some of the same difficulties as Marx's hypothesis about the immiserization of the working classes in capitalism. Were the Indian critics of British imperialism asserting that India had become worse off absolutely because of British rule or that it was worse off than it would have been if it had been governed by Indians? Did the British depress the economy or hold back its rate of advance? And related to both of these questions, how could there have been a drain if the basic form of economic organization furthered by British governance was the market whose very purpose was to maximize exchange?

With respect to the last question, the orthodox economic view, which we discussed in Chapter 1, conceives of markets as institutions for facilitating the exchange of equivalent values so that the notion of a drain without a return does not seem plausible. But what was at issue in India in the nineteenth century was the impact of British rule on exchange. That is to say, what did Indians receive for the presence in India of the viceroy and his subordinate governors? Sir John Strachey, an eminent Anglo-Indian governor, answered the question as follows:

> It is an inevitable consequence of the subjection of India that a portion of the cost of her government should be paid in England. The maintenance of our dominion is essential in the interests of India herself, and, provided that she is not compelled to pay more than is really necessary to give her a thoroughly efficient Government, and in return for services actually rendered to her, she has no reason for complaint.[45]

This vague assertion made without any reference to the Indian position on the matter which at the time of writing was readily available to Strachey hardly settled it. The Indian critics charged, to use the expenditure categories of income analysis, that the structure of output changed as government expenditures and net foreign investment expanded at the expense of consumption and investment. This constituted a drain because, while government expenditures may have provided more efficient government than in the previous century, they also provided unwanted public goods such as the military expeditions and occupations that we enumerated earlier in this chapter. Moreover, if net foreign investment increased with the diversion of resources from domestic consumption because the apparatus of Indian government was staffed in its upper reaches by Europeans without permanent commitment to India, this too constituted a drain. To the Indians, then, the drain was an unwanted reallocation of resources brought about by the subjection of India by England. To Strachey and

Englishmen of like mind, the reallocation of resources benefited India and so was an exchange rather than a drain. Clearly, these different perspectives spring from different values. Equally clearly, however, in the ambiguous and conflicting world of interests, Indians had a more credible claim for expressing what it was that they wanted than did the British. The Strachey position that 'the maintenance of our dominion is essential in the interests of India herself' may have been sincerely held, but except for those inside the imperial establishment who cannot believe that it was self-serving?

As for economic growth, the Indian critics of British imperialism were on less sure ground. It does not follow that if there had been no drain the Indian economy would have autonomously and naturally entered into the stream of industrial development that transformed European economies in the nineteenth century. They seemed to have assumed that there were leading sectors in the economy that were held back for lack of capital or by being fatally weakened by the failure of the Indian government to protect them against the competition of more advanced European industry. There was indeed evidence of Indian industrial activity in Bengal in the first half of the nineteenth century and a modern textile industry emerged in Bombay in the second half of the century. Moreover, the Tata family whose members had been leaders in the development of textiles subsequently turned their entrepreneurial talents to the establishment of an iron and steel industry in Bihar and by 1913 had built with Indian capital and were operating one of the largest steel mills in the world.[46] Yet these and other industries were slight extrusions in a vast agrarian plain. If their eruption demonstrated that there were active, entrepreneurially vigorous Indian communities, they also showed that most communities did not respond to these indigenous industrial impulses.

There were many reasons for the industrial inertia of India. We have already pointed out that in the seventeenth century when the British first came to India its Mughal governors and the ruling classes had little interest in the technological and marketing problems that so absorbed English society. These were given little internal, natural, or innovative support in Indian communities beyond the mercantile centers that serviced the traditional household manufacturing industries. The cultural, religious, and social basis of Indian life, however well adapted to the grim reality of scarcity in the subcontinent, did not bring on the inventive faculties. And, of course, in the eighteenth century the disintegration of Mughal authority and the resulting anarchic conditions of political life inhibited the formation of a stable environment that might have encouraged experimentation and entrepreneurial efforts to transform local resources for human purposes. Moreover, unlike England where tastes and consumption norms facilitated an expansion of external and a reorganization of internal markets, Indian tastes seemed to perpetuate traditional markets. The desire of the ruling classes in Mughal India to hoard precious metals or to use them for ornamentation did not set standards that had dynamic benefits for the growth of Indian markets. The export surplus, occasioned by the sale of Indian textiles in Asian and European markets, was more sterile than it would have been had it been used for financing the marketing in India of foreign goods which might have shaped Indian tastes and opened up opportunities for the growth of Indian firms.

It is unlikely in the extreme that, had the British never acquired Indian dominion, India would have developed a more vibrant economy better equipped to take advantage of the international specialization of function that was injected into the world economy by the industrialization of Europe. To repeat what we have observed in a previous chapter, there is no evidence that in the early nineteenth century there was an Indian political community capable of establishing order in the subcontinent or that there were widespread entrepreneurial energies waiting to be released by the reëstablishment of order. The British indubitably established order and probably strengthened the force of the industrial impulse in India if only because they constructed railroads and other transportation and communication facilities without which it is difficult to organize industrial markets. Having said this, however, it does not follow that there was no such thing as a drain or that there could not have been a better outcome for India than in fact occurred in the period between the Great Revolt and World War I.

For one thin, if Indian society did not engender the kind of behavior that autonomously stimulated industrial growth, why should it have bothered about it. We know that as Gandhi came to have such great, charismatic authority in the Indian National Congress early in the present century, his hostility to industrial society and support of household manufacturing in village India influenced its policy and struck a responsive note with the Indian people. And from the vantage point of the late twentieth century when the warts of industrial societies have become uglier and we respond nostalgically to the maxim that small is beautiful, we may have sympathy for anyone who wished to resist the arrogant demands of industrialization. Yet the early Indian critics of British imperialism were not opposed to industrial development. On the contrary, this small coterie of English-speaking and westernized Indians was persuaded that it held the answer to the poverty of India. No doubt there would have been fewer of them had the British never come to rule India because there would not have been the same emphasis on western education in India. But an independent India in the nineteenth century could not have avoided the impact of industrialization whose worldwide thrust and thirst for markets would have been a problem with which Indian government would have had to cope. It could not have retreated into a Japanese-like seclusion.

For another thing, *pax Britannica* affected the rate of population growth from the rebellion to World War I with unanticipated and unintended consequences in rural India more ominous than the aborted or diminished rate of growth in an industrial sector. Because of the elimination of war and banditry with the imposition of political order, the more effective control of famine after the turn of the twentieth century, and still later the restricting of epidemic diseases, the population of India grew at a greater rate than hitherto. How much greater is not easy to determine. The first census was taken in 1871 but subsequently there were changes in the methods of enumeration and in the territories included. When these are adjusted for, the estimated population in 1871 was 255 million and in 1911, 303 million. Prior to 1871, population data do not have a census base and they very probably were underestimated. For example, the estimate of 175 million for 1855 would show a more than 45 percent increase in population between that date and 1871, a demographic feat that strains credulity. If the population in 1855 were of the order of 225 million, then the increase to 1911 would have been 78 million or 34 percent, an average annual increase of less than one-half of one percent. While this rate of increase in population was low by the standards of industrializing societies in the nineteenth century, it was high by the standards of pre-British India.[47]

In any case, an addition to population of approximately 75 million people, superimposed on a traditional order already disrupted by the extension of markets and the establishment in the land settlements of new legal entitlements, exacerbated landlord–tenant relationships and increased rural indebtedness. The price of land rose as the population–land ratio rose during the half-century preceding World War I and, since there was now a market in land supported in law, it could be bought and, of course, sold when owners could not meet their obligations to the state or the moneylenders. How the structure in the ownership of land changed is difficult to ascertain, but there appears to have been a fragmentation of land holdings with an increase in poor cultivating owners and poor undertenants, even as there was a concentration of large property-holdings among a small élite. Moreover, the rural proletariat began to increase and the moneylender increasingly became an opprobrious figure bound less by the constraints of traditional obligations than by the contractual rights assured him in the courts. The latter did, indeed, often become the parasitical landlord that, ironically enough, the British thought they were exorcizing in the land settlements in the years before the rebellion.

The conjuncture of population increases with the changes introduced by the British in the law and the economic system and the persistence of hierarchical social relationships, now somewhat less cohesive because of the weakening bonds of mutual obligation, increased the coercive burden of subsistence on the landless peasants and the poor undertenants, whether they lived in *zamindari* or ryotwari provinces. The matter of the drain and the other issues debated by the emerging national Indian leadership could not have penetrated far into their world circumscribed as it was by the headman, moneylender, and landlord. And the efforts by the British Raj, as in the Bengal Rent Act of 1859, to protect them against the grasping landlord and to reinforce their occupancy rights were diluted by the economic consequences of a growing population. Had there been tangible evidence in overwhelmingly agrarian India that the changes introduced by the British raised standards of subsistence, the burden might have been justified. It seems, however, that surplus agricultural output tended to enrich those who had neither the inclination nor the need to use capital productively. British imperialist governance may have thwarted its own purpose in agriculture by nurturing parasitic rather than improving landlords.[48]

British rule in India, then, and European industrialization, imposed an allocation of resources on India that, while first-best for England, was second- or third-best for India. We may well imagine a better organization of resources for Indian interests in the nineteenth century. A different structure of public investment with greater priority on canals and less on railroads; construction of transportation facilities with greater attention to the potential of indigenous Indian markets; a reduction of the tax burden on the Indian peasant with a concomitant reduction in expenditures on the maintenance of the military establishment; a more careful adjustment of the tariff structure to the development of Indian industry; the establishment of credit institutions for agricultural improvements and industrial innovation, all may have stimulated agricultural productivity and encouraged the growth of manufacturing and industry. The Indian critics supported many of these measures and, early on, many of them thought that the British government in India was the appropriate authority for carrying them out. In fact, the British Raj responded to a different set of priorities manifested in the public expenditures and policies at which the critics railed.

But what do we imagine in the absence of the British Raj? We have already asserted that Indian society did not possess those propensities which fostered growth autonomously in private markets. Whoever might have governed, they would have had to take initiative in accommodating the Indian economy to the changing reality of world markets, if they were to improve upon the historical record under the British. What indigenous rulers in India had the motivations, the skills, and the access to the administrative resources for accomplishing more than could have been accomplished by private initiative? Industrialization was a western invention; so too were the institutional and administrative supports for it. Had India been independent and governed by progressive rulers, they no doubt would have turned to the west for counsel and the skills they lacked at home. At best they would have established a Japanese-like connection with the outside world. More likely, they would have developed a Chinese-like connection with treaty ports harboring enclaves of foreign merchants, bankers, advisers, soldiers of fortune, a mélange of characters with ambiguous commitment to anything but their own interests. There would not have been a good prospect for achieving a better development of India's economic potential in that sort of setting.

If we have implied in this discussion of the economics of British imperialism that, though India's economic interest was not the primary goal of British rule, it may not have been much better served in other systems of governance, we do not mean to depreciate the force of the Indian critics' arguments. While their arguments may not have rested easily on the intransigent substance of economic reality, they expressed the anguish of people who were coming to believe that economic conditions ought not to have been as grim as they were. The normative force of their arguments had greater consequences than their analytical validity. They expressed a point of view that brought the disparate experiences of Indian communities held fast in the coercive grip of scarcity into focus as the burden of British rule.

There is an illusory element to imperialist oppression because if perceived as such it implies a better, freer life when the foreign devil is expelled. Few societies have suffered greater oppression than India and none have so systematically sublimated them in their social order. Historically it survived or mastered many invaders. It was not until the last of these that there began to form in the minds of a few the idea of India which both rendered the British superfluous and called into question the norms of the stabilizing social order. India as a nation cut across castes, subcastes, and communities, and embodied values which competed with the parochial, particularistic standards of life in village India.

The economics of British imperialism in India weakened the belief held by many of the early nationalist leaders that Indian goals could be achieved under British rule. It strengthened the commitment to independent India at the locus in the society where the national norm took roots. And it was all the more effective because the somber, quantitative nature of the economic arguments had such strong implications about justice and fairness as an Indian outlook related them to imperialism as a world phenomenon. We have already noted that Naoroji distinguished economic development in the self-governing white colonies from its absence in India. By the same token the early nationalists appreciated the affinity of their position with the plight of Ireland and the civil and military apparatus of English rule. Moreover, the opium trade whose heinous denouement in China was more destructive than it was on the Indian producers of the poppy revealed the pretentiousness of the disinterested welfare claims of British imperialism. And with the diaspora of Indian migrants, their mistreatment in various parts of the empire further tarnished the luster of English rule. Gandhi's formative years as an Indian nationalist were spent in South Africa using his legal and organizational skills in representing the oppressed Indian minority who worked there.

If the half-century between the Great Revolt and World War I marked the high tide of British imperialism in India, it was partly because of the stirring of these anti-imperialist, pro-Indian sentiments. An imperialism that is not resented has not reached full strength. Resentment, however, is contagious and it is more apt to say of British imperialism in India than of Lenin's capitalist development that its highest was also its moribund stage. In one short generation after World War I India had become independent and had to deal with the aspirations of a free people.

Notes

1 Thomas R. Metcalf, *The Aftermath of Revolt, India 1857–1870*, Princeton, Princeton University Press, 1964, 55.

2 In a letter to Colonel Edwardes quoted by John W. Kaye, *A History of the Sepoy War in India, 1857–58*, London, W. H. Allen, 1878, II, 401.

3 Metcalf, op. cit., 81.

4 S. B. Chaudhuri, *Civil Rebellion in the Indian Mutinies, 1857–1859*, Calcutta, World Press, 1957, 258–99, for the view of the rebellion as an early freedom struggle; R. C. Majumdar, *Three Phases of India's Struggle for Freedom*, Bombay, Bharatiya Vidya Bhava, 1961, 2–4, for the view that it was the stand of conservative vested interests against change; Eric Stokes, *The Peasant and the Raj: Studies in Agrarian Society and Peasant Rebellion in Colonial India*, London, Cambridge University Press, 1978, for detailed case studies of the Indian reaction.

5 Brian Gardner, *The East India Company*, New York, McCall, 1972, 296–8.

6 Romesh Dutt, *The Economic History of India in the Victorian Age*, 7th edn, London, Routledge & Kegan Paul, 1950, 232.

7 'We hold ourselves bound to the Natives of our Indian territories by the same obligations of duty which bind us to all our other subjects, and these obligations, by the blessing of Almighty God, we shall faithfully and conscientiously fulfill. It is our further will that, so far as may be, our subjects of whatever race or creed, be freely and impartially admitted to offices in our service, the duties of which they may be qualified by their education, ability, and integrity, duly to discharge.' From the Queen's Proclamation, quoted by Dadabhai Naoroji, *Poverty and Un-British Rule in India*, Delhi, Government Publications Division, 1962, 83.

8 Vincent A. Smith, *The Oxford History of India*, Percival Spear (ed.), 3rd edn, Oxford, Clarendon Press, 1967, 675.

9 Dutt, op. cit., 229.

10 Stephen P. Cohen, *The Indian Army, its Contribution to the Development of a Nation*, Berkeley, University of California Press, 1971, 35–45.

11 When open examinations was first used in recruiting civil servants, the examinations were held in England. It was not until 1864 that an Indian qualified for the Indian Civil Service.

12 The covenanted service originated in Clive's requirement that servants of the Company sign a covenant pledging themselves not to engage in private trade or to accept gifts. The Charter Act of 1793

then stipulated that 'no office with a salary higher than £500 was to go to any one who had not worked in India for three years as a covenanted servant': H. H. Dodwell (ed.), *The Cambridge Shorter History of India*, Delhi, S. Chand, 1964, 763.

13 Donald E. Smith, *India as a Secular State*, Princeton, Princeton University Press, 1963, 276.

14 Bipan Chandra, *The Rise and Growth of Economic Nationalism in India*, New Delhi, People's Publishing House, 1966, 172–7.

15 Vincent A. Smith, *The Oxford History of India*, 678.

16 A. J. Sargent, *Seaways of the Empire*, London, Black, 1918, 49. There was not the same saving in time over the route to India which took passengers to Alexandria by boat, overland to Suez by stage coach, and then boat again to India.

17 David S. Landes, *Bankers and Pashas, International Finance and Economic Imperialism*, Cambridge, Mass., Harvard University Press, 1958.

18 Afaf Lutfi Al-Sayyid, *Egypt and Cromer, a Study in Anglo-Egyptian Relations*, New York, Praeger, 1969. The Egyptian involvement was a 'persistent irritant to Britain'. A. P. Thornton, *For the File on Empire*, London, Macmillan, 1968, 254. It was complicated by the sub-imperialism of Egypt in the Sudan and its abortive efforts to crush the uprising of the Mahdi, an Islamic Sudanese nationalist. The reluctant British in 1884 dispatched General 'Chinese' Gordon to the Sudan to evacuate the Egyptian army and westerners resident in Khartoum. The general, however, stayed in Khartoum, which was besieged and assaulted by the Mahdi's troops whose victory was authenticated by the presentation to their leaders of the general's severed head. Gordon became a Victorian hero and still later the subject of one of Lytton Strachey's biographical essays in *Eminent Victorians*, New York, Harcourt Brace, 1918.

19 John McLane, 'The drain of wealth and Indian nationalism at the turn of the century', in T. Raychaudhuri (ed.), *Contributions to Indian Economic History*, Calcutta, K. L. Mukhopadhyay, II, 1963, 33. Aside from Egypt and the northwest frontier, the Indian army was used in the annexation of Upper Burma 1885–6, the Sikkim expedition 1888, the Chitral expedition 1895, and in South Africa in 1899–1900 and China 1900–1. Chandra, op. cit., 508–88.

20 Chandra, op. cit. 217–70.

21 ibid., 360–70.

22 ibid., 323.

23 ibid., 636–8.

24 H. M. Hyndman, 'The bankruptcy of India', *The Nineteenth Century*, 4 (20), 585–608; Naoroji, op. cit., 1–124.

25 Naoroji, op. cit. viii.

26 The openness of English society nurtured support for India. Naoroji himself served a term in the House of Commons following the election of 1892 and gained a forum for publicizing his views. Almost forty years before his election an Indian Reform Society with at least thirty-five members of the House of Commons was formed in order to bring 'public opinion to bear on the Imperial Parliament in the case of India so as to obtain due attention to the complaints and claims of the inhabitants of that vast Empire': ibid., 510. Annie Besant, an early Fabian, was an active proponent of the Indian National Congress and in *How India Wrought Freedom*, Madras, Theosophical Publishing House, 1915, reported the work of its annual meetings. And William Digby supported Naoroji's views in a biting attack on British policy in India: *'Prosperous' British India, a Revelation from Official Records*, London, T. Fisher Unwin, 1901.

27 As Bernard Porter put it, 'It had been a notable feature of Indian protest in the last decades of the nineteenth century that it had been generally moderate, constitutional, almost fawning in its insistent loyalty to the British connexion: a tribute to the esteem in which the protestors held the British, from whom they learnt how to criticize autocracy as well as how to suffer it': *The Lion's Share*, New York, Longman, 1975, 215.

28 Chandra, op. cit., 238.

29 ibid., 211.

30 ibid., 208.

31 B. M. Bhatia, *Famines in India, a Study in Some Aspects of the Economic History of India, 1860–1946*, Bombay, Asia Publishing House, 1963, 3–7.

32 Vincent A. Smith, *The Oxford History of India*, 688. As always, the roundness of the estimated number of deaths suggests it was a guess rather than hard, empirically based datum.

33 Bhatia, op. cit., 181.

34 The data for the Irish famine are somewhat better than for Indian famines. In 1841 the population of Ireland was 8,175,124 and in 1851 6,552,385. If it had grown at a normal rate, it would have been 9,018,799. Cecil Woodham-Smith, *The Great Hunger, Ireland, 1845–1849*, London, Hamish Hamilton, 1962, 411. Of the lost two-and-a-half million people perhaps as many as one million died. M. K.

Bennett, 'Famine', in D. L. Sills (ed.), *International Encyclopedia of The Social Sciences*, New York, Macmillan, 1968, v, 324. Again the roundness of the estimate invites doubt but, if it were reduced by 50 percent, the incidence of death during the Irish famines would still have been greater than during the Indian famines of 1876–8.

35 At various times and places, cooked food was distributed to the starving in poor houses, a grain dole was distributed through villages, or work relief was organized through village projects or larger centralized projects. Whatever the method, the English were influenced by the principle of less eligibility that governed relief in England after the passage of the Poor Law Amendment in 1834. As J. S. Mill argued, 'If the condition of a person receiving relief is made as eligible as that of the labourer who supports himself by his own exertions, the system strikes at the root of all individual industry and self-government, and, if fully acted up to, would require as its supplement an organized system of compulsion for governing and setting to work like cattle those who have been removed from the influence of motives that act on human beings': quoted by Bhatia, op. cit., 112.

36 Vincent A. Smith, *The Oxford History of India*, 728.

37 Bhatia, op. cit., 39.

38 Quoted by Chandra, op. cit., 506.

39 Naoroji, op. cit., 22.

40 ibid., 27.

41 In the days of the Company, the home charges included the expenses of the Board of Control, the Court of Directors, and Haileybury College and the dividends paid to proprietors. After 1858, the administrative expenses of the Company in England were absorbed in the expenses of the Secretary of State for India. Pramathanath Banerjea, *Indian Finance in the Days of the Company*, London, Macmillan, 1928, 329–36; Chandra, op. cit., 636–708.

42 Quoted by B. N. Ganguli, *Dadabhai Naoroji and the Drain Theory*, London, Asia Publishing House, 1965, 23.

43 On debates over the economic aspects of Indian nationalism the same names come up again and again: in addition to Naoroji, they are Surendranath Banerjea, R. C. Dutt, G. K. Gokhale, G. V. Joshi, M. G. Ranade, B. G. Tilak, and D. E. Wacha. For an assessment from a modern economic analytical standpoint of the arguments of the Indian nationalists, particularly with respect to the drain, see K. N. Chaudhuri, 'India's international economy in the nineteenth century:

an historical survey', *Modern Asian Studies*, II (1), 31–50.

44 Alexander Hamilton, 'Report on the subject of manufacturers', in F. W. Taussig (ed.), *State Papers and Speeches on the Tariff*, Cambridge, Mass., Harvard University Press, 1893, 1–107; Friedrich List, *The National System of Political Economy*, London, Longmans, Green, 1885. The four parts of List's book were originally published between 1841 and 1844.

45 Sir John Strachey, *India, its Administration and Progress*, 3rd edn, London, Macmillan, 1903, 192–3.

46 Vincent A. Smith, *The Oxford History of India*, 712. For a comprehensive, objective, and inevitably inconclusive review of the literature and problems of economic development during the last century of British rule in India see W. J. MacPherson, 'Economic development in India under the British Crown, 1858–1947', in A. J. Youngson (ed.), *Economic Development in the Long Run*, London, Allen & Unwin, 1972, 126–91.

47 Kingsley Davis, *The Population of India and Pakistan*, Princeton, Princeton University Press, 1951, 25–7. From 1921 to 1941 population increased from 306 to 389 million, an overall increase of 24 percent or 1.2 percent per annum. The full impact of British governance on Indian population growth was not felt until after World War I.

48 Barrington Moore, Jr, *Social Origins of Dictatorship and Democracy, Lord and Peasant in the Making of the Modern World*, Boston, Beacon, 1966, 353–70. Moore notes that in researching the Indian chapter of this monumental and impressive book he at one point 'suspected that the parasitic landlord might well be a lengendary social species created by Indian nationalists and semi-Marxist writers', (356). The evidence that he assessed, however, persuaded him that the parasitic landlord was very real indeed.

6

England out of India: 1947 and after

On 15 August 1947, India became independent, Pakistan was created from Baluchistan, Sind, and part of the Punjab in the west of India and from the division of Bengal in the east, and both new states entered the British Commonwealth of nations. After two centuries of direct rule, the British relinquished the reins of power, leaving behind governmental institutions that already were partially staffed by Indians and rankling problems that had been bottled up in the colonial relationship. That the British departed India reflected the persistent force of the independence movement which emerged out of the Indian National Congress that first met in 1885. Committed initially to achieving Indian objectives within the British empire, the Congress gradually became the focus and fulcrum of Indian nationalist aspirations. Dadabhai Naoroji had been in advance of his peers, but by 1929 they had made independence the goal above all others which they would not compromise. Led by Gandhi and Nehru and using civil disobedience selectively to bring the pressure of the Indian masses on their British rulers, the Congress raised the cost of imperialism and filled the prisons with protesting, non-compliant nationalists.[1] It became increasingly difficult for the British to maintain that their rule in India was acceptable to Indians and the visibility of the Congress in the nationalist struggle strengthened the hand of the opponents in England of the imperial connection.

The departure of the British, however, also was occasioned by the relative decline of the British economy. At the time of the Sepoy Revolt, it dominated the international order. Industrial growth was in full stride when its European and North American rivals were just beginning to develop their industrial potential. By the end of the nineteenth century, the German and United States economies had surpassed the British and in the Far East the Japanese were on the edge of the industrial age. In the twentieth century, the world wars imposed shocks on an already faltering economy which made the imperial commitment an increasing burden. If there was a drain in the nineteenth century, there was little evidence in 1945 that Indian resources could help the British economy in its postwar adjustment.

Its problems, ironically enough, were a consequence of that industrial preeminence in the nineteenth century which made it the dominant power in the world. The British economy developed in advance of other economies by harnessing steam power and applying mechanical inventions to the production of a narrow range of output – textiles, transportation, coal, iron and steel, and metal and engineering products. Its industrial revolution, moreover, was a triumph of mechanics and engineers with little formal training but much energy and initiative and a strong intuitive and empirical sense about how to break the production bottlenecks that were holding back economic expansion. By virtue of being first in the order of industrialization it became committed to an intractable organization of resources that subsequently was less suited to the demands emanating from world markets as income rose in western economies. One difficulty, first noted by Thorstein Veblen, inhered in the construction of assets with one kind of technology having strong complementary components which rendered it extremely expensive to change when a later and better technology became available.[2] The classic example of this immobility was a railroad system whose engines, rolling stock, tunnels, bridges, stations, and loading platforms were built to specifications constrained by the gauge of the track. When larger engines with greater traction became technologically feasible, their use was inhibited economically by the required wider-gauged track that also entailed the rebuilding of the other complementary equipment of the railroad system. The railroads initially laid down in the follower economies were not beholden to an older, but still usable capital stock.

Whether or not the technology of the first industrial revolution was immobilizing. British entrepreneurial capabilities were stunted by the achievement. It was a remarkable accomplishment of individuals who received little systematic support from government. The men who made the industrial revolution, perhaps understandably, came to feel that they had invented enduring methods for producing and marketing industrial output and subsequent generations of English businessmen traded on the pioneering reputation that the industrial founders so richly deserved. The follower economies, however, sought the goal of industrial expansion outside the pale of the founders' influences. In both Germany and the United States, there was greater willingness to experiment with forms of business organization, managerial and business education, productive techniques, and the application of science in industry. The result was that, as new technology based in applied chemical science, for example, began to supplement mechanical technology, the British business community was less able or less willing to take advantage of it. While England pioneered in the development of organic chemistry and even produced some of the first synthetic dye-stuffs that eventually undermined the market for indigo, it was Germany that employed its organizational skills in mobilizing capital and training workers for the growth of an industry that has been called 'Imperial Germany's greatest industrial achievement'.[3] And before the triumph of the German dye-stuff industry, the American economy had given the mechanical age an extraordinary boost with the invention of interchangeable parts which reduced the dependence of manufacturers on highly skilled artisans and prepared the way for mass-production methods of which Henry Ford took such great advantage. Already in 1851 at the Crystal Palace Exhibition in London, the apotheosis to the industrial might of England, Englishmen were talking about the 'American System of Manufacturing'.[4]

While the British economy was less mobile and adaptable than its younger rivals, its greater investment capacity was largely exported, especially to the regions of recent settlement, the United States, Argentina, Australia, and Canada. In the half-century before World War I, England invested an average of 4 percent of her national income overseas and in the period immediately preceding the war the rate reached 7 percent.[5] It was the return on this investment that for a time made it a mature creditor nation with an import balance of goods and services on current account. It also represented a use of resources in the expansion of young economies at the cost of the modernization of England's domestic capital stock. Had there been a reallocation of investment from overseas to the British economy, it might have retained the productive flexibility that would have allowed it to compete more effectively with the economies it was helping to industrialize.

Had the world wars not taken their toll on the British economy, it would have been in a better position to address the problem of the relative decline in its productivity. But their capacious and enervating demand on scarce resources compelled England to sell many overseas assets to acquire the foreign exchange that during the wars was no longer generated by exports. Moreover, in World War II England was so close to the brink of defeat that it maximized current military and related output by allocating resources to strategic industries that otherwise would have gone to a proper replacement of depreciated or obsolete assets in export industries. By 1945 its earnings from foreign investment were depleted when the export sector of the economy needed to be modernized in order to resume its traditional role in international trade.

Indian independence then was not simply a recognition by the British of the merits of the demands of Indian nationalists or a belief that they had fulfilled their responsibilities as trustees of Indian welfare. Notwithstanding Winston Churchill's contemptuous dismissal of the British Labour Party's transfer of power to the Congress as 'operation scuttle', it was required by the grim condition of the British economy. It was to the credit of the English, however, that necessity was recognized and that they did not make a quixotic stand in defense of the old colonialism as the French did in southeast Asia and later in North Africa. The willingness to yield, it should be stressed, always was implicit somewhere in the imperial relationship between England and

India. The Macaulay Minute on Education, arrogant though it was, implied that Indians potentially had the capacity for self-government and many of the British reformers in India in the first half of the nineteenth century no doubt believed it, all the more so since at that time it appeared to be a far distant goal. Though the Great Revolt set back the cause of enlightened reform and ushered in the period of high Victorian imperialism in which many of the British proconsuls in India assumed that they were there to stay, the continuing evolution of democratic institutions in England was inconsistent with the repression of self-government in India.

The election of a Liberal government in Great Britain in 1906 was a portent of the growing recognition among the Congress's English allies of self-government as a legitimate goal for India. Concrete evidence of this was contained in the Morley–Minto Reforms of 1909 in which in British India (as opposed to the princely states of India) Indians were admitted to executive offices and were allotted a majority of the seats in the provincial legislatures that were to be elected by a limited constituency.[6] While the ultimate legislative power remained with the viceroy, since the provincial legislatures only had advisory power on the actions of the central government, the principle of Indians holding elected offices had been conceded, foreshadowing the transfer of political power in 1947 to a central Indian parliamentary body. In 1917 when the outcome of World War I was still uncertain and England, with the other European combatants, was suffering a prodigal and insensate slaughter of a generation of young men, the Secretary of State for India, Samuel Montagu, announced that the policy of his government in India would be 'the gradual development of self-governing institutions with a view to the progressive realization of responsible government as an integral part of the British Empire'.[7] Two years later, in the year of Amritsar, the British government passed the Government of India Act, known as the Montagu–Chelmsford Reforms, which increased the jurisdiction of the provincial legislatures, allowing them to enact laws dealing with education, agriculture, and health (but not finance, taxation, or police), and extending the franchise for the elections to these bodies from some 30,000 to 5 million.

Though the central government remained responsible to the British government in Westminster, the viceroy was advised by a council of eight members, which now included three Indians. Moreover, an Imperial Legislative Council was enlarged and made into a bicameral legislature – the Legislative Assembly elected on limited franchise for three years and a Council of State for five years – with powers to initiate legislation and deliberate on proposals originating in the viceroy's office without having the power to turn him out of office.

Sixteen years later in the last constitutional reform before World War II, another Government of India Act was passed. The 1935 Act increased the autonomy of provincial legislatures so that they were fully responsible for local issues, extended the franchise to 30 million Indians, made provisions for separate constituencies, reserved seats in legislative bodies for the so-called scheduled castes, that is untouchables, and created a federal framework for the political integration of the provinces and for bringing the princely states into the system, if they so desired. As for the central government, the size of the legislative assemblies was increased as was the number of ministers responsible to them, though the viceroy retained full authority in foreign and internal affairs.[8]

The transfer of the authority in 1947 to govern India from Great Britain to Indians may be viewed as a consistent development of tendencies already apparent in the imperial relationship but very much accelerated by the debilitating consequences of the world wars on an already weakening British economy.

Indian rule and the articulation of Indian interests

What difference did the departure of the British Raj make for the coercive burden of poverty and scarcity experienced by Indian society? If this question is close to being unanswerable, it none the less must be asked in order to place the transformation of economic imperialism in perspective. On the morrow of independence the peasants of village India lived with those traditional constraints that had always ordered their lives. The shifting of command at the apex of society, however, allowed the more forceful expression and pursuit of Indian interests which, in the light of their luxuriant variety, were no easy matter to reconcile. Two hundred years of British imperial rule had brought institutional changes that had created élites with conflicting attitudes about economic development and modernization, but with strong nationalist aspirations. The reception of English law and legal institutions stimulated the growth of the legal profession, as did government the rise of civil servants and constitutional reform politicians. Moreover, the order imposed on India by the British as well as their construction of railroads and investment in other kinds of infrastructure encouraged the development of an entrepreneurial class. There were, then, cadres for staffing governmental and political positions and managerial resources for expanding the private economy. More than most colonial countries that followed India to independence, it had a leadership capable of confronting the problems of economic development. Yet the fragmentation of the society and the conflict of indigenous interests made them awesomely difficult.

The partition of the subcontinent between India and Pakistan at the outset of independence released the most tragic of these conflicts. Communal rioting, pillage, and slaughter among Hindus, Muslims, and Sikhs may have taken the lives of as many as one million people and led to the counter migrations of 12 to 15 million between West and East Pakistan and India.[9] However difficult it may be to comprehend the horrors visited upon the families whose lives and homes were destroyed, it is no less difficult to make a judgment about responsibility for the Hobbesian world they revealed. One may argue that this was precisely what British imperialism had given India surcease from following its succession to Mughal rule in the eighteenth century; the hostility between Hindu and Muslim had not been eliminated, but had been contained by the maintenance of law and order. Or it may be argued that British rule created vested interests and jealousies that exacerbated communal enmities so that when the imperial lid was lifted the explosions were worse than they otherwise would have been. Or perhaps the British were not sufficiently ingenious or patient in devising institutional means for transferring power from the Crown to the new states of the subcontinent.[10] Or, as the Indian Nationalists felt, the British should have fulfilled their pledge of World War I with greater alacrity in the years before the outbreak of World War II. In any event, the frenzy of killing, apprehended most sorrowfully in the west in the assassination of Gandhi in January 1948 by a fanatical Hindu who detested his efforts to abate communal conflict, was a cost of the transfer of power from imperial rulers to India and Pakistan.

Also fraught with danger to the political stability of independent India were the princely states whose rulers' prerogatives had been protected by the British in the establishment of Crown rule following the Great Revolt. Most of them, however, had been induced by the Mountbatten Plan for independence to grant either to India or to Pakistan control over foreign affairs, defense, and communications, leaving for themselves control of wholly internal matters. Hyderabad and Kashmir were the only large states that had not acceded to the terms of the Mountbatten Plan by 15 August 1947. The former, completely surrounded by Indian territory, was brought into the new state by force of Indian arms. The latter, precariously positioned atop north Pakistan and India, was predominantly Muslim but governed by a Hindu maharaja who agreed to accede to India when his territories were invaded by tribesmen from Pakistan. Thus did Kashmir become a continuing source of friction between India and Pakistan which was not appreciably diminished by its partition between the two. Here again these problems were, in the colorless phrase of economics, the transfer costs of independence, some of which were externalized in the international relations of India and others internalized on the agenda of the development of Indian federalism.

The Indian leadership which survived the trauma of independence contained in the Congress a wide range of values that reflected not only the varied economic, caste, language, and communal interests of India but the force of democratic and socialist ideals which had flourished so vigorously during the previous century in the international environment. Some, though hardly a majority, of these leaders held deeply to a belief that the inequities of the social–economic order in India needed to be expunged if it were to become a modern state. Gandhi was not a socialist, and in matters of economic policy was anti-modern, if not reactionary, but no one could have been more distraught by the way caste Indians treated untouchables or by the communal hostility between Hindus and Muslims. Nehru was a Kashmir brahman whose socialist outlook, fashioned out of the clay of Fabianism and Marxism, placed great store in systematic planning for economic development. Leaders of his persuasion anticipated the penetration of Indian society in a conscious effort to change ancient customs and practices that were thought to be incompatible with modernization. The relationships between political leaders of society, however, may operate in two directions. By virtue of the greater interest in penetrating society, the political system itself was to become more responsive to the sources of fragmentation in India. Conflicts that had been submerged in the social order or acted upon in local communities were now more likely to acquire a political incarnation at the level of the national state.

This was symbolized at the creation of independent India by the appointment of B.R. Ambedkar, the leader of the untouchables, to the chairmanship of the drafting committee of the Constituent Assembly whose members had been elected in 1947 by the provincial legislatures. The Indian Constitution of 1950 was uniquely a document of the twentieth century. Ambedkar argued in the Constituent Assembly that 'it would be impossible to frame an absolutely new or original constitution at this point in history. The only innovations possible in a constitution framed so late in the day would be the variations needed to adapt it to the peculiar conditions prevailing in India.'[11] Few constitutions have been written which drew more explicitly on political and legal values and institutions developed in other countries.[12] In framing the fundamental law of the land on the structure of government and the values it should represent, the Constitution, like all constitutions, attempted to legitimize governing institutions and to inculcate in Indian society beliefs about the kind of civil community it aspired to be.

Constitutions typically encounter more difficulties, or at any rate more glaring inconsistencies, in the performance of their normative than of their positive functions. The Indian Constitution was no exception. So far as the latter was concerned, the government established by the Constituent Assembly was a federal structure with union, state, and concurrent powers specified in the Constitution and residual legislative powers residing in the Union Parliament. The parliament was bicameral, the upper house, the *Rajya Sabha* or Council of States, being largely chosen by state legislatures, and the lower house, the *Lok Sabha* or House of the People, being elected by universal suffrage. As in Great Britain, the lower house was more powerful. When conflicts occurred, it met jointly with the upper house and with twice its membership could outvote it. Again like Great Britain, the cabinet whose members were elected to the Union Parliament were responsible to it and the prime minister was the leader of the party or coalition of parties that commanded a majority. In the judicial branch of government a Supreme Court replaced the Privy Council as the court of last resort, though its power was not so great as the power of the US Supreme Court. The Constitution made it relatively easy for the Parliament to amend it and overturn adverse judicial decisions.

If parliaments, cabinets, and courts could be duly formed according to procedures established by the Indian Constitution, it was not so easy to realize the ideals enshrined in it. Nehru and people of his persuasion wanted to express in the Constitution of newly independent India its commitment to the rule of law and individual right as understood in secular society in the western tradition, values, of course, that were wildly at variance with a social order based on a hierarchy of castes and horizontally on different communities. The Indian Constitution was immensely detailed as it tried to deal with the particularistic problems of the social structure as well as lay down general standards of behavior for the state and individuals. Article 15 (1) asserted that: 'The state shall not discriminate against any citizen on grounds only of religion, race, caste, sex, place of birth or any of them.'[13] Since the Constituent Assembly numbered among its members strong and influential advocates of eliminating the condition of untouchability, it was not satisfied to rest with this negative statement on the rights of citizens, but wanted positively to express support for those people who traditionally had been depreciated by the social order. Article 15 (4) stated: 'Nothing in this article or in clause (2) of article 19 shall prevent the state from making any social provision for the advancement of any socially and educationally backward classes of citizens or for the Scheduled Castes and the Scheduled Tribes'. Subsequently, after specifying that there should be no communal electorates, Article 330 (1) stated that 'Seats shall be reserved in the House of the People for – a) the Scheduled Castes; and b) the Scheduled Tribes' and Article 332 (1) that 'Seats shall be reserved for the Scheduled Castes and Scheduled Tribes.' Subsequently, after specifying that there

One does not have to examine more provisions of the Constitution to appreciate the problems articles like these raised. On the one hand, the Constitution was committed to the idea that the state should deal with individuals as individuals and not as members of communities. On the other hand, in the interests of making amends for the inequities of the social order, it had explicitly reserved for disadvantaged groups privileges – and legislative seats were not the only ones – that provided a strong rationale for their continued existence. One consequence of this was that the burden on the courts increased because it was a judicial problem to determine what constituted membership in a caste or community for the purposes of the benefits they may have had under the Constitution. The means for achieving social justice was a type of public good whose importance depended on the weight attached to it by those people in a position to articulate the normative values of society. Nehru and his followers in the Congress Party acted on standards of justice that had evolved gradually in the development of the western world and in the mid-twentieth century put them in competition with other values critical in modernization. Social justice held equal rank with economic development, and if it were to be pursued the limited resources of the political and judicial system had to be devoted to the labyrinthian task of working through the claims of caste and community in the face of a formal commitment to the rule of law.

In twentieth-century India, the international environment transmitted to Nehru and many Congress leaders a set of values that put them out of phase with the dominant values of village India. They heard the 'cry for justice' if the latter did not and hence could not ignore its claims when addressing the problems of economic and political modernization.[15] In this respect late-twentieth-century India differed from late-eighteenth-century England where the vast majority of the people were not constitutionally incorporated in the political community and it did not occur to its rulers that it was part of their function to reduce inequities of a class society. A sense of public responsibility for social welfare developed very late in the game, after industrialization and urbanization had concentrated poverty and made it visible and had precipitated the organization of a wide variety of movements which insinuated the social question into the consciousness of society.[16] Over the centuries of modernization in Great Britain, then, there was a rough and ready rationing of public goals which had the effect of easing the burden imposed on the political system. Autonomous economic development in the private sector restructured society which led to demands for the reform of political institutions. As these were gradually accommodated to democratic pressures, the range of issues managed by the political system widened until social–economic inequities were formally taken on in the welfare state.

While many of the Congress leaders wished to use the authority of the newly independent Indian state to press on society the values of social–economic justice in an abstract, universal sense, there were many more who viewed the political system as a vehicle for furthering the more concrete interest of their constituents. While the lofty aspiration of righting the centuries of injustice visited upon the untouchables received constitutional blessing, linguistic and regional interests worked through the federalism of the states to acquire more pronounced political identities and bases. The central government yielded to the demand for linguistic states and, following a report submitted in 1955 by the States Reorganization Committee, redrew the boundaries of the states so that each of the languages had, as it were, a political home. In the then four states of the north, Hindi was the official language; in each of the remaining thirteen a regional language was dominant. There may well have been no other way to deal with a problem the national solution to which was so terribly threatening to those whose native language would have put them at a disadvantage in education and employment. None the less, the political autonomy of different languages increased separatist tendencies in India and so compelled the national government to use a greater portion of its scarce political capital to hold the system together. The language policy that Britain imposed in the nineteenth century no longer was feasible in the twentieth century.

It would be a task for a person of Promethean courage to assess the change in the coercive burden of Indian life occasioned by the replacement of the British Raj by Indian rulers. If the imperialist connection between Britain and India passed into the dustbin of history, its coercive consequences were internalized, now wearing indigenous garb rather than the colors of the British viceroy and his district commissioners. This may have made the policeman or the tax collector a less threatening representative of the state, though not perhaps in the view of the Muslim in predominantly Hindu territory or of the Hindu in predominantly Muslim territory. None the less, after the mass migrations immediately following independence and the partition of the subcontinent, there cannot have been many Indians who would have preferred a return to the paternalism of British imperial rule. If they felt the burden of subsistence and governance as they did in the days of imperial rule, they now had better representation to vent their frustration on devils who at least were their own.

The burden of economic development in independent India

The complexity of these problems was demonstrated in the tasks of economic development that confronted India after 1947. Unlike Britain at the headwaters of industrialization in the eighteenth century, India embarked on its quest for an end to poverty when the awareness of and the expectations for economic performance had been heightened by two centuries of industrialization and economic commentary and ideology about it. In India, the discussion and controversy about the drain initiated by Dadabhai Naoroji had disseminated the view that India's own economic development had been held in thralldom to England's economic interest. Even before independence, the Congress Party in the 1930s under Nehru's leadership had established a planning committee to assess the appropriateness for an India in charge of its own destiny of the planning methods that the Soviet Union was then using to accelerate industrial growth. The establishment of a Planning Commission in 1950 was an earnest of his intent to strive consciously for a better economic future while realizing the civil and social rights so painstakingly adumbrated in the Constitution. And in the first five-year plan formally inaugurated the next year the Planning Commission revealed its great expectations in the statement that

> planning even in the initial stages should not be confined to stimulating economic activity within the existing social and economic framework. That framework itself has to be remoulded so as to ensure progressively for all members of the community full employment, education, security against sickness and other disabilities and adequate income.[17]

The planners, then, brought into the open conflicts over social and economic priorities that in the imperial age either had been acted upon unilaterally by the British or left to their traditional resolution in the functioning of society and economy.

It was perhaps anomalous that at the outset the planners should place such great emphasis on industrialization in a society with such a massive agrarian population so strongly anchored in ancient village and caste traditions. At the time of independence, the industrial sector was small, geographically restricted, and confined to a few business communities and castes – the Parsis, Gujaratis, and Marwaris – and did not, as one Indian economist facetiously put it, 'even produce domestically such rudimentary items as pencils'.[18] Nehru was committed to rectifying this situation through planning a more rapid rate of industrial growth. As prime minister, he sat on the National Development Council which in addition to himself consisted of the chief ministers of the states and members of the Planning Commission. The duties of the Council were to review the performances of the National Plan, consider issues of social and economic policy important for national development, and recommend policies relevant to the aims and targets of the National Plan.[19] Though Nehru's views of industrialization as influenced by the members of the Planning Commission prevailed in the Council, the latter contained the representatives of regional interests some of whom were little more interested in planned industrialization than they were in changing the existing social and economic framework of India.

These potential conflicts of interest did not prevent an increased stress on industrialization in the second five-year plan, the first year of which was 1956. The rate of net saving and investment was to be raised and a greater proportion of investment allocated to the industrial sector, including the expansion of steel capacity with the construction of three new plants. Since the Indian economy was a mixed private–public sector system and there was no commitment to a command economy of the Soviet type, investment allocations were divided between the public and private sectors with the former, however, planned to grow faster. The policy instruments for achieving these planning purposes 'consisted mainly of a powerful and comprehensive industrial licensing system, occasionally combined with price and distributional controls'.[20]

The results of industrialization since the start of the second five-year plan have not been compellingly dramatic. One of the characteristics of planning procedures that periodize the economic process in blocks of five years, however, is that it creates expectations that are hard to fulfill. There is, of course, nothing magic about the number five or any other number that might have been selected as the appropriate period for measuring performance. Whatever the number, it becomes a norm which requires an accounting. While the rate of net domestic investment did rise during the second five-year plan and thereafter remained at the higher level – from 1956 to 1957 it rose from 9.9 to 14.7 percent and in 1965 it was 14.3 percent – over the eighteen-year period from 1952 to 1970 industrial output as a proportion of net domestic output changed very little. Between those years industrial output doubled, but increased proportionately only from 16 to 17 percent. In the same period the proportion of agricultural output in net domestic product decreased from 48 to 42 percent while the proportion of trade, transport, communication, and other services increased from 34 to 41 percent.

These priorities in resource utilization manifested at the level of national economy the burden of economic growth which in the nineteenth century had been seen as an external drain which aborted growth and whose domestic burdens were laid at the feet of British imperial rulers. Now the distributive counterpart of these priorities, the winners and losers in the claims to net output and influence, could less easily attribute their fortune, good or bad, to the machinations of a foreign power. Consider, for example, the problems of the agricultural sector. However strong the commitment to industrialization, the role of agriculture in facilitating it is critical. If the structure of output is to change with economic growth so that the secondary and tertiary sectors expand relative to the primary sector, productivity in the latter must increase so that it can provide the raw materials and food for the former. Moreover, if a country is dependent on the international market for the importation of capital goods needed for industrialization, rising agricultural productivity helps hold off the balance-of-payments deterrent to growth. Faltering productivity not only reduces foreign exchange earnings from agricultural exports, but may, in conjunction with population growth, absorb scarce foreign exchange in the importation of food stuffs. Even with a strong agricultural sector, the developing country intent upon economic growth inevitably runs into balance-of-payments constraints because its demand for the output of the advanced economies grows more rapidly than the demand of the latter for the output of the former.

In India, much was expected of the Community Development Program which was designed to raise agricultural productivity and to carry out the egalitarian objectives, so important to Nehru, in the organization of social and economic life in the countryside. On the one hand, it was concerned 'with the development of agriculture, village industries, health, sanitation, education, mostly on a self-help basis with resources available within the village'.[21] On the other hand, it attempted to provide peasants with technical assistance, cheap credit facilities and 'the highest priority was assigned to rapid implementation of land reforms, including security of tenure, lower rents, transfer of ownership rights to tenants, and redistribution of land.'[22] The Community Development Program focused its resources on the whole village and was designed to mobilize the mass of peasants in the struggle to overcome poverty.

By the third five-year plan, however, there was a shift in agricultural policy that implicitly at least acknowledged the difficulty of simultaneously achieving egalitarian and productivity objectives in a society with such deeply embedded conservative landed interests. From the outset the Community Development Program had been hampered by resistance to the institutional changes that were proposed in the organization of agriculture. The union government whose political leaders and planners were the most enthusiastic proponents of community development did not constitutionally have the power in certain areas – agriculture, education, and health – to effect the policies its program required. In consequence, technical advisory services were inadequate and the pace of land reform was extraordinarily slow, the latter being a predictable result of the strong representation of landowners in the state legislatures. While the *zamindari* system was abolished by many states in which it was entrenched, for example in West Bengal, Orissa, and Bihar, the *zamindars* were permitted to retain the land that they cultivated directly. Moreover, the enabling legislation tended to make it difficult for cultivating tenant peasants to acquire proprietary rights in land.[23] The democratic political process in the states became an effective forum for organizing those agrarian interests that, rightly or wrongly, feared they would suffer from the egalitarian values of community development.

In 1960 the Union Government adopted an Intensive

Agricultural Districts Program (IADP) which marked a shift from the general, village approach to one stressing the allocation of investment to responsive districts, i.e. to areas with water and other resource characteristics that assured maximum increase in output with the application of increased inputs. Fifteen such IADP districts throughout India were selected and were to receive, among other things, adequate credit and fertilizer, price support for major food grains, technical assistance in water management and farm planning, and public works for the unemployed and under-employed. The agricultural planners had turned away from the egalitarian emphasis on the development of the institutional capabilities of the Indian village to an emphasis on the productivity of major crops.

The planners committed themselves to IADP before the so-called green revolution began to raise hopes that Asia could at last be delivered from the specter of famine. This technological breakthrough in the development of food-grain seeds dramatically increased land productivity if they were cultivated with the appropriate volume of water and fertilizers.[24] It was the outcome of cooperative research efforts sponsored by states and private organizations – the Rockefeller and Carnegie Foundations – experimenting in agricultural farm stations in Mexico, the Philippines, Taiwan, and India. The shift in the production functions for wheat and rice, the most important of the food grains, could not have occurred had there not been a sector in the world economy with the resources, genetic knowledge, technical skills, and the time necessary for experimentation in raising seeds of the required quality. Yet the new seeds could not be used without a substantial increase in complementary inputs which raised the capital requirements for optimal farm productivity. The new production function squarely confronted Indian authorities with the conflict between productivity and equality which had been implicitly resolved in favor of the former with the shift from the Community Development Program to IADP during the third five-year plan. The green revolution was a boon to the medium and large landowners who had access to the capital necessary for growing the new wheat and rice. As Wolf Ladejinsky observed:

'The green revolution affects the few rather than the many not only because of environmental conditions but because the majority of the farmers lack resources, or are "institutionally" precluded from taking advantage of the new agricultural trends.'[25]

The impact of the green revolution began to be felt in the late 1960s and in the fourth five-year plan (1969–74) it was proposed 'to bring approximately 60,000,000 acres under high-yielding varieties of wheat, rice, maize, jowar, and bajra. Yet, while this area represents less than 30 percent of the total acreage under these crops, over two-thirds of the additional production of food grains targeted for the Fourth Plan is expected to come from it.'[26] Such concentrated production is visible and 'many farmers in areas of great potential are now pointing enviously to better production, higher income and better living conditions "over there" in their neighbors' fields.'[27] In view of the egalitarian values formally expressed by the state and embodied in the language of the early five-year plans it is not surprising that the green revolution has not been easily accommodated in the countryside. Even before the failure of the monsoons in the early 1970s threatened its productivity gains, it was seen as having a polarizing influence that might 'ultimately undermine the foundations of rural political stability'.[28]

The proposals initially designed to raise subsistence in India – agricultural planning in the Community Development Program – unleashed participatory and clamorous forces that have not been stilled by the promise of the green revolution. Indeed, that import from the external world has had to compete with another import, the increase in population which had reached 303 million by 1911. Since then, population has grown more rapidly. According to the 1971 census, it amounted to 548 million. By 1979 the World Bank reported that it was 659 million, an increase in eight years of 20 percent.[29] Unlike the increase induced by the growth of output, in India population has increased because of the decline in death rates brought about by public-health technology and more adequate stocks of food grains, both of these originating in the world economy. The control of malaria, for example, through mosquito-abatement programs and the dissemination of malarial pills were in part responsible for raising life expectancy from 32 to

57 years in the quarter-century following 1951.

The consequences of population growth in India are relentless. From 1960 through 1970 gross domestic product at constant prices increased 45 percent but only 12.6 percent when adjusted for increases in population. In Britain where the rate of increase of population was below 0.5 percent during the same period, gross domestic product at constant prices increased 31.4 percent and on a per-capita basis 21.9 percent. In the next decade, although India experienced higher annual average growth rates in the agricultural, industrial, and service sectors than Great Britain, by 1979 its per-capita gross national product measured in current dollars was only 190, while Britain's was 6320.[30] Moreover, the population growth that diluted output increases further fragmented land holdings, making it more difficult to form optimal-sized farms and exacerbating the delicate issues of equity and justice that inhere in the relationship of peasants to land. It also has caused the rate of urbanization to increase ahead of the capacity of the cities to provide jobs, housing, and other essential urban services. The consequences for Calcutta have been vividly described by Ved Mehta:

> Although parts of New York and parts of Tokyo have a population density comparable to that of parts of the Calcutta Metropolitan District, it, unlike the two other metropolises, has few buildings more than three stories high, and most of its people are housed in one- or two-storey structures. Few of the houses are *pukka* structures. Rather most are *kutcha* made of bamboo, mud, or unbaked bricks. Except for the palatial quarters of the rich, most houses, *pukka* and *kutcha*, have no inside plumbing and the *pukka* structures are often in disrepair. Many of these structures were originally intended only as temporary shelters for migrant workers, but they now house big families. Even so, a large number of people must sleep in and around the dockyards, in factories, in offices, in shops, on construction sites, in railway stations, in hallways, and on stairways of buildings. More than half the Calcutta Metropolitan District is taken up by streams or by the marshland that is

unreclaimable for reasons of cost or technology; the demands on the remaining land are so intense that several hundred thousand people sleep out on the pavements and tens of thousands of people now live, as a matter of course, on low, undrained, disease-infested land bordering the salt marshes. All available public or private land is occupied by colonies of squatters. There is no place – not even the border of Calcutta's refuse dump – that is left unoccupied.[31]

If Calcutta is an egregious case of the consequences of a high rate of population growth, it none the less dramatizes the burdens imposed on India by forces which originated in the external world. Moreover, the external world is no longer as receptive to what was once a solution to the problems of excess population – emigration. Indians historically had emigrated to southeast Asia, Ceylon, and South and East Africa in search of better employment opportunities. Now either because these regions suffer themselves from overpopulation or, in their newly independent status and nationalistic fervor, are hostile to Indians, they no longer welcome them as immigrants. Indeed, in East Africa, Uganda expelled Indians who had been resident for two or three generations and had greater attachment to Africa than to India.

So the problem must be faced internally. On the one hand, the state may attempt to assuage it by encouraging family planning and disseminating information about contraceptives and other means for preventing conception. India does so, but its success is inhibited by high rates of illiteracy, the inferior status of women, the lack of ideal contraceptive techniques for the conditions of peasant life, and the continuing high value placed on children as a familial guarantee of security. There is no realm of public policy that penetrates society more deeply than family planning, the very sensitivity of which makes it extremely difficult for a democratic government to enforce. Not the least of the reasons for the fall of Mrs Gandhi's authoritarian regime following the national emergency from June 1975 to March 1977 was the vigorous and arbitrary role played by her son Sanjay in the promotion of population control through the enforcement of sterilization in clinics established for the purpose.[32]

On the other hand, the state must contend with the threat of violence that may occur when population grows ahead of the resources needed to service it. The emergency itself was a product of this dilemma. A correspondent writing in 1973 two years after the Bangladesh War when Mrs Gandhi's popularity was at a spectacular high noted that, since the war,

> India has suffered two severe droughts, and Mrs. Gandhi has come under bruising attacks from critics of the right and left for failing to carry out her stated policy of abolishing poverty. Beyond this there is a perceptible, almost melancholy, sense of disillusion and gloom that has emerged in recent weeks in a nation torn by food riots, by a policy of rebellion in one state that involved a violent confrontation with the army, and by bitter charges of Government bungling.[33]

Even before the Bangladesh War, the evidence of rural discontent had become manifest in the Naxalite movement which originated in the northern districts of West Bengal. Clashes between a landless peasantry and the owners of large tea plantations stimulated the activist imagination and fervor of impatient students and intellectuals in urban areas and gave a boost to the ideological appeal of Maoist versions of Marxism. For a time the Naxalites made inroads into the support normally given to the orthodox Marxist party and had followers in states as geographically removed as Punjab and Tamil Nadu. In consequence, 'sporadic terrorism . . . including raids on the homes of landlords, murder and arson, and more spectacular attacks on police stations, occurred in widely separated parts of the country.'[34] It would be too simple an explanation to attribute the upsurge of violence solely to the growth of a population whose expectations had been stimulated by the promise of an end to poverty. None the less it poured fuel on an already combustible political environment.

Who can tell whether the aggrieved peasants in the Naxalbari regions of West Bengal felt more or less oppressed by poverty and injustice than their peers, for example, in the indigo-producing regions of Bengal in the previous century? Perhaps the disaffected intellectuals in Calcutta were more willing to encourage violence than were their predecessors who took up the cause of the oppressed indigo workers. Could it have seemed less endurable to them that the continuing burden of poverty in rural India was embedded in states whose prescriptions and proscriptions were the work of their own leaders? Were the frustrations of independent India the more galling because they could not so easily be laid at the feet of the British Raj? I do not wish to imply by asking these rhetorical questions that the momentous problems of the economy and polity were challenges that Indian leadership would have been pleased to see repressed in an imperial relationship or managed by imperial proconsuls. Economic development has never been a finely balanced, equilibrium process in which the benefits and costs of the growth of output are equitably distributed. For India to be in charge of its own development was its own reward for those men and women who participated in the struggles to set Indian priorities and the means of achieving them. But in a population of more than 650 million people *that* kind of reward was experienced by a small minority, those privileged to have the knowledge, skills, and persuasions to engage in the struggles and dialogues of politics and administration.

But the Naxalites, too, represented a small minority of the population and we cannot leave the impression that the violence associated with them expressed the normal reaction of Indians to the ancient burden of subsistence. Indeed, from what has been said in previous chapters about the fragmented dimensions of India, it is hardly possible to speak of a normal reaction. It is therefore salutary to be reminded of traditional India which persists in symbiotic relationship in its occasional contiguity with the industrial world V. S. Naipaul has described sensitively and perceptively a small village in the state of Maharashtra, east of Poona and the industrial hinterland of Bombay and across India from West Bengal whence arose the Naxalite movement. He had gone there to observe the work of a hydrologic engineer in improving the local irrigation system. His observations about the village merit extensive quotation.

The village had had so little, had been left to itself for so long. After two decades of effort and investment simple things had arrived, but were still superfluous to daily life, answered no established needs. Electric light, ready water, an outhouse: the Patel was the only man in the village to possess them all, and only the water would have been considered strictly necessary. Everything else was still half for show, proof of the Patel's position, the extraordinariness which yet, fearing the gods, he took care to hide in his person, in the drabness and anonymity of his peasant appearance.

It was necessary to be in the village, to see the Patel and his attendants, to understand the nature of the power of that simple man, to see how easily such a man could, if he wished, frustrate the talk from Delhi about minimum wages, the abolition of untouchability, the abolition of rural indebtedness. How could the laws be enforced? Who would be the policeman in the village? The Patel was more than the biggest landowner. In that village needs were still so basic, the Patel, with his house of grain, ruled; and he ruled by custom and consent. In his authority, which in his piety he extended backward to his ancestors, there was almost the weight of religion.

The irrigation scheme was a cooperative project. But the village was not a community of peasant farmers. It was divided into people who had land and people who hadn't; and the people who had land were divided into those who were Masters and those who weren't. The Patel was the greatest Master in the village. The landless laborers he employed (out somewhere in the fields now) were his servants; many had been born his servants. He acknowledged certain obligations to them. He would lend them money so that they knew they had a claim on the grain in his house. Their debts would wind around them and never end, and would be passed on to their children. But to have a master was to be in some way secure. To be untied was to run the risk of being lost.

And the Patel was progressive. He was a good farmer. It was improved farming (and the absence of tax on agricultural income) that had made him a rich man. Not everyone in his position was like that. There were villages, the engineer said later, when we were on the highway again, which couldn't be included in the irrigation scheme because the big landowners there didn't like the idea of a lot of people making more money. The Patel wasn't like that; and the engineer was careful not to cross him. The engineer knew that he could do nothing in the village without the cooperation of the Patel. As an engineer, he was to help increase food production; and he kept his ideas about debt and servants and bonded labor to himself.[35]

In achieving independence, India shouldered the burden of governance which had been the responsibility of the British. While the burden of scarcity and poverty endured by society continued as before, they acquired a higher ranking on the national agenda as it took shape in New Delhi. For some people – the ruling élite whose understanding of poverty was mediated by their governing responsibilities – this simultaneously created a challenge and raised expectations that they could do for themselves what the British did not do. For many others – those who lived with poverty as if it were an aspect of nature – the plans and intentions of the leaders at the center, as so often in Indian's history, may have made little impression. Or they may have raised hopes that were frustrated in the continuing strength of the traditional social order in village India. But the coercive consequences of the scarcity of resources remain, perhaps redistributed by national policy, but now wholly administered, as it were, by Indians. India has outlasted British imperialism, but not the problems to which the latter was an unwanted solution.

Notes

1 Civil disobedience reached a peak during World War II when under the influence of Gandhi the Congress inaugurated a 'quit India' movement which led to the imprisonment of most of the Congress leaders. Beatrice P. Lamb, *India – A World in Transition*, 3rd edn, New York, Praeger, 1968, 85.

2 Thorstein Veblen, *Imperial Germany and the Industrial Revolution*, New York, Viking, 1939, 129–33.

3 David Landes, 'Technological change and development in western Europe, 1750–1914', in *The Cambridge Economic History of Europe*, Cambridge, Cambridge University Press, VI, Pt I, 503.

4 Nathan Rosenberg, *Technology and American Economic Growth*, New York, Harper & Row, 1972, 90.

5 Ragnar Nurkse, *Equilibrium and Growth in the World Economy*, Gottfried Haberler and Robert M. Stern (eds), Cambridge, Mass., Harvard University Press, 1966, 135.

6 After John Morley, the Secretary of State for India in the Liberal government of 1906, and Lord Minto, the viceroy of India.

7 Lamb, op. cit., 74.

8 Percival Spear, *India, a Modern History*, 2nd edn, Ann Arbor, University of Michigan Press, 1972, 386–94.

9 Lamb, op. cit., 91–2; Spear, op. cit., 423.

10 Noone could have been more skillful and patient in coping with the excruciating problems of the transfer of power in 1947 than Lord Louis Mountbatten, the last British viceroy of India. Stanley Wolpert, *A New History of India*, 2nd edn, New York, Oxford University Press, 1982, 344–9.

11 Donald E. Smith, *India as a Secular State*, Princeton, Princeton University Press, 1963, 100.

12 Japan, too, in drafting the Maiji Constitution adopted in 1889, drew heavily on the experience of western states, especially Prussia. The Japanese administrative élite, who governed in the name of the emperor Maiji following the overthrow in 1867 of the two-and-a-half-centuries' rule of the Tokugawa clan, sent a mission in 1882 to the west to study constitutions. It spent close to three months in Prussia absorbing Rudolph von Gneist's defense of the authoritarian state but only one day in England listening to Herbert Spencer on representative government. Unlike India, Japan did not hold a constituent assembly for framing its constitution. Rather it was drafted by a committee of four and then debated in the Privy Council over a period of nine months with the emperor in attendance. Its legitimacy inhered in its acceptance by the emperor Maiji and thus was not a document grounded in individual rights and values that were held to be the function of the state to preserve and protect. Hugh Borton, *Japan's Modern Century*, New York, Ronald, 1955, 131–49.

13 Smith, op. cit., 136.

14 ibid., 137.

15 *The Cry for Justice* is the title of an anthology of the literature of social protest edited and published by Upton Sinclair in 1951 with an

introduction by Jack London.

16 The paternalism of the old Poor Law in England did not survive the passing of the mercantilist age, its substitute as outlined in the Poor Law Amendment Act of 1834 being a good deal more punitive and harshly utilitarian.

17 Quoted by T. Scarlett Epstein, *South India, Yesterday, Today, and Tomorrow*, London, Macmillan, 1973, 243.

18 Subramanian Swamy, 'Economic growth in China and India, 1952–1970, a comparative appraisal', *Economic Development and Cultural Change*, 1973, 21 (4), Pt 2, 52. Swamy noted the existence of the steel and textile industries at independence, but somewhat vaguely said their growth 'has a historical specificity'.

19 Jagdish N. Bhagwati and Padman Desai, *Indian Planning for Industrialization, Industrialization and Trade Policies since 1951*, London, Oxford University Press, 1970, 111–13; Francine R. Frankel, *India's Political Economy, 1947–1977, and the Gradual Revolution*, Princeton, Princeton University Press, 1978, 113–17.

20 Bhagwati and Desai, op. cit., 120.

21 Dorris D. Brown, *Agricultural Development in India's Districts*, Cambridge, Mass., Harvard University Press, 1971, 4.

22 Francine R. Frankel, *India's Green Revolution, Economic Gains and Political Costs*, Princeton, Princeton University Press, 4.

23 Frankel, *India's Political Economy*, 190–1.

24 The new hybrid grains were short-strawed (so that they could bear a heavier burden of fruit), more nutritious and resistant to disease.

25 Wolf Ladejinsky, 'Ironies of India's green revolution', *Foreign Affairs*, 1970, 48 (4), 763.

26 Frankel, *India's Green Revolution* . . . , 6.

27 Ladejinsky, op. cit., 764.

28 Frankel, *India's Green Revolution* . . ., 8–9.

29 World Bank, *World Development Report 1981*, New York, Oxford University Press, 1981, 134.

30 ibid., 134–7.

31 Ved Mehta, 'City of the dreadful night', *The New Yorker Magazine*, 21 March 1970, 57.

32 Frankel, *India's Political Economy* . . ., 565–6.

33 Bernard Weinraub, *New York Times*, 8 June 1963, 2.

34 Frankel, *India's Political Economy* . . ., 379.

35 V. S. Naipaul, 'India, new claim on the land', *New York Review of Books*, 23 (11), 15.

7

Imperialism as inequality

The imperial history of England in India is a story about changing inequality, how England rose above India and how India, in its turn, recaptured its sovereignty. At the beginning in 1608, England was not an imposing power. William Hawkins went to India not as a conqueror in quest of the Mughal throne, but as a supplicant seeking trading opportunities. In retrospect, we realize that his presence there manifested some strengths or assets that in time allowed England to assume the imperial mantle of the Mughal emperors. The commercial drive that led to the formation of the East India Company and the knowledge of navigation and shipbuilding which enhanced its naval and maritime strength gave it command of the ocean approaches to India whose orientation toward the threats to its security from the northwest and the interior of Asia had ill-equipped it for coping with aggressors from the sea. When the Mughal empire declined in the eighteenth century, the Company became a formidable competitor for political power that was initially acquired in Bengal at the end of the century.

In the nineteenth century with the industrial revolution well under way, England asserted its interests in India with increasing effectiveness and the Company became less a commercial and more a governing body. It was able to do this because its assets grew relative to Indian assets. Wealth, military power, knowledge, organizational capacity, and ideology combined to further the capacity of the British to achieve their private and public purposes. The society that invented industrial growth in the private sector at home was equally adept at attaining public and private purposes abroad. British imperialism in India was palpably the consequence of India being unable, unwilling, or uninterested in asserting a common or public interest against the British interest in extending its rule there.

That an Indian public purpose did not take shape until the end of the nineteenth century underscores the peculiar importance of ideology. Unlike the other assets, it is wholly subjective or cerebral, consisting of beliefs, values, and theories, often implicit, ill-formed, or inchoate, through which the objective world reaches the mind and rationalizes one's conduct in it. Ideology may be imposed by religious or secular authorities or, at the other extreme, behavioral norms may emerge more or less spontaneously as ideology from primary social institutions. Individuals react with varying degrees of self-consciousness to imposed or spontaneous ideology, ranging from indifferent acquiescence, on the one hand, to militant acceptance or rejection, on the other. The sources of ideology are as abundant as the human imagination is fertile: Christianity, Islam, Hinduism – democracy, socialism, nationalism; positivism, materialism, transcendentalism. In India the religious, linguistic, social, and geographical fragmentation of society inhibited the formation of commonly held values that would make the British purposes in India repugnant to its own purposes.

That British imperialism receded so abruptly in the twentieth century points up the pliance of belief and ideology in the relative strength of contemporary societies. The accumulation of wealth through economic growth is a slow process whose visibility in expanding per-capita output requires years, perhaps centuries, of institutional development that cultivate the propensities to save, innovate, take risks, and work hard. So protean a substance as ideology, however, need not wait upon the development of the material conditions of society. The idea of India as a national political community with which individuals of diverse linguistic, communal, or caste characteristics could identify began to take shape in the nineteenth century among those Indians who were most involved with the British, especially in Bengal where the imperial history of the latter had originated. By the end of World

War I those western values – democracy, nationalism, or socialism – that were beginning to raise self-doubts in the minds of some of the English about their imperial role in India had so far permeated an all-India leadership that it no longer doubted its own national destiny. Continuing British rule became increasingly intolerable and 'the calm assurance of always being in the right' – the attitude that so irritated Nehru as he tells us in his autobiography – no longer carried conviction among those Indians who had come to believe the British were in the wrong.[1] And with the growth of Indian self-awareness an organizational capacity to express Indian interests developed whose dramatic and portentous denouement in 1947 was no less important for having been hastened by the decline of British economic and organizational strength.

Imperialisms in the twentieth century

There have been as many imperialisms as there have been pairs of societies so engaged. Some of these have been more coerced and brutalizing than others, often in cases where there has been a pronounced inequality of assets or an asset with the dominant society unconstrained in its conduct by a moderating ideology. When in 1441, Antam Gonçales seized ten Africans and forcibly took them to Portugal, he had arms and sufficient mastery of the sea to make African resistance difficult and pursuit impossible. Moreover, if he had doubts about violating their rights as human beings, he did not let them interfere with the carrying out of Prince Henry's instructions. Vasco da Gama's hanging of the Calicut fishermen presumably was made easier for him by their being infidels, just as the garroting in 1537 of Atahualpa, the last Inca monarch, seemed to Pizarro an appropriate punishment for his failure to convert to the true faith.

But the scale of these brutalizing acts was infinitesimal compared with the wanton slaughter of human beings made possible by technical advances in weapons and transport with the industrialization of the west. For all its liberal and democratic stirrings, its evangelical denunciation of slavery, and its equivocal view of imperialism, symbolized by the contrasting personalities of

Disraeli and Gladstone, Great Britain still unleashed Lord Kitchener's relentless and brutal conquest of the Upper Nile with an Anglo-Egyptian army in 1898. Systematically laying down rail transportation behind his advancing troops who were equipped with breech-loading rifles and maxim machine-guns and copiously supported by artillery and naval gunboats, Kitchener had little difficulty in subduing the dervishes who not long previously under the Mahdi had besieged Khartoum and early in 1885 captured it, while martyring General Charles Gordon. In the bloodiest section of the campaign at the Battle of Omdurman outside Khartoum, some 13,000 dervishes were killed at the cost of 48 lives in the allied army and 434 wounded.[2] It was, as one war correspondent noted, 'not a battle, but an execution', 'a torrent of death' that 'no white troops would have faced'.[3] The Mahdi's successor, Khalifa Abdullah, led troops who were armed with inferior weapons obtained in secondary markets and inspired by a commitment to Islam which seemingly made them indifferent to death.

In the twentieth century, a profound shift in relative power across all societies has caused the nineteenth-century imperialist powers to disengage from their colonial relationships. The shift has been occasioned less by the narrowing of economic inequalities than by the emergence of ideological outlooks in new political settings which have advanced the expression of interests once submerged in the imperial relationship. Where the evolution of an Indian political identity may have been held back by an amorphous, weakly ideological world community, today international organizations, formed, ironically enough, by the most active imperialist states, symbolize those values – independence, nationality, economic and political rights – that spread during the modernization of the western world. The Colonel Blimps who never did feel comfortable with these changes no doubt must feel their reforming peers have been hoist with their own petard.

The rush to independence, either forcibly seized or begrudgingly granted, following India, in both British and non-British empires, expanded the number of sovereign states at an uncommonly rapid rate. The membership in the United Nations has risen from the original 51 in 1945 to 154 in 1981. Many of these new states reflect in their territorial boundaries the conflicts of expanding European imperialists in the nineteenth century and the settlements reached amongst themselves more than local, social, linguistic, or ethnic conditions which might have cohered in viable political communities.

This was especially true in sub-Saharan Africa which in its long isolation from the Eurasian continent was not subject to the immense, continental political and military forces that gradually shaped many nation–states out of smaller parochial communities. Nor was there in consequence as rich or literate a tradition or memory that could serve as the mortar for constructing the historical foundations of the state. Neither Nigeria nor Ghana in West Africa nor Tanzania or Kenya in East Africa with their tribal divisons and oral traditions of rivalries and conquests had the depth or reach of the histories of societies on the Eurasian land mass. History in Europe was surely tailored to the needs of monarchs, but historical cloth existed in abundance for dressing emerging civil personae in the colors of the state, however remote rulers may have been from them. If the English and the French as pieces in the fabric of the nation–states appeared on the world scene before Indians, this in no way belied the history of the latter. In Africa, however, the past had to be transmogrified more consciously into history, a task that was complicated by the drawing of state boundaries by European imperialists rather than these having emerged in the coalescence of various communities against the aggression of other communities.

In Latin America, independence had been achieved more than a century before the formation in the twentieth century of the new states and the reassertion of the sovereign independence of old states in Asia and Africa. Beset by the mercantilist restrictions of metropolitan governance from Spain (and Portugal) which were attenuated but in some cases reinforced during the years of the Napoleonic Wars in Europe and inspired in varying degrees by the example of the British colonies in North America in the previous century, the Spanish colonies in Argentina and Colombia rebelled in 1810, an example soon followed by the other colonies in Latin America. In the working out of these rebellions, however, the

European colonists became subimperialists in the sense that the dominance they had always exerted over the indigenous Indian populations now no longer was mitigated by the metropolitan government. The liberation movements were mounted in the name of the white colonists whose Indian peons and black slaves were not brought inside the constitutional pale of the Latin American states.

The changing structure of inequalities that marked the proliferation of independent states in the twentieth century had its most dramatic consummation in the physical withdrawal of the imperial presence. Lord Louis Mountbatten was the last viceroy of India and negotiated the conditions for the transfer of power from the Crown to India, thus symbolizing the departure of the British. It was characteristic of the British empire and other empires that had similarly been acquired through the strength of naval and maritime forces that, when the time came for departure, their formal imperial emissaries returned to their distant metropolitan homelands. If the oceans had been the avenues of approach for the expanding west from the sixteenth through the nineteenth centuries, they were in the twentieth century the convenient exit for the imperial presence. In many imperialisms, however, departure of the historical aggressors was impossible, because there was no place for them to go or they had no wish to leave. People of European origins dominated, exploited, and destroyed Indians in the settlement of the North American continent as, we noted above, they did in Latin America. Russia expanded eastward in Siberia by conquering those populations in the interior of Asia who themselves had once been the fount of conquests throughout the Eurasian land mass. The Boers and the British in southern Africa dispossessed Bantu peoples. While the English relinquished Irish rule shortly after World War I, the long tortuous process was rendered more painful by the propinquity of Celtic and Anglo-Saxon peoples and the colonization of northern Ireland by Protestants. There are, indeed, precious few societies in the world that are not touched by the economic and political claims of groups in their midst to restitution or independence based on what they believe are the injustices visited upon them by imperialist rulers.

Nor have coercions like these in the history of western expansion been laid to rest by the withdrawal of the west from its overseas colonies. We have seen that in India the departure of the British led to the internalization of the coercive burden of imperialism, both with respect to economic policy affecting the allocation of resources and the distribution of income and with respect to the maintenance of order. But in India there had been a long tutelage under the British Raj that, whatever its intentions towards its subjects, facilitated the emergence of an Indian governing class capable of assuming these responsibilites. If the new Indian government could not solve the riddle of poverty it could address it preeminently as an Indian problem constrained by the welter of Indian interests. Moreover, there was already in place an infrastructure – transportation facilities, educational institutions, a civil service, governmental physical plant – that potentially could support experimentation and changing directions in economic growth.

Elsewhere former colonial territories were not so fortunate. Unlike Japan in its isolation, they had not been able to evolve indigenous institutions for accommodating their polities and economies to the changing world. Unlike India, they had not been governed by societies as ready as the British to transfer the skills and institutions of western modernization. When, for example, the Congo (now Zaire) became independent in 1960, there were only ten Congolese with university degrees.[4] In its colonial policy, Belgium stressed primary education to the extent necessary for training indigenous workers needed for the development of the prodigious natural resources of the Congo, most of which were found in the Katanga province.[5] Before World War II higher education had been restricted to Catholic theological training. It was not until 1949 that the University of Louvain established an overseas extension in Leopoldville, its curriculum, not surprisingly under the circumstances, initially serving a small number of students in technical training in agriculture and health services at the secondary-school level. In 1956, Louvanium was joined by a state university at Elisabethville, but the returns to education mature slowly and take unpredictable forms. Belgian education stressed pragmatic skills and Christianity with little or no attention paid to the arts of governance or self-rule. The Leopoldville riots in January 1959 were the prelude to independence in 1960 and a tortured history of conflicting tribal and western economic interests. These might not have been averted by a greater willingness on the part of Belgian officials to prepare the Congo for self-rule. One suspects, however, that unknowingly their educational policy was designed for disaster: enough education to raise aspirations for independence, too little education and too recent to have encouraged the growth of a Congolese governing class.

The charges of neocolonialism and neoimperialism, outlined briefly in Chapter 1, with which the old imperial states have been belabored acquire whatever merit they have from the extraordinarily varied imbalances of economic and political assets in the Third World, Zaire being but one egregious variant. The withdrawal of the west from colonial territories has left behind a congeries of states with varying objectives that appear to be out of phase with their capability of achieving them. Mrs Gandhi's slogan to eradicate poverty touches the quick of any society which, whatever it might have wished, has come in contact with people that have demonstrated that low income, hunger, and disease are not preordained human conditions. The preferences of Third World peoples have changed and simultaneously imparted to them a cosmopolitan sense of injustice. While independence has given them the opportunity to express new values and, in the international forums that abound in the contemporary world, to formulate demands and programs designed to satisfy them, the ineluctable fact of scarcity at low levels of income limits their effectiveness. For the latter condition has been intensified by the success of industrial societies in raising themselves above the primordial economic struggle and the difficulty of transmitting the secret of their success to countries that have to struggle to keep output abreast of population increases. In their new self-consciousness, Third World countries not only are aware of having been left behind but suspect, rightly or wrongly, that international economic inequalities have been widened at their expense.

Unlike nineteenth-century imperialists, Curzon, Cromer, Milner, and Rhodes for example, who ruled in foreign lands unambiguously, with relish, and, to greater or less extent, openly, the sources of Third World economic problems in the era of fading colonialism cannot be so pejoratively personified. This, of course, is partly because foreign rulers have been replaced in the old imperial territories by local rulers. It also is because the economic and political relationships among the proliferating states of the world are constrained by increasingly dense and complex institutions, some of which, as indicated above, have the purpose of preserving their independence and integrity. The United Nations and the international organizations associated with it symbolize the formal commitment of states to non-imperial behavior, a stance that at least has rhetorical value and is reflected in the frequency with which the charges of imperialism are leveled by states or communities against whom aggression is aimed and the equally frequent denials of imperialist intent by the supposed aggressors. Even when aggression is as overtly militaristic as the intervention of the United States in Vietnam or more recently in 1980 of the Soviet Union in Afghanistan, the dominant powers do not care to describe their actions with nineteenth-century candor. But when the use of power is not so gross, the newly independent states none the less feel aggrieved by the international economic interdependence revealed in their resolute efforts to overcome poverty.

If the former colonies wish to increase per-capita real income, they have no choice but to seek in world markets the resources, skills, and knowledge, the lack of which has held them back. And a link between them, that has become a rogue for those who find the persistence of international inequality prima-facie evidence of neoimperialism, is the multinational corporation (MNC).[6] The MNC has indeed come a long way since the East India Company first ventured into Asian waters early in the seventeenth century. The technological revolutions in transportation, communication, and the organization and utilization of knowledge have made it possible for corporations to maximize net income by responding rapidly to relative prices of resources, labor, and capital throughout the world. International extensions of the conglomerate corporation, they operate inside and outside many states whose laws relating to tax liabilities, property entitlements, and international trade influence the sites where they choose to make direct investments. Seemingly without any territorial commitments, in the view of their detractors they bargain with hosts for tax and operating advantages which are hard to withhold because elsewhere there are governments anxious for their presence, or they bribe a local clientele who become an élite identified with the profit-maximizing objectives of the MNC more than the development needs of their own country. The technology embodied in the assets constructed, the charge continues, more frequently reflects the resource availabilities of the advanced economies than local resource patterns. Capital-intensive rather than labor-intensive investment maximizes output at the expense of employment, rendering more painful the duality of a modern sector, staffed by foreign technicians and experts, in the midst of a subsistence economy with a surfeit of population and unemployment. Moreover, the use of transfer pricing and accounting allows the MNC to manipulate the net income of its subsidiaries and branches in various countries in order to minimize local tax liability. Finally, to the extent that the MNC is staffed by high-salaried foreign executives, a larger proportion of income generated within the firm is expatriated than if local executives were employed.

It should be noted that the greater part of the direct investment of the MNCs is not in developing economies, but in advanced economies, a consequence of the higher growth rates of the latter and their more assured profit rates. Whatever the soundness of the argument in the previous paragraph – and we shall return to it shortly – the flow of private investment in the twentieth century is not as effective a transmitter of economic growth to those regions that lag behind as it was in the nineteenth century. The high rate of foreign investment by Great Britain during the half-century before World War I facilitated the transfer of resources to the areas of recent settlement – North America, Argentina, Australia, New Zealand – the utilization of which was abetted by the complementary migration of a skilled and hard-working population. These new countries increased their productivity to the extent necessary to pay their obligations on their borrowings and to have a residual increase in output that could be allocated to growth. Industrialization in the new territories was perhaps caused not so much by the transfer of financial resources as by the presence there of a population with the necessary behavioral values for using them productively.

The relative weakness of private international investment in the Third World during the years of decolonization in the twentieth century has led to the expansion of public investment for development, either bilaterally from one country to another, as for example in the activities of the Agency for International Development of the United States Department of State (AID), or multilaterally through the International Bank for Reconstruction and Development (the World Bank). Here again, it has been alleged that the allocation of public funds for this purpose harbors neoimperialism for it has permitted the wealthy countries to exert control over the way funds are used in poor countries. Bilateral aid especially has been seen as an instrument of foreign policy granted less on the economic merits of project or program designs than on the necessity of cultivating or admonishing clients in a world sharply divided on matters of ideology and security. Writing in the latter years of the United States military involvement in southeast Asia, Gustav Ranis noted that

> special interest programs as aid to Southeast Asia or to Israel, for American schools and hospitals, and other specialized programs which have powerful lobby support, have become an ever larger portion (nearly two-thirds) of a steadily declining aid total (now .3 percent of our Gross National Product).

Moreover, he lamented that

> when President Richard Nixon and Senator Frank Church agree (one implicitly, one explicitly) that aid should be cut back in retaliation for dancing in the aisles of the United Nations; when individual countries are punished for their position in trade, on fishing rights, on Vietnam, on Bangla Desh; and when we are rapidly approaching the day of twenty-five different (small) aid bills by which countries can be voted 'up' or 'down' depending

on their current Congressional 'report card' – how can any one expect aid officials to do that other job which all our rhetoric and our legislation call for?[7]

Even with multilateral aid where the link between the political interests of advanced economies and economic needs of recipient countries is very much weaker, it has been argued that prevailing economic orthodoxy among the dominant contributors of capital for development has influenced the way funds are used. The World Bank, to which the United States contributes twice as much capital as the next largest contributor, has been supportive of loans for infrastructure investment that it hopes will stimulate the growth of the private sector, but less willing to support a state goods-producing sector.

Investment programs, public or private, for transferring technology and growth to Third World countries can only be minimally effective if the markets for their output do not grow correspondingly. The industrial economies by virtue of being the first of the modernizing states have played the dominant role in the creation of the international trade system which has evolved in response to their mutual and conflicting interests, the less developed economies having had little leverage to influence the structure of tariffs and other trade impediments that shaped world markets. Following World War II, in 1948 the United Nations established the General Agreement on Tariffs and Trade (GATT), the members of which were committed to reducing barriers to international trade. As the membership in the United Nations and GATT expanded, the range of interests represented in the latter increased and, more particularly, a Third World bloc emerged that was manifestly dissatisfied with GATT's failure to respond to the interests of the poor, primary-producing economies. As they saw it, the rich nations were a good deal more intent on increasing trade amongst themselves than in opening their markets to the manufactured goods of the poor nations. Subsequently, the United Nations Conference on Trade and Development (UNCTAD) was formed as a suborganization of these countries within GATT and in 1964 in Geneva held its first meetings to formulate their objectives so that they could be more effective in pressing on the larger body Third World claims in trade negotiations.

What, then, remains of the coercive face of imperialism in the contemporary world which at once has begotten so many states and so many international organizations to further their common, and mediate their conflicting, interests as well as gargantuan business firms that are cause and effect of the increasing interdependence of the world's economies? An approximate answer to this question follows from the historical and analytical emphasis in this book on Great Britain and India over the close to four centuries of their mutual involvement. It may strike some as a non-answer, for it evades generalizations that cut across societies by stressing the idiosyncratic historical conditions of the countries at issue. There is, however, the common element of the scarcity of resources that runs through them. Scarcity has always given rise to the systematic (and unsystematic) use of coercion by governors who establish or administer the laws or other means that affect the production and the distribution of output. In its economic manifestation, imperialism may render such coercion more severe and harder to endure or, conceivably, more benign. The East India Company was aggressively monopolistic in the latter half of the eighteenth century in Bengal during the years immediately following the assumption of the *diwani*. In the second half of the nineteenth century, the British Crown in India governed more even-handedly, more austerely, and more distantly, but, paradoxically, it was during this period of the rule of law that an Indian élite began to view the British presence as an unwanted intrusion and a growing impediment to their national aspirations.

As for the charge that the MNC is an instrument of neoimperialism, there is no easy response. This is because the resource endowments, the demographic and cultural characteristics, and the historical backgrounds of the newly independent states are so disparate that their asset strengths are equally varied. The terms, therefore, on which a MNC conducts business in a country – the extent to which it may exert monopoly or monopsony power locally and bribe or otherwise manipulate political authorities – also vary. However much the poorer countries differ from one another, they none the less have political independence in a world order that recognizes its legitimacy. It is now difficult to imagine that a MNC could extort from a Third World country the type of contract that, for example, Rhodes's agents negotiated in 1888 with King Lobengula of the Matabele and Mashone tribes in what subsequently became Rhodesia and now is Zimbabwe. For the 'complete and exclusive charge over all metals and minerals situated and contained in [his] kingdom, principalities and dominions', with the right to 'exclude from [his] kingdom all persons seeking land, metals, minerals, or mining rights therein', Lobengula received 1000 rifles, 100,000 ball cartridges, 1200 pounds sterling for life, and a second-hand river steamer.[8] Even if that exchange had been voluntary – and it was not – at the time it was consummated, it would not have taken long for the extraordinary inequality in knowledge that made it possible to reveal itself. Today a MNC has command of technological and capital resources that many developing countries need more urgently than the MNC needs to invest in the Third World. But the countries there now have organizational capacity far beyond Lobengula to seek out the knowledge that is relevant to their needs and *potentially* to have an independent judgment about what they might do to improve their economic well-being.

I have underscored 'potentially' because the issue of the MNC and neoimperialism is hopelessly enmeshed in the economics of development, which relies heavily on theoretical, institutional, and historical analysis and does not lend itself to facile answers. Does the MNC increase the coercive burden in Third World countries beyond that already occasioned by the scarcity of resources? The answer partly depends upon the prospects for economic growth and the capacity for development in particular countries. If these are positive, then the MNC not only may transfer much-needed technology to develop a country's resource endowment, but the conditions collateral to its investment may generate external economies with backward, forward, and lateral linkages to other sectors that strengthen the national economy. If, however, the behavioral propensities for economic development are weak, these linkages will not be so easily forged and the MNC may exacerbate the duality referred to above, productivity may not increase rapidly enough to offset a rising negative current balance on international account, and the burden of an increasing population may become heavier.

Much hangs on the natural endowment of a country, not only its subsurface mineral resources, but its size and location relative to the world centers of economic activity. Pitcairn Island may have been a splendid hideaway for Fletcher Christian and the mutineers of the *Bounty* but, one supposes, it is not now likely to excite the interest of a MNC. Elsewhere small countries closer to industrial markets but limited in agricultural and other primary resources – Guatemala, Sierra Leone, or Somaliland, for example – may be dependent on external markets and less able independently to affect the allocation of resources for economic growth. Moreover, if they possess an environment that is especially suited to the raising of a single commodity – bananas, sugar, cotton – in demand in world markets, the MNC may increase their dependence on it.

Yet as the older industrial world has discovered to its great discomfort in the past decade, Third World countries, large and small, can do very well indeed if they have the right resources and the organizational strength to increase their share of the benefits in marketing them. Since the beginning of the oil age towards the close of the last century, oil has been used prodigally in the United States, its low price, seemingly not reckoning with its exhaustibility, encouraging the extraordinary growth of the automobile industry and the outputs – roads, service stations, garages, motels, vacation resorts, and the endless gee-gaws of the well-endowed motorist – complementary with it.[9] The discovery of major oil fields in the Persian Gulf shortly before World War II maintained the illusion that the supply of this mineral so essential for the power and lubricating needs of industrial economies would always increase at 'reasonable' prices, an illusion perhaps inhering in the monopsony power of the petroleum MNCs that initially developed the Middle East oil fields. As oil production in the United States fell behind domestic demand in the great economic expansion following World War II, the Middle Eastern oil fields became a more important source of supply. The west at first was not hesitant in a traditional assertion of its economic interest there. If, however, the role of the United States in the overthrow of Prime Minister Mossadegh of Iran in 1953 for having nationalized the oil industry in 1951 was an imperialist action worthy of the nineteenth century, the formation of the Organization of Petroleum Exporting Countries (OPEC) in 1960 was a more telling portent. By 1972 Saudi Arabia had negotiated an agreement with the Arabian American Oil Co. (ARAMCO) in which its share of oil-producing profits increased to 60 percent, and in the following year it took the first steps towards acquiring full ownership of the assets of ARAMCO in Saudi Arabia. In 1974 OPEC dramatically exerted its monopoly power in the marketing of petroleum by raising the average price of a barrel of its members' crude oil to more than $10, about four times the 1973 price.[10] Given the inflationary impact of this action on the importing countries, it is hardly surprising that OPEC meetings now are front-page news and never fail to cause a stir in security markets.

Who, then, is coercing whom? The MNCs in the Middle East, so far as they continue to perform production and maintenance functions there, appear to be conduits for transmitting the impact of rising prices of crude oil throughout world markets. Yet the very process has induced complex changes in the structure of production and consumption that for the early years of the 1980s have turned an excess demand for petroleum into an excess supply. The spot prices for various grades of oil have diverged from OPEC prices, leading the countries in the cartel to lower prices even while they restrict output. These changes may be easier to accommodate where the opportunities for substitution in production and consumption are greater. In the United States the market for small, fuel-efficient automobiles has grown at the expense of the commodious, overweight, energy-prodigal automobile so beloved in Detroit. Households have discovered myriad ways of conserving energy in home heating and the price of petroleum has encouraged the exploitation of alternative sources of energy. All these changes have employment effects, the coercive impact of which can be severe as, for example, in the automobile industry where plant capacity has shrunk in the face of Japanese and

European competition. Yet the burden may be greater in Third World countries whose need for oil is occasioned less by the imperious demands of the automobile than by petroleum derivatives used in the production of fertilizers that feed the green revolution. Moreover, the high price of crude oil increases their international indebtedness more threateningly than in the high-income countries. One cannot suppose that Saudi Arabia is especially solicitous of American families' burdens in maintaining a second automobile, though there is no reason to believe that the sheikhs, at least, have an aversion to automobiles, even big ones. Nor can one suppose that they wish to undermine the green revolution.

The reverberations of OPEC price and output policies throughout the world economy are instances of the diffuseness of economic coercion – the disjuncture of intent and consequence – that makes the image of imperialism very much less sharp than during the century and a half before World War I. The green revolution itself is another instance. If, as suggested in the previous chapter, it has widened inequalities in India so that some communities have become less cohesive and more difficult to govern, does that mean the members of the consortium from the western world that initially conducted the research and experiments that made the green revolution possible are culpable of oppressing poor Indian peasants? Or, so far as population growth is concerned, are the scientists and public-health experts who exported to Third World countries the techniques and knowledge for reducing death rates in advance of birth rates responsible for the consequent growth of unemployment and malnutrition? Would, for that matter, the subsistence struggle have been less grim had the industrial revolution and its enabling technology never been invented?

It is doubtful that many people would answer the last question affirmatively, least of all those who have yet to benefit from it. The charges of neoimperialism continue to be directed at the advanced economies precisely because the poor countries feel they have been deprived of their fair share of the rewards of industrial development. The ethics of equality, however, agitate the spirit of the deprived more intensely than it motivates their ability to develop their productive potential. The animus thus generated may be directed against many targets, not only the old imperialists, but the leaders of the many new states who now are responsible for coping with poverty. And that responsibility is not made simpler by the increasing size of the international political community in a world economy that has become more interdependent.

If the coercive burden of the old imperialism has become internalized in, and diffused among, many states, who can say that it has become lighter? When more is expected of the world and less time is allowed for performance, either rulers or ruled can easily become impatient. It is a combustible mixture as those living in the closing decades of the twentieth century have every reason to know from the harsh events reported in the world news: the killings in Uganda before and after the downfall of Idi Amin; the destruction of Beirut in civil war; terrorists raids in Israel and Israeli reprisals; the Islamic revolution in Iran and the enforcement of conservative Islamic values on a divided society; the expulsion of population from Vietnam and its invasion of a self-eviscerated Cambodia; the fratricidal struggles of the ruling classes in South Korea; tribal massacres of Bengali immigrants to the Indian state of Tripura; Russian intervention and tribal resistance in Afghanistan; the overthrow of the dictator Somoza in Nicaragua and unrest in Central America; as well as terrorist assassinations throughout the globe wherever there are refugees from the world's disorders who seek haven from their own battlefield so they may plot and plan ways of getting back into the action. Are these the price we pay for modern ideals, for the growth of too many autonomous centers with legitimate interests that must be expressed? Or are they the short-run costs of the world's search for the equitable system for accommodating these diverse interests? Can such a system be fashioned without some states being more equal than others? These questions undoubtedly are only susceptible to Delphic answers. One must hope that in the struggle for equity and justice, the world's states do not in their name impose more appalling restrictions on individuals and groups than did the nineteenth-century imperialists in the maintenance of foreign rule.

Notes

1 Jawaharlal Nehru, *An Autobiography*, London, Bodley Head, 1949, 428.

2 Daniel R. Headrick, 'The tools of imperialism, technology and the expansion of European colonial empires in the nineteenth century', *Journal of Modern History*, 51 (2) 231–63; Philip Magnus, *Kitchener, the Portrait of an Imperialist*, London, John Murray, 1958, 126–32; Bernard Porter, *The Lion's Share*, London and New York, Longman, 1975, 163–5. For Winston Churchill's account of his part in a cavalry charge at the battle of Omdurman see *My Early Life, a Roving Commission*, London, Thomas Butterworth, 1930, 203–10.

3 Alan Moorehead, *The White Nile*, New York, Dell, 1962, 366.

4 Marjory Taylor, 'The Belgian Congo today', *The World Today*, 15 (9), 357. In the latter quarter of the nineteenth century Leopold II of Belgium with the considerable assistance of Henry Stanley had acquired the Congo as a private investment preserve, unhampered by the restrictions of the Belgian government. As described by D. K. Fieldhouse, Leopold was 'the conceptual economic imperialist of the late nineteenth century whose acquisitive instincts were uncomplicated by humanitarianism, the pressure of domestic public opinion or strategic considerations': *Economics and Empire, 1830–1914*, Ithaca, Cornell University Press, 1973, 343.

5 In 1961 it was estimated that the Katanga province contained 8 percent of the world's copper, 60 percent of the west's uranium, 73 percent of the world's cobalt, 80 percent of the world's industrial diamonds and, in addition, substantial deposits of gold, zinc, cadmium, manganese, columbium, and tantalum. Colin Legum, *Congo Disaster*, Baltimore, Penguin, 1961, 44.

6 The literature on the MNC is vast and seemingly growing at an exponential rate. The references that follow barely scratch the surface. David Apter and Louis W. Goodman (eds), *The Multinational Corporation and Social Change*, New York, Praeger, 1976; Michael Clapham, *Multinational Corporations and Nation States*, London, Athlone Press, 1975; Benjamin J. Cohen, *The Question of Imperialism, the Political Economy of Dominance and Dependence*, New York, Basic Books, 1973; Charles T. Goodsell, *American Corporations and Peruvian Politics*, Cambridge, Mass., Harvard University Press, 1974; Colin Leys, *Underdevelopment in Kenya, the Political Economy of Neo-Colonialism*, Berkeley, University of California Press, 1974; Theodore H. Moran, *Multinational Corporations and the Politics of Dependence, Copper in Chile*,

Princeton, Princeton University Press, 1974; Richard L. Sklar, *Corporate Power in an African State, the Political Impact of Multinational Mining Companies in Zambia*, Berkeley, University of California Press, 1975; Franklin Tugwell, *The Politics of Oil in Venezuela*, Stanford, Stanford University Press, 1975; Raymond Vernon, *Storm over the Multinationals, the Real Issues*, Cambridge, Mass., Harvard University Press, 1977.

7 Gustav Ranis, 'Foreign aid, dead or alive', *Yale Review*, 62 (2), 162.

8 Parket T. Moon, *Imperialism and World Politics*, New York, Macmillan, 1926, 169.

9 According to the industry itself, 'one American worker in six is directly or indirectly involved with Detroit's principal products, and the Motor Vehicle Manufacturing Association says that Americans spent $91 billion in 1978 – almost 5% of the nation's . . . gross national product – on automobiles and auto parts and accessories': 'Business and Finance', *New York Times*, 22 June 1980, 1. Even if one discounts these data for the bias of the organizations reporting, they are impressive.

10 Khodada Farmanfarmaiam *et al.*, 'How can the world afford Opec oil?', *Foreign Affairs*, 53 (2). 201. Selling prices of crude oil ranged from $9.40 in Saudi Arabia and $9.70 in Iran to $14.13 in Venezuela and $14.65 in Libya. By June 1980 the price of Saudi crude, still the cheapest in OPEC, was $28 per barrel.

Bibliography

Ali, M. A. (1968) *The Mughal Nobility under Aurangzeb*, Bombay, Asia Publishing House.

Al-Sayyid, A. L. (1969) *Egypt and Cromer, a Study in Anglo-Egyptian Relations*, New York, Praeger.

Apter, D. and Goodman, L.W. (eds) (1976) *The Multinational Corporation and Social Change*, New York, Praeger.

Arrow, K. J. (1951) *Social Choice and Individual Values*, New York, Wiley.

Arrow, K. J. and Scitovsky, T. (eds) (1969) *Readings in Welfare Economics*, Homewood, Irwin.

Banerjea, P. (1928) *Indian Finance in the Days of the Company*, London, Macmillan.

Baran, P. A. and Sweezy, P. M. (1966) *Monopoly Capital, an Essay on the American Economic and Social Order*, New York, Monthly Review.

Barat, A. (1962) *The Bengal Native Infantry, its Organization and Discipline*, Calcutta, K. L. Mukhopadhyay.

Barber, W. J. (1975) *British Economic Thought and India 1600–1858 – A Study in the History of Development Economics*, Oxford, Clarendon Press.

Bell, C. (1974) *Portugal and the Quest for the Indies*, London, Constable.

Bennett, M. K. (1968) 'Famine', in D. L. Sills (ed.), *International Encyclopedia of the Social Sciences*, v, New York, Macmillan, 322–5.

Bergson, A. (1938) 'A reformulation of certain aspects of welfare

economics', *Quarterly Journal of Economics*, 52 (2), 310–34.
Berlin, I. (1959) *Karl Marx, his Life and Environment*, New York, Oxford University Press.
Berlin, I. (1958) *Two Concepts of Liberty*, Oxford, Clarendon Press.
Bernier, F. (1916) *Travels in the Mogul Empire, 1656–1668*, trans. A. Constable, 2nd edn, London, Oxford University Press.
Besant, A. (1915) *How India Wrought Freedom*, Madras, Theosophical Publishing House.
Bhagwati, J. (ed.) (1972) *Economics and World Order*, New York, Macmillan.
Bhagwati, J. and Desai, P. (1970) *Indian Planning for Industrialization, Industrialization and Trade Policies since 1951*, London, Oxford University Press.
Bhatia, B. M. (1963) *Famines in India, a Study in Some Aspects of the Economic History of India, 1860–1946*, Bombay, Asia Publishing House.
Bodelsen, C. A. (1924) *Studies in Mid-Victorian Imperialism*, Copenhagen, Glydendap Forlagstrykkeri.
Borton, H. (1955) *Japan's Modern Century*, New York, Ronald.
Brown, D. D. (1971) *Agricultural Development in India's Districts*, Cambridge, Mass., Harvard University Press.
Burn, R. (ed.) (1922) *The Cambridge History of India*, IV, New York, Macmillan.
Chandra, B. (1966) *The Rise and Growth of Economic Nationalism in India*, New Delhi, People's Publishing House.
Chang, Hsin-pao (1964) *Commissioner Lin and the Opium War*, Cambridge, Mass., Harvard University Press.
Chaudhuri, K. N. (1968) 'India's international economy in the nineteenth century: an historical survey', *Modern Asian Studies*, II (1), 31–50.
Chaudhuri, K. N. (1978) *The Trading World of Asia and the English East India Company, 1660–1760*, London, Cambridge University Press.
Chaudhuri, S. B. (1955) *Civil Disturbances during the British Rule in India, 1765–1857*, Calcutta, World Press.
Chaudhuri, S. B. (1957) *Civil Rebellion in the Indian Mutinies, 1857–1859*, Calcutta, World Press.

Churchill, W. (1930) *My Early Life, a Roving Commission*, London, T. Butterworth.

Clapham, J. H. (1951) *A Concise Economic History of Britain – From the Earliest Times to 1750*, Cambridge, Cambridge University Press.

Clapham, M. (1975) *Multinational Corporations and Nation States*, London, Athlone Press.

Clive, J. (1973) *Macaulay, the Shaping of the Historian*, New York, Knopf.

Cohen, B. J. (1973) *The Question of Imperialism, the Political Economy of Dominance and Dependence*, New York, Basic Books.

Cohen, S. P. (1971) *The Indian Army, its Contribution to the Development of a Nation*, Berkeley, University of California Press.

Cohn, B. S. (1969) 'Structural change in Indian rural society, 1596–1885', in R. E. Frykenberg (ed.), *Land Control and Social Structure in Indian Society*, Madison, University of Wisconsin Press, 53–121.

Cole, G. D. H. (1948) *A Short History of the British Working-Class Movement*, 2nd edn, London, Allen & Unwin.

Cromer, Earl of (1910) *Ancient and Modern Imperialism*, London, Longmans, Green.

Davis, K. (1951) *The Population of India and Pakistan*, Princeton, Princeton University Press.

de Schweinitz, K. Jr (1969) 'Growth, development, and political monuments', in M. Sherif and C. Sherif (eds), *Interdisciplinary Relationships in the Social Sciences*, Chicago, Aldine, 209–24.

de Schweinitz, K. Jr (1979) 'The question of freedom in economics and economic organization', *Ethics*, 89 (4), 336–53.

de Schweinitz, K. Jr (1981) 'What is economic imperialism?', *Journal of Economic Issues*, 15 (3), 675–701.

Digby, W. (1901) *'Prosperous' British India, a Revelation from Official Records*, London, T. Fisher Unwin.

Dilke, C. W. (1869) *Greater Britain*, New York, Harper.

Dodwell, H. H. (ed.) (1964) *The Cambridge Shorter History of India*, Delhi, S. Chand.

Dutt, R. (1950) *The Economic History of India in the Victorian Age*, 7th edn, London, Routledge & Kegan Paul.

Elliott, J. H. (1963) *Imperial Spain, 1469–1716*, New York, St Martin's Press.

Epstein, T. S. (1973) *South India, Yesterday, Today, and Tomorrow*, London, Macmillan.

Farmanfarmaian, K., et al. (1973) 'How can the world afford Opec oil?', *Foreign Affairs*, 53 (2), 201–22.

Fieldhouse, D. K. (1973) *Economics and Empire, 1830–1914*, Ithaca, Cornell University Press.

Foster, W. (ed.) (1899) *The Embassy of Sir Thomas Roe to the Court of the Great Mogul, 1615–1619*, London, Hakluyt Society.

Frank, A. G. (1969) *Capitalism and Underdevelopment in Latin America*, New York, Monthly Review.

Frankel, F. R. (1971) *India's Green Revolution, Economic Gains and Political Costs*, Princeton, Princeton University Press.

Frankel, F. R. (1978) *India's Political Economy, 1947–1977, and the Gradual Revolution*, Princeton, Princeton University Press.

Friedman, M. (1962) *Capitalism and Freedom*, Chicago, University of Chicago Press.

Froude, J. A. (1886) *Oceana*, London, Longmans, Green.

Frykenberg, R. E. (1969) 'Village strength in south India', in R. E. Frykenberg (ed.), *Land Control and Social Structure in Indian Society*, Madison, University of Wisconsin Press, 217–47.

Furneaux, R. (1963) *Massacre at Amritsar*, London, Allen & Unwin.

Galanter, M. (1968) 'The displacement of traditional law in modern India', *Journal of Social Issues*, 24 (4), 65–91.

Ganguli, B. N. (1965) *Dadabhai Naoroji and the Drain Theory*, London, Asia Publishing House.

Gardner, B. (1972) *The East India Company*, New York, McCall.

Goodsell, C. T. (1974) *American Corporations and Peruvian Politics*, Cambridge, Mass., Harvard University Press.

Griffiths, P. (1972) *The British Impact on India*, 2nd edn, Ann Arbor, University of Michigan Press.

Guha, R. (1963) *A Rule of Property for Bengal, an Essay on the Idea of Permanent Settlement*, Paris, Mouton.

Habib, I. (1963) *The Agrarian System of Mughal India, 1556–1707*, Bombay, Asia Publishing House.

Habib, I. (1969) 'Potentialities of capitalistic development in the economy of Mughal India', *Journal of Economic History*, 29 (1), 32–78.

Hall, J. W. (1968) 'Foundations of the modern Japanese daimyo', in John W. Hall and Marius B. Jansen (eds), *Studies in the Institutional History of Early Modern Japan*, Princeton, Princeton University Press.

Hamilton, A. (1893) 'Report on the subject of manufacturers', in F. W. Taussig (ed.), *State Papers and Speeches on the Tariff*, Cambridge, Mass., Harvard University Press, 1–107.

Hart, H. H. (1950) *Sea Road to the Indies*, New York, Macmillan.

Hart, H. H. (1942) *Venetian Adventurer*, Stanford, Stanford University Press.

Headrick, D. R. (1979) 'The tools of imperialism, technology and the expansion of European colonial empires in the nineteenth century', *Journal of Modern History*, 51 (2), 231–63.

Hilferding, R. (1923), *Das Finanzkapital*, Wien, Verlag der Wiener Volksbuchhandlung.

Hobson, J. A. (1948) *Imperialism, a Study*, 3rd edn, London, Allen & Unwin.

Hymer, S. H. (1970) 'The efficiency (contradictions) of multinational corporations', *American Economic Review*, 60 (2), 441–8.

Hymer, S. H. (1972) 'The multinational corporation and the law of uneven development', in J. Bhagwati (ed.), *Economics and World Order*, New York, Macmillan.

Hyndman, H. M. (1878) 'The bankruptcy of India', *The Nineteenth Century*, 4 (20), 585–608.

Ilbert, C. (1922) *The Government of India*, Oxford, Clarendon Press.

Irish University Press Series (1970) *Parliamentary Papers, 1852–53*, 15, Shannon, Irish University Press, 313–32.

Islam, S. (1979) *The Permanent Settlement in Bengal: A Study of Its Operation 1790–1819*, Dacca, Bangla Academy.

Kaye, J. W. (1877 and 1878) *A History of the Sepoy War in India, 1857–1858*, I & II, London, W. H. Allen.

Kaye, J. W. (1867) *Lives of Indian Officers*, I, London, Strachan.

Keynes, J. M. (1965) *A Treatise on Money*, London, Macmillan.

Keynes, J. M. (1936) *The General Theory of Employment, Interest, and*

Money, New York, Harcourt Brace.
Kling, B. B. (1966) *The Blue Mutiny, the Indigo Disturbances in Bengal, 1857–1862*, Philadelphia, University of Pennsylvania Press.
Kling, B. B. (1976) *Partner in Empire, Dwarkanath Tagore and the Age of Enterprise in Eastern India*, Berkeley, University of California Press.
Koebner, R. (1965) *Empire*, New York, Grosset & Dunlop.
Lach, D. F. (1965) *Asia in the Making of Europe*, I, Chicago, University of Chicago Press.
Ladejinsky, W. (1970) 'Ironies of India's green revolution', *Foreign Affairs*, 48 (4), 758–68.
Lamb, B. P. (1968) *India – A World in Transition*, 3rd edn, New York, Praeger.
Landes, D. S. (1958) *Bankers and Pashas, International Finance and Economic Imperialism*, Cambridge, Mass., Harvard University Press.
Landes, D. S. (1970) 'Technological change and development in western Europe, 1750–1914', in *The Cambridge Economic History of Europe*, VI, Pt I, Cambridge, Cambridge University Press, 374–601.
Lane, F. C. (1966) *Venice and History*, Baltimore, Johns Hopkins University Press.
Langer, W. L. (1968) *The Diplomacy of Imperialism, 1890–1902*, 2nd edn, New York, Knopf.
Legum, C. (1961) *Congo Disaster*, Baltimore, Penguin.
Lenin, V. I. (1939) *Imperialism, the Highest Stage of Capitalism*, New York, International Publishers.
Leys, C. (1974) *Underdevelopment in Kenya, the Political Economy of Neo-Colonialism*, Berkeley, University of California Press.
List, F. (1885) *The National System of Political Economy*, London, Longmans, Green.
Longford, E. (1971) *Wellington, the Years of the Sword*, London, Panther.
Luxemburg, R. (1951) *The Accumulation of Capital*, trans. A. Schwarzschild with an introduction by J. Robinson, London, Routledge & Kegan Paul.
McLane, J. R. (1963) 'The drain of wealth and Indian nationalism

at the turn of the century', in R. Raychaudhuri (ed.), *Contributions to Indian Economic History*, II, Calcutta, K. L. Mukhopadhyay, 21–40.

McLane, J. R. (1977) 'Revenue farming and the zamindari system in 18th-century Bengal', in R. E. Frykenberg (ed.), *Land Tenure and Peasant in South Asia*, New Delhi, Orient Longman, 19–36.

McLellan, D. (1970) *Marx before Marxism*, New York, Harper & Row.

MacMunn, G. F. (1911) *The Armies of India*, London, Adam & Charles Black.

MacPherson, W. J. (1972) 'Economic development in India under the British Crown, 1858–1947', in A. J. Youngson (ed.), *Economic Development in the Long Run*, London, Allen & Unwin, 126–91.

Magdoff, H. (1969) *The Age of Imperialism*, New York, Monthly Review.

Magnus, P. (1958) *Kitchener, the Portrait of an Imperialist*, London, John Murray.

Majumdar, R. C. (1961) *Three Phases of India's Struggle for Freedom*, Bombay, Bharatiya Vidya Bhava.

Mantoux, P. (1952) *The Industrial Revolution in the Eighteenth Century*, trans. M. Vernon, 2nd edn, London, Jonathan Cape.

Marlow, J. (1969) *The Peterloo Massacre*, London, Rapp & Whiting.

Marshall, P. J. (1976) *East Indian Fortunes, the British in Bengal in the Eighteenth Century*, Oxford, Clarendon Press.

Marshall, P. J. (1968) *Problems of Empire, Britain and India, 1757–1813*, London, Allen & Unwin.

Marx, K. (1906) *Capital*, I, trans. S. Moore and E. Aveling from 3rd German edn, Chicago, Charles H. Kerr.

Mayer, A. C. (1966) 'The caste system', in D. L. Sills (ed.), *International Encyclopedia of Social Sciences*, II, New York, Macmillan, 339–44.

Mehta, V. (1970) 'City of the dreadful night', *The New Yorker Magazine*, 21 March, 47–112.

Meilink-Roelofsz, M. A. P. (1962) *Asian Trade and European Influence in the Indonesian Archipelago between 1500 and 1630*, The

Hague, Martinus Nijhoff.

Metcalf, T. R. (1964) *The Aftermath of Revolt, India 1857–1870*, Princeton, Princeton University Press.

Mill, J. (1840) *The History of British India*, 4th edn, London, J. Madden, 8 vols.

Mill, J. (1975) *The History of British India*, abridged by William Thomas, Chicago, University of Chicago Press.

Mill, J. S. (1947) *On Liberty*, New York, Appleton-Century-Crofts.

Mill, J. S. (1883) *Principles of Political Economy*, 5th edn, New York, Appleton.

Moon, P. T. (1926) *Imperialism and World Politics*, New York, MacMillan.

Moore, B. Jr (1978) *Injustice – The Social Basis of Obedience and Revolt*, White Plains, M. E. Sharpe.

Moore, B. Jr (1966) *Social Origins of Dictatorship and Democracy, Lord and Peasant in the Making of the Modern World*, Boston, Beacon.

Moorehead, A. (1962) *The White Nile*, New York, Dell.

Moran, T. H. (1974) *Multinational Corporations and the Politics of Dependence, Copper in Chile*, Princeton, Princeton University Press.

Moreland, W. H. (1923) *From Akbar to Aurangzeb – A Study in Indian Economic History*, London, Macmillan.

Moreland, W. H. (1920) *India at the Death of Akbar – An Economic Study*, London, Macmillan.

Morgan, E. S. (1975) *American Slavery, American Freedom – The Ordeal of Colonial Virginia*, New York, Norton.

Morris, J. (1973) *Heaven's Command, an Imperial Progress*, New York, Harcourt Brace Jovanovich.

Morris, M. D. (1963) 'Towards a reinterpretation of nineteenth-century Indian economic history', *Journal of Economic History*, 23 (4), 606–18.

Morris, M. D. (1969) 'Trends and tendencies in Indian economic history', *Indian Economy in the Nineteenth Century: A Symposium*, Delhi, Indian Economic and Social History Association, 101–70.

Morse, H. B. (1926) *The Chronicles of the East India Company Trading to China*, II, Oxford, Clarendon Press.

Mueller, D. C. (1976) 'Public choice, a survey', *Journal of Economic Literature*, 14 (2), 395–433.

Murphey, R. (1977) *The Outsiders*, Ann Arbor, University of Michigan Press.

Naipaul, V. S. (1976) 'India, new claim on the land', *New York Review of Books*, 23 (11), 11–18.

Naoroji, D. (1962) *Poverty and Un-British Rule in India*, London, Swan Sonnenschein.

Nehru, J. (1949) *An Autobiography*, London, Bodley Head.

Nurkse, R. (1961) *Equilibrium and Growth in the World Economy*, G. Harberler and R.M. Stern (eds), Cambridge, Mass., Harvard University Press.

Owen, D. E. (1934) *British Opium Policy in China and India*, New Haven, Yale University Press.

Philips, C. H. (1940) *The East India Company, 1784–1834*, Manchester, Manchester University Press.

Popper, K. R. (1966) *The Open Society and Its Enemies*, 5th edn, Princeton, Princeton University Press.

Porter, B. (1975) *The Lion's Share*, London and New York, Longman.

Rae, J. (1895) *Life of Adam Smith*, London, Macmillan.

Ranis, G. (1973) 'Foreign aid, dead or alive', *Yale Review*, 62 (2), 161–7.

Rawls, J. (1971) *A Theory of Justice*, Cambridge, Belknap Press.

Raychaudhuri, T. (1969) 'A re-interpretation of nineteenth-century Indian economic history', *Indian Economy in the Nineteenth Century: A Symposium*, Delhi, Indian Economic and Social History Association, 77–100.

Reischauer, E. O. and Fairbank, J. K. (1958 and 1960) *East Asia – The Great Tradition*, Boston, Houghton Mifflin.

Ricardo, D. (1953) *On the Principles of Political Economy and Taxation*, P. Sraffa and M. H. Dobb (eds), Cambridge, Cambridge University Press.

Robinson, J. (1966) *An Essay on Marxian Economics*, New York, St Martin's Press.

Robinson, J. (1953) *On Re-reading Marx*, Cambridge, Students' Bookshops.

Robinson, R. and Gallagher, J. (1961) *Africa and the Victorians, the*

Official Mind of Imperialism, London, Macmillan.
Robson, W. (1935) *Civilisation and the Growth of the Law*, New York, Macmillan.
Rosenberg, N. (1972) *Technology and American Economic Growth*, New York, Harper & Row.
Rousseau, J. J. (1947) *The Social Contract*, trans. C. Frankel, New York, Hafner.
Sansom, G. (1963) *A History of Japan, 1615–1817*, Stanford, Stanford University Press.
Sargent, A. J. (1918) *Seaways of the Empire*, London, Black.
Schumpeter, J. A. (1950) *Capitalism, Socialism, and Democracy*, 3rd edn, New York, Harper.
Schumpeter, J. A. (1974) *The Sociology of Imperialism*, trans. H. Norden, New York, New American Library.
Seal, A. (1968) *The Emergence of Indian Nationalism: Competition and Collaboration in the Later Nineteenth Century*, Cambridge, Cambridge University Press.
Seeley, J. R. (1883) *The Expansion of England*, London, Macmillan.
Simmel, B. (1970) *The Rise of Free Trade Imperialism*, Cambridge, Cambridge University Press.
Sklar, R. L. (1975) *Corporate Power in an African State, the Political Impact of Multinational Mining Companies in Zambia*, Berkeley, University of California Press.
Smith, A. (1937) *An Inquiry into the Nature and Causes of the Wealth of Nations*, E. Cannan (ed.), New York, Modern Library.
Smith, A. E. (1947) *Colonists in Bondage – White Servitude and Convict Labor in America 1607–1776*, Chapel Hill, University of North Carolina Press.
Smith, D. E. (1963) *India as a Secular State*, Princeton, Princeton University Press.
Smith, V. A. (1919) *Akbar, the Great Mogul, 1542–1605*, Oxford, Clarendon Press.
Smith, V. A. (1967) *The Oxford History of India*, Percival Spear (ed.), 3rd edn, Oxford, Clarendon Press.
Spear, P. (1972) *India, a Modern History*, 2nd edn, Ann Arbor, University of Michigan Press.
Spear, P. (1963) *The Nabobs – A Study of the Social Life of the English*

in Eighteenth-Century India, London, Oxford University Press.

Spear, P. (1951) *Twilight of the Mughals*, Cambridge, Cambridge University Press.

Srinivas, M. N. (1966) *Social Change in Modern India*, Berkeley, University of California Press.

Steensgaard, N. (1973) *Carracks, Caravans, and Companies – The Structural Crisis in the European–Asian Trade in the Early Seventeenth Century*, Copenhagen, Studentlitteratur.

Stokes, E. (1978) *The Peasant and the Raj: Studies in Agrarian Society and Peasant Rebellion in Colonial India*, London, Cambridge University Press.

Strachey, Sir John (1903) *India, its Administration and Progress*, 3rd edn, London, Macmillan.

Strachey, L. (1918) *Eminent Victorians*, New York, Harcourt Brace.

Swamy, S. (1973) 'Economic growth in China and India, 1952–1970, a comparative appraisal', *Economic Development and Cultural Change*, 21 (4), Pt 2, 1–83.

Sweezy, P. M. (1946) *The Theory of Capitalist Development*, London, Dennis Dobson.

Talmon, J. L. (1952) *The Rise of Totalitarian Democracy*, Boston, Beacon.

Taylor, M. (1959) 'The Belgian Congo today', *The World Today*, 15 (9), 351–64.

Thomson, G. M. (1976) *Sir Francis Drake*, London, Futura.

Thompson, E. P. (1963) *The Making of the English Working Class*, London, Victor Gollancz.

Thornton, A. P. (1968) *For the File on Empire*, London, Macmillan.

Thornton, A. P. (1959) *The Imperial Idea and Its Enemies, a Study in British Power*, London, Macmillan.

Tinker, H. (1974) *A New System of Slavery, the Export of India's Labour Overseas, 1830–1920*, London, Oxford University Press.

Trevelyan, G. M. (1943) *English Social History*, London, Longmans, Green.

Tugwell, F. (1975) *The Politics of Oil in Venezuela*, Stanford, Stanford University Press.

Veblen, T. (1939) *Imperial Germany and the Industrial Revolution*, New York, Viking.

Vernon, R. (1977) *Storm over the Multinationals, the Real Issues*, Cambridge, Mass., Harvard University Press.

Wakefield, E. G. (1929) *A Letter from Sydney, the Principal Town of Australasia*, New York, Dutton.

Weber, M. (1978) *Economy and Society*, G. Roth and C. Wittich (eds), Berkeley, University of California Press.

Wolpert, S. (1982) *A New History of India*, 2nd edn, New York, Oxford University Press.

Woodham-Smith, C. (1962) *The Great Hunger, Ireland 1845–1849*, London, Hamish Hamilton.

Woolf, L. (1961) *Growing, an Autobiography of the Years 1904–1911*, London, Hogarth Press.

World Bank (1981) *World Development Report 1981*, New York, Oxford University Press.

Index